"Where were you, Colin, when my brother, Jeff, and I took the decision to leave our family sports footwear business to found Reebok? Your book *Start. Scale. Exit. Repeat.* could have saved us a lot of pain. But we also had a lot of fun, which as you point out, came from being in *love* with our mission."

—**JOE FOSTER,** cofounder, Reebok; author of *Shoemaker*

"Colin has started, scaled, and exited many businesses successfully. He has survived many mistakes and thrived with even more successes. He will inspire you and guide you with golden nuggets to navigate and succeed in your own unique journey to start, scale, exit, and repeat."

—**PATRICK THEAN,** *Wall Street Journal* and *USA Today* best-selling author; CEO, coach, guide

"Through his one-of-a-kind storytelling, zestful, energetic learning spirit, and engaging humility, Colin C.Campbell has created a masterful gem. *Start. Scale. Exit. Repeat.* is a must read for any entrepreneur or leader passionately looking for a learning edge to better performance."

—**LEE SCHRAM,** former CEO, Deluxe Corporation

"Colin's journey, combined with insights from successful experts and serial entrepreneurs, unveils the code to achieve startup success."

—**VERNE HARNISH,** founder Entrepreneurs' Organization (EO), author of *Scaling Up: How a Few Companies Make It…and Why the Rest Don't (Rockefeller Habits 2.0 Revised Edition)*

"Building a company from start to exit—and doing it all over again—is not easy. This book provides you with the formula to do just that."

—**ERIC MALKA,** founder, Art of Shaving

"Colin's theories are incredibly simple and applicable to a wide range of company types, including SaaS, real estate, manufacturing, and e-commerce businesses. His step-by-step approach makes the entire process appear effortless from the very beginning to the very end."

—**LIL ROBERTS,** founder and CEO, Xendoo

"Colin Campbell is a true master of entrepreneurship. Having founded and scaled several successful companies, his approach to business can be summed up in four simple words: start, scale, exit, and repeat."

—**LANCE TRACEY,** serial entrepreneur; president, Lanebury Growth Capital

"This book provides a captivating insight into the tech journey from the 1990s to the present, highlighting patterns of success. Colin has seen a lot in his thirty-plus years as a serial entrepreneur!"

—**SHEEL MOHNOT,** cofounder, Better Tomorrow Ventures; cohost, *The Pitch* Podcast

"Colin has thrived across many businesses by understanding customers and how businesses make money."

—**ELLIOT NOSS,** CEO, Tucows

"Never accept business advice ... unless the advisor has built a track record of personal successes based on their own advice! Colin Campbell's *Start. Scale. Exit. Repeat.* provides a pithy and practical road map for entrepreneurs. If you want to be a successful entrepreneur, get your hands on this indispensable guide."

—**GEORGE WALTHER,** Hall of Fame speaker; acclaimed author

START.
SCALE.
EXIT.
REPEAT.

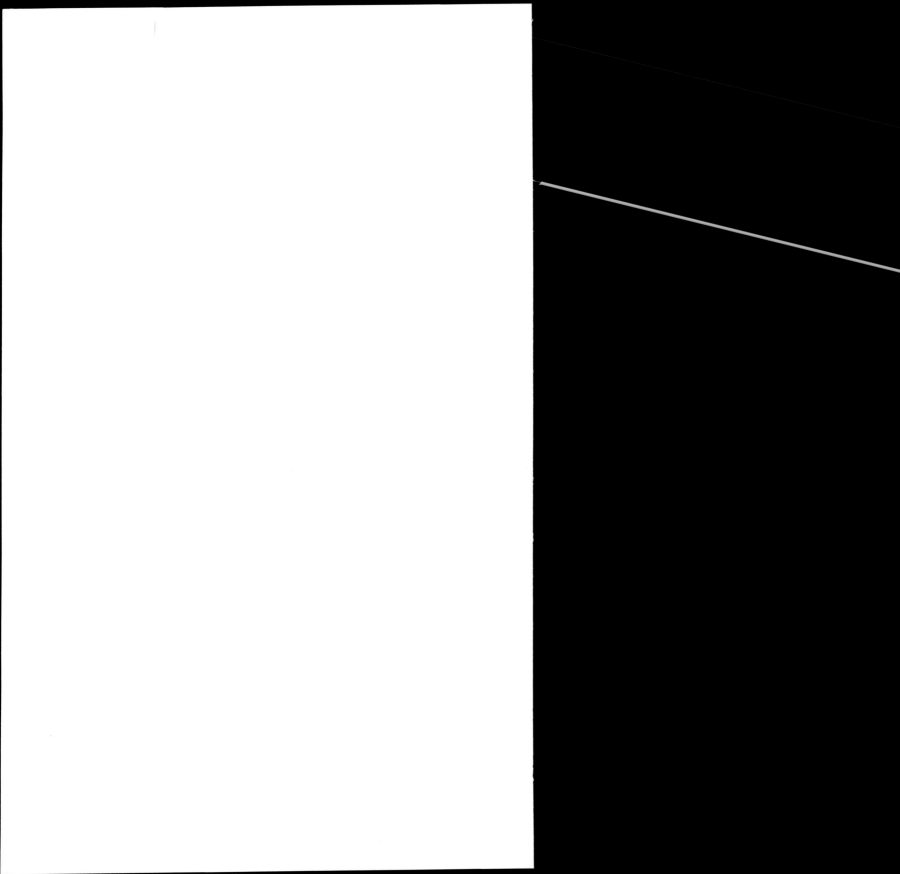

Colin C. Campbell

START.
SCALE.
EXIT.
Serial
Entrepreneurs'
Secrets
Revealed!

REPEAT.

"No book has come closer to cracking the code of what it takes to make a startup successful."

—MICHELE VAN TILBORG,
CEO STARTUP CLUB, 1 MILLION MEMBERS

Forbes | Books

Published by Forbes Books, Charleston, South Carolina.
Member of Advantage Media.

Forbes Books is a registered trademark, and the Forbes Books colophon is a trademark of Forbes Media, LLC.

Printed in the United States of America.

10 9 8 7 6 5 4 3 2 1

ISBN: 978-1-95588-496-9 (Hardcover)
ISBN: 979-8-88750-614-2 (Paperback)
ISBN: 978-1-95588-497-6 (eBook)

LCCN: 2023907626

Cover design by Danna Steele and Olivia Valdés.
Illustrations by Erica Francisco, Olivia Valdés, and Michele Van Tilborg.
Layout design by Wesley Strickland.

This custom publication is intended to provide accurate information and the opinions of the author in regard to the subject matter covered. It is sold with the understanding that the publisher, Forbes Books, Come Together LLC, or Colin C. Campbell, is not engaged in rendering legal, financial, or professional services of any kind. If legal advice or other expert assistance is required, the reader is advised to seek the services of a competent professional.

Since 1917, Forbes has remained steadfast in its mission to serve as the defining voice of entrepreneurial capitalism. Forbes Books, launched in 2016 through a partnership with Advantage Media, furthers that aim by helping business and thought leaders bring their stories, passion, and knowledge to the forefront in custom books. Opinions expressed by Forbes Books authors are their own. To be considered for publication, please visit **books.Forbes.com**.

Dedicated to:

All the entrepreneurs and aspiring entrepreneurs who want to learn

Contents

EXIT 335

Introduction

WHAT MAKES A STARTUP SUCCESSFUL? Is it dumb luck? Hard work? Or is there a winning formula?

Those are the questions I've been working to answer for over thirty years as a serial entrepreneur.

Back in 2012, I went skiing, and as much as I would love to regale you with stories of how I dominated the snowy mountainsides, the truth is that the mountain got the best of me, and I ended my trip with a broken tibia and fibula. Not good! It took the surgeons eight hours to put my leg back together. Needless to say, it put a damper on the trip by making it memorable in the worst kind of way.

A few months later, I was still in a cast and healing when I got a call from my CEO coach, Patrick Thean: "Colin, I'd like for you to come to MIT and speak at the masters of entrepreneurship program. I want you to share with them exactly what you're doing that's making you successful over and over again."

For starters, I was flattered by the invitation. After all, Patrick is someone I really admire, and at the time he was also partners with Verne

Harnish, the author of the must-read books *Mastering the Rockefeller Habits* and *Scaling Up*. But I understood why he had asked me. By this point, I had successfully started, scaled, and sold businesses several times over: Internet Direct Canada, Tucows Interactive, Hostopia, .CLUB, and GeeksForLess are among those success stories.

But what interested me most about his invitation was that it gave me the opportunity to really think about the answer to his question: "What was it that I was doing so right over and over again?" Answering this question meant I had to analyze the patterns in my successes to see if there was a formula that could be repeatable by other entrepreneurs. Was there an actual repeatable formula?

So I agreed to do the talk at MIT before I had the chance to fully think about what I was agreeing to. See, the MIT masters of entrepreneurship program is one of the most select in the world, as they accept only sixty entrepreneurs a year, and one of the qualifications for acceptance is that you have to run a company generating at least $1 million in annual revenue. These were already top entrepreneurs, people I looked up to—and I had agreed to teach them *what* exactly?

I'm not one to back out of a commitment, so I flew to MIT, and I'm sure I was a sight to behold as I hobbled into that lecture hall with my crutches, sweaty and nervous, catching my breath as I began to share my story and what I had learned along the way. And I didn't focus just on the successes. There had been plenty of failures as well.

The first thing I discovered in my analysis was that for every business I had been involved in, there had been a new wave, a macro change, or a paradigm shift that presented an opportunity for the business to uniquely solve a problem rather than to simply replicate what someone else was already doing. Second, I found that I was asking myself, "How can I defend this company? How can I build a moat of protection around it?" And third, I realized that all my successful ideas had been scalable.

But was it just me? Was I just lucky?

In trying to figure this out, I started having conversations with other serial entrepreneurs about whether they had observed similar patterns in their own successes. Through Startup Club on Clubhouse, I also found myself learning from our members and discovering new ingredients that needed to be added to the recipe, things I had never noticed or experienced before.

In the journey of serial entrepreneurship, you're going to need others around you for counsel, whether in vetting your idea, getting legal or financial advice, or negotiating the sale of your company. This book is a guide to point you in the right direction on your unique journey and to help you answer the questions you'll encounter.

All this is to say that I'm not here to proclaim, "I have all the answers" or "I am the expert at everything in this book"; rather, it's to share what I have experienced in life starting, scaling, exiting, and repeating—both the right way *and* the wrong way. I present not only my experiences but also what I've learned from the dozens of serial entrepreneurs and experts we have spoken with in over hundreds of Startup Club interviews in the hopes that it will help you and other entrepreneurs find and accelerate your success—with fewer mistakes along the way.

Before we dive deeper, though, it will be helpful to explain how this book is organized and what you can expect. First, it's divided into four primary sections that reflect what I see as the four essential stages of entrepreneurship. In some ways, you could see these as four mini books put together:

START

Every business begins with an idea. Then you have to Start by building a business around the idea, including assembling a successful team and taking your idea to market. Obviously, this is what lays the foundation for every other stage of business, since nothing else can happen if you never get your startup going to begin with. It's like taking two rocks and smashing them together to make a spark. Ever tried it? It's not easy!

SCALE

Success often comes down to whether or not you can Scale the business. Growing your business—or what I call scaling in zeros—means adding zeros to your revenue and profits. This will be the longest section of the book, as we identify and take advantage of what sets you apart and then track those benchmarks, key performance indicators, and goals to measure and drive results. In this stage it's all about throwing gasoline on the fire. Ever tried that? It's pretty easy!

EXIT

When you've successfully scaled your business, you'll attract the interest of potential buyers. Knowing when it's time to sell, expanding your efforts for maximum valuation, and navigating the negotiation are all complex but essential skills for an entrepreneur. Also, how do you make the most out of an exit you didn't ask for? What do you do when things go bust? One way or another, eventually you will be faced with an Exit.

REPEAT

Having been through a number of both challenging and highly successful exits, this is perhaps my favorite part of the journey, and it's the stage where you get to define yourself as a serial entrepreneur. Finding your next business venture and taking key learnings and assets with you are essential to being able to Repeat. Even if you're not at this stage (yet), you can learn many lessons from serial entrepreneurs that can be applied in your startup today.

While every business venture is unique, it's my intent to walk you through each stage, from Starting, Scaling, Exiting, and Repeating the process, to provide you with useful tips and big takeaways—or Golden Nuggets—along the way.

On that note, this book is meant to be read chronologically, not like an encyclopedia where you just flip to the entry of interest. In other words, you might be at the stage of entrepreneurship where you're looking to sell your business, so there may be a temptation to skip ahead to the Exit section. This is fair warning that if you do so, you'll be missing a lot of the foundational information you need that provides context for later concepts.

I believe that every small business can grow if the owner so chooses and if they have a clear map or strategy. But it's not just about knowing the formula. You must also apply it through *action*. The actions needed to grow your company will be very difficult, maybe too difficult for some, but I've seen how success is a direct result of the right decisions and actions based on using best practices.

> **❝ I've seen how success is a direct result of the right decisions and actions based on using best practices. ❞**

That being said, let me start with a caveat.

Is the path outlined here 100 percent foolproof? No, nothing in life is 100 percent. As we'll discuss later, changes can occur outside of your control to derail your best efforts and plans. I'd consider myself foolish if I didn't admit that luck *can* play a role. But ultimately it's not luck alone that makes you successful. Instead, it's about knowing how to position yourself for good luck and then capitalizing on it when it comes around—what we usually refer to as your big break. But it also means being prepared to mitigate bad luck when it comes around, which can prove just as valuable in the long run.

Yes, we all read every day about companies that have experienced astronomical growth—so-called unicorn companies that simply explode and don't appear to go through the natural growth stages of most businesses. We live in a unicorn nation where many believe that less than a billion just doesn't cut it anymore.

So let me be clear: if you want to read a book on how to create the next unicorn and "get rich quick," this is the wrong book for you. I have seen countless tech startups fail because the entrepreneurs chase the big win without properly building a solid foundation. Unfortunately, this occurs more often than not in Silicon Valley—what I've nicknamed Silicon Valley Disease. While I applaud the innovation and success that's come from Silicon Valley, that environment can also have its negatives.

Just know that success doesn't mean you have to give up control of your company or reach a billion dollars. The language of Silicon Valley can be dangerous and lead you down the wrong path. Companies like Google, Facebook, Uber, Chewy, Zoom, and Clubhouse are extremely rare, hence unicorns. Letting them define *your* path for success is unrealistic at best and dangerous at worst. Plus, it should be noted that almost all these unicorns took in venture funding in their past, with almost all such funding presenting risk to the ownership status of the founders and early investors. With some exceptions, this is a risk not every founder needs to endure.

For every one unicorn, we don't hear about the dozens—even hundreds—of entrepreneurs who failed to make a successful exit, leading to carnage on the entrepreneurial highway. Venture capital can help drive unicorns and empower their ability to scale, but it can also drive founders out of their company and their ownership.

I don't pretend to be the next Steve Jobs, Bill Gates, or Elon Musk—and I don't want to be. What I am, though, is a small business entrepreneur who has done it successfully over and over again. And like many other serial entrepreneurs, I've had wins *and* losses. But even the losses have helped me figure out what makes this formula different. By focusing on building a solid foundation and knowing what to look out for, I believe this strategy can dramatically increase your chances of success.

If you need your company to grow from $100,000 in sales to $1 million, or $1 million to $10 million, or $10 million to $100 million, I believe the insights here *can* walk you down the pathway to success. Or if you want to launch a startup and then scale it to sell for millions—or even tens of millions—then this *is* the right book for you.

I'm grateful now that I accepted Patrick's invitation to nervously hobble up to talk to those sixty entrepreneurs at MIT, because it started the process of creating this book as well as *Serial Entrepreneur: Secrets Revealed!*, our Startup Club podcast on Clubhouse. Each chapter is short and pragmatic and presents an approach backed up by real-life experience. Time is valuable, so I want to give you actionable steps that you can take now to Start, Scale, Exit, Repeat.

Get ready, strap yourself in, and let's go for a ride.

START.
SCALE.
EXIT.
REPEAT.

I've really enjoyed running sessions with new founders. I tend to start the session by asking one question: "What makes a startup successful? Isn't this what we all want to know?" I'm fascinated by all the different responses. Those responses, my experiences, and the lessons from other serial entrepreneurs are the basis for Start.

What if there was a method, system, or set of philosophies that could dramatically improve a startup's chance of success? Can we break the code of what serial entrepreneurs do over and over again to Start, Scale, Exit, Repeat?

You've probably heard before that 9 out of 10 startups will fail. In fact, Startup Genome's 2019 report found 11 out of 12 startups fail, and Shikhar Ghosh's analysis found that 7.5 out of 10 venture-backed startups fail.[1]

This begs the question of whether serial entrepreneurs have a higher rate of success. Well, research shows that they do—and this is great news for anyone who wants to learn the trade of entrepreneurship.

Harvard Business School researchers found that entrepreneurs who had success in a prior venture (i.e., started a company that went public) had a 30 percent chance of succeeding in their next venture. In contrast, first-time entrepreneurs showed only an 18 percent chance of succeeding with their startup.[2]

You might say, "Thirty percent still doesn't sound so great," but you have to think of it a bit like baseball. Outfielder Ty Cobb holds the record for the highest batting average ever, with a .366 (or 36.6 percent) over his twenty-four seasons in Major League Baseball. So if you've got a batter who gets on base 36 percent of the time, they're a keeper! My own entrepreneurial batting average is around .466, as I've had about seven successful exits from fifteen businesses I've started over the last thirty years.

Will more than 50 percent of my new ventures fail? Yes, they will. Which is why the skill of mitigating failure is just as important.

So that's really what's at the heart of Start: How can you improve your chances of getting on base and maximize your entrepreneurial batting average? Entrepreneurship is not just a mysterious God-given talent. It takes the right personality and the willingness to learn. So let's Start.

1   Nicolás Cerdeira and Kyril Kotashev, "Startup Failure Rate: Ultimate Report + Infographic 2021," Failory.com, March 25, 2021.

2   Paul Gompers et al., "Performance Persistence in Entrepreneurship and Venture Capital," *Journal of Financial Economics* 96, no. 1 (April 2010): 18–32.

STORY

CHAPTER 1:

Ideas Are Everywhere

I HATE HOTEL ROOMS more than anything else. I know that sounds extreme, but it's the truth. I traveled for thirty years, practically living in hotels. So whenever my wife and I go somewhere, we've always opted for vacation rentals, because the experience is so much better.

However, the problem we face with vacation rentals is that while the experience is nicer, they always seem to have the cheapest beds, beat-up old furniture, and worn-out cookware that looks disgusting. It gave me the impression that these landlords must think, "Hey, they're just renters and will destroy it anyway, so let's leave them the junk."

It ain't going to work.

In contrast, I enjoy the cleanliness and comfort of hotels, but I hate the environment. I couldn't help but be bothered by this problematic trade-off: either have a better bed and cleanliness at a hotel without the fun of travel or have a nice vacation experience with a bad night's sleep. Why couldn't we have both?

Which gave me an idea. Why not offer hotel quality combined with the vacation rental experience? Since then, we've bought nineteen properties in South Florida to run as hotel vacation rentals under the brand Escape Club. The beds are luxurious Westin Heavenly mattresses, the kitchens are stocked with Williams-Sonoma cookware, and we've strived to create a better vacation rental experience by combining the best of both worlds. The end results are top ratings on Airbnb, which drive more rentals—and more income—our way.

It all boils down to this: we had a problem, and it gave me an idea. We figured we weren't the only people in the world bothered by those things, and we were right. There are others out there willing to pay a higher price for a better experience, and now we're meeting that need for them.

Ideas begin with why.

The strongest ideas always begin with why. I know it sounds obvious, and a lot of people will probably roll their eyes at the whole start-with-why concept because they've heard it over and over again, but it simply can't be overstated—it will be extremely difficult to be successful if there's not a clear purpose driving your idea. Too many would-be entrepreneurs pursue ideas that they think will get them rich quick, or whatever the latest trend is, but they have no real belief in or purpose backing up that pursuit.

First, if you're looking to get rich quick, then running a startup probably isn't for you. Because what happens is that when things get tough or you hit your first roadblock, if you don't have a *why* pushing you forward, you end up calling it quits, and all you've done is waste your own time and money in the process.

Second, you'll often find that your purpose is connected to a problem that needs to be solved (more on that in a minute). But even if you don't know what problem you want to solve yet, having a clear picture of what really motivates you, what excites you, and what gets you up in the morning—or even what keeps you up at night—is never a bad place to start.

And it doesn't have to be a big thing—it just has to be something you really care about. Is our vacation rental business going to solve climate change or world hunger? No. But I can promise you that it's coming from a place of purpose because it's something I really care about, and it's something I wholeheartedly believe will create a better experience for people and add value to their lives. Everyone deserves a great vacation. That's still a purpose.

So always start with the why behind your idea. Because if you don't have one, then you probably don't have anything at all.

Opportunities are everywhere, but you must be looking for them.

One day my son found a twenty-dollar bill on the ground and told me he was lucky. I responded, "But you were also smart enough to be observant."

Ideas are ad hoc in nature—they come when they come, and forced ideas rarely come with a built-in purpose. As my friend and podcast cohost, Michele Van Tilborg, once said, "It's almost impossible to force yourself to come up with a new idea. More likely, you'll stumble across it, but take the time to develop it and find solutions." In other words, you need to practice the following action steps:

1. When you have an idea, write it down.

2. Create mini business plans for your ideas.

3. Start proving the concept by vetting your ideas with others.

We all have friends and family we might trust, but we're also surrounded by a lot of naysayers whose negativity can hold us back from moving forward. It's also dangerous to share with the yea-sayers in your life who will only tell you what they think you want to hear. Instead, surround yourself with the right people you can trust to vet your idea. This won't just help your business but also your mental health. Entrepreneurship has its challenges, and we don't need the extra stress that comes from those who always want to shut us down.

It may seem like some people come up with business ideas more easily than others, but from what I've experienced, it's not because they have any magical ability but because they consciously look for them. They're looking for that twenty-dollar bill. As another colleague of mine, Jeff Sass, puts it: "Be aware of what's happening in the world." By doing so, you not only see available opportunities but also can start filtering which ideas have an audience (a.k.a. potential customers) and which ones don't.

Ideas come from your own experiences.

One of our Startup Club members, Marcia Reece, once said, "Ideas come from an unfilled need in our lives." In the 1970s, her daughter loved doing arts and crafts and enjoyed drawing with chalk, but Marcia didn't want her daughter using regular chalk because of the toxic ingredients, not to mention there was a creativity limit with having only one color option.

So Marcia decided to create something called sidewalk chalk. You might have heard of it. She figured out how to make nontoxic chalk in different colors. Eventually, she started selling it at craft fairs, which became her focus groups. She learned what the right pricing was, what colors people wanted, how many should come in a package, and so on. Fast-forward a bit, and Walmart came knocking on her door, eventually carrying her product in all sixty-six stores they had at the time. The rest is history.

Ideas may be everywhere, but that doesn't mean your idea will be for everyone. Marcia also had a business idea in the early days of TSA traveling requirements. She came up with a document portfolio that could save time by presenting your boarding pass, passport, or other ID all in one convenient place. Great idea, but it never made it to first base. Presenting documents to security personnel was just not seen as a big enough problem for enough people, so it wasn't worth spending the time and money marketing it, no matter how good of an idea it was.

Ideas come from solving problems.

The best ideas solve problems. Marcia's sidewalk chalk idea was also solving a problem she had, as was another business idea she developed. If you've ever seen an older computer, the keyboards used to be very thick and clunky, and a day filled with typing caused her considerable wrist pain. She

❝ The best ideas solve problems. ❞

quickly realized that she wasn't the only one experiencing this problem, so she created a gel-filled wrist rest, which became a popular office accessory for a long time.

This is the mental shift that needs to happen when looking at a problem: instead of complaining about the problem, find a solution to it. And because problems are everywhere, it means that ideas can be everywhere too.

Take Cindy Santa Cruz, who won the P&G Ventures Innovation Challenge in 2022. She founded her company, Lady Patch, around the idea of helping women find a safe and effective way to solve the all too common problem of accidental urination that couldn't be comfortably addressed with existing personal care products.

In fact, it all started with her desire to help her mother, who was struggling with incontinence but was embarrassed to discuss it with others. By looking for solutions to this problem, she not only started a business but also created an incredible product that could help restore dignity and confidence for women—including her mother.

Ideas come from transforming problems into opportunities.

Sometimes you get ideas by turning a problem into a resource. Rocket scientist Bill Birgen developed a product that could help food keep fresher longer because he was having problems keeping his lunch fresh. After tossing out too many soggy salads, he developed a prototype for his invention SAVRpak to keep his lunch fresh.

After being its sole user for five years, he heard others expressing their frustration with the same problem, and he realized that he had already solved the problem for himself—and could help others not only save their lunches but also reduce food waste on a larger scale in the agriculture industry. He transformed his problems into an opportunity.

Or Richard Hanbury, who, at the age of nineteen, was in a head-on collision that led to spinal cord injuries and a ripped aorta that nearly killed him. Afterward, the nerve damage and resulting chronic pain were so bad that he was told he would have only five years to live and a diminishing quality of life. But a series of circumstances—including a Bruce Willis movie—led him to research meditation and to utilize audiovisual modulations to repair nerve damage. In three months, he was able to recover from his nerve damage, and for nearly three decades, he has been helping others do the same through his company, Sana Health.

Not every good idea is a slam dunk, and not all ideas are equal. Since the idea itself has a huge impact on whether or not you will be successful, it's not simply a matter of whether the idea is good. If you want it to really take off as a business, it must answer the following questions:

- ➔ Does it solve a real problem?

- ➔ Is it scalable? That is, does it solve a problem for enough people to grow the business?

- ➔ Is it protectable? Can you create a moat that defends your idea long enough for the business to grow?

We'll talk more about scaling and protecting your ideas soon, but these questions will at least help you know whether you're on the right track or whether your idea can provide real value to others, allowing it to grow into a viable business.

You need to love your idea.

There's a lot to be said about loving your idea. Startups tend to be a roller coaster, so when you are weighing different ideas, my advice is to go with the one you love most, because love is what will sustain you through the low periods and give you the motivation to keep going.

As long as it's an idea you love, you will be committed to see it through when you might otherwise be tempted to quit too soon. In my experience, loving your idea is also key in leading others to love your idea too.

It can also help you know when you need to move on from an idea or to prioritize one over another. In college, my brother, Bill, and I ran a successful BBS (bulletin board service) called Computer-Link. In fact, we had grown into the second largest BBS in Canada at the time.

But people were starting to talk about this thing called the internet. Even though I had never used the web myself, I was fascinated with it and fell in love with the idea of ISPs (internet service providers). As a couple of college kids, we knew that we couldn't do both a BBS and an ISP at the same time, so we had to make a choice. Even though we were getting good cash flow from the BBS, we loved the ISP idea more, so we decided to close down ComputerLink, repurpose the phone line resources we had, and launch Internet Direct, which went on to become the largest ISP in Canada during its heyday.

ComputerLink wasn't a bad idea, but sometimes love for another idea can direct you to your next business, and I'm glad we didn't just stick with what was comfortable. Eventually, ComputerLink would have been forced out of business by the internet. Instead, we were able to close it on our own terms and use that success to take action on our next idea.

Which leads us to one more important idea …

Ideas can come from your current job or business.

You don't have to come up with a brand-new, earth-shattering idea. It's also okay to take an existing idea and improve upon it. After all, I didn't come up with the idea of vacation rentals—I simply found a way to improve upon it. And the same thing for Internet Direct—it evolved out of the work and resources we'd built with ComputerLink.

I remember being called in 1998 by a gentleman at Sasktel in Canada who was interested in licensing the web hosting platform we had built for the ISP. The bells went off. If this company wanted to license out our platform, then it was likely that other telecoms would as well. So we launched a new company—Hostopia—offering private label web hosting and email solutions to small businesses. Today, it remains a successful company and continues to provide services to the largest telecoms in the world.

Maybe you're still working for someone else and don't know what idea you'll pursue. You can still put yourself in the right environment to identify opportunities like Bill Birgen did when he created SAVRpak. At the very least, get yourself into an industry you enjoy, and do something you love.

That's why I think it's essential to be on the lookout for new ideas wherever you are right now. Listen to what's going on in that industry, learn from the experiences you have in that job, and find the bottlenecks or the problems within the industry so that you can start brainstorming solutions, which can then turn into a product or service. You are a product of your environment, so be in an environment that allows you to see the twenty-dollar bill lying on the ground.

> **Ideas are everywhere if you're looking for solutions.**

Ideas are everywhere if you're looking for solutions. Once you have an idea you love, one that solves a problem or improves upon a solution, don't stop there. Because the next step is to start taking actions that transform your idea into a reality.

CHAPTER 2:

From Idea to Action

AT HOSTOPIA, MY business partners and I traveled all over the world selling our platform to telecoms like AT&T, Vodafone, British Telecom … you get the idea. In 2008, we were sitting in a Ukrainian dacha (cabin) during one of our trips there and lamenting the fact that it was so hard to find a taxi when we traveled. It drove us nuts. We just could not figure out how to get around and instead found ourselves stranded in remote office parks in foreign countries.

Then eureka—we had an idea! What if we created an app that could use GPS technology to find the nearest taxi and hail it for you and then you could watch its progress on the app so that you could get in as it arrived?

We decided to call this new app MyYellowButton and even bought the domain name for it. But that's where the idea ended. Instead, we spent our time and resources on another business idea, Brisk Mobile, where we were developing game apps for mobile.

So while Brisk Mobile ended up as one of my business ideas that didn't pan out, Uber came along and reinvented ride hailing with their app while our MyYellowButton idea remained just an idea. I can finally laugh about it now, but at the time when Uber was really blowing up, I felt like we'd been so stupid for not taking action on our own idea years before Uber launched.

The moral of the story is this: don't be one of those people who talks about ideas but never acts on them and then later on says, "That was my idea!"

Ideas are worthless; acting on them is what is valuable.

Serial entrepreneurs can find themselves plagued with the problem of finding ideas everywhere but then never stop *thinking* about their new ideas. They struggle to filter through them and then find the right ones to take action on.

In the last chapter, we talked about the importance of starting to prove your ideas by talking about them with others. Vetting an idea must go beyond simply seeing if others think it's good too, though that's part of it. After all, if you're the only one who thinks it's a good idea, it's better to kill it fast rather than spend more time on it. And if it's a good idea, then it's better to strike hard and act swiftly.

A common misconception I see in some entrepreneurs is the notion that you can only take action on an idea that helps solve a major social good, like global warming. If your idea does that, great. But I would argue that even if your idea is solving small problems, it's still making the world a better place.

Share your new ideas with everyone.

Now don't share with literally everyone—you don't want someone running off with your great idea. Just ask the Winklevoss twins how that worked out for them with Facebook.

We also already discussed caution with approaching both the naysayers and the yea-sayers in your life. But once you've weeded those groups out, sharing your ideas with others is the first practical action you can take. In fact, I would go as far as to say that sharing *increases* your chances of success.

> **Sharing your ideas with others is the first practical action you can take.**

A good way to look at it is that you're consulting with those who are closest to your idea. When bringing an idea to launch, my colleague Jeff once said, "You want those advisors to be people who have an understanding of and interest in the space you're going into." Also, consider who the end customers will be, and see if you can get their advice and feedback as well.

For one thing, it may help you improve upon your idea. Others may have suggestions that strengthen the idea, make it more viable, or even provide your next action steps. You need to accept early on that you may not have all the answers.

For another thing, sharing with others may help you determine those you need to bring your idea to life, whether it's finding the right business partner to join you, an investor, or even a mentor who can help propel your idea to the next level.

For example, you might want to build a rocket ship, but do you have the expertise to do so? No? Then you might need to partner with someone who does. A classic example of this is the Steve Jobs-Steve Wozniak partnership. You had Jobs, the idea man, but he needed

Wozniak, the technical man who could bring the idea to life. As an idea guy myself, early on I have been fortunate to partner with my brother, Bill, who understands the plumbing and wiring behind technology better than I ever could.

Sharing your idea with others can also help you perform your first bits of market research and answer these questions: Is someone else already doing this? If not, then why not? Is there no market or no demand? If yes, then what makes your idea different and gives you a fighting chance?

Look for idea incubators and accelerator programs.

Maybe you've never heard of this concept before, but if you're wary of getting feedback from people you know, or you simply want to expand your circle of support, then consider joining an incubator or accelerator. I think you'll be absolutely amazed by how much effort and time volunteers will put in to help you launch your startup. Here you test and refine your idea alongside other entrepreneurs, practice your pitch, find sources of capital, and make contacts you never would have if you were just flying solo. And here's the best part: most of them are free—or nearly free!

An example comes from one of our Startup Club guests, John Wensveen, who heads up the Alan B. Levan Center of Innovation at NSU Broward. He compares their work as being like a "theme park for entrepreneurs," describing how there's no shortage of entrepreneurs who are devoted to their ideas—that's the common denominator among all their participants. So the focus of incubation is not to create love for an idea but to remove the common barriers faced by startup entrepreneurs and help set them up for success. Leaning into his theme park analogy, John says that they "identify rides, if you will, and at every twist, every turn throughout that founder's journey, there's some kind of return on investment, not just for the entrepreneur but for all of the stakeholders that make them successful throughout that journey."

They set up entrepreneurs for success through a number of avenues, from virtual events, to pitching ideas to intake committees, to mapping out a specific plan, to helping people set up their LLCs, and even to providing introductions to strategic partner companies. But the main purpose behind such incubator programs is to give entrepreneurs a safe place to test things out, receive honest and helpful feedback, and obtain assistance from others with the knowledge and skills to get a strong start.

Carrie Purcell, CEO and cofounder of Tech-Adaptika, is taking idea incubation to the next level by providing a metaverse space where entrepreneurs can test out and grow their ideas before launching them into the real world. Her key advice is striking in its simplicity: "If you wait until you have everything you think you need in place, you probably won't get there." By allowing entrepreneurs a virtual environment to interact within, they can build lots of small test cases, minimize risk, and make key adjustments based on the input received.

These are just two examples of such programs—many entrepreneurs simply aren't aware of their existence and offerings. But a good place to start is by looking into local universities and colleges, as there are several offering similar incubator and accelerator programs for local entrepreneurs, and they may offer other resources for startups or even networking options for local investors. And don't think that it's just for college students—I've done incubator cohorts where some of the participants were in their sixties!

Visualization is key.

This may not sound like an action step, but in my own experience, it can prove the most powerful. I often find that I take actions on those ideas that I can visualize the best. To connect this to the previous point, maybe you can visualize your idea, but can others visualize it as well?

This can be a great way to test the strength of the idea, and it ties in well with utilizing an incubator program where you're compelled to paint a picture for others. Most incubators will help you work on your pitch—one that takes no more than a thirty-second elevator ride to convince a potential investor to understand and care about what you do, what problem it solves, and how you can drive sales.

Visualization can also factor into your vetting process by helping you define the purpose of the business by doing the following:

➔ Picturing your target market: "Who am I selling to?"

➔ Establishing your brand: "What space do I want to own?"

➔ Providing a solution: "What problem am I solving?"

Coming up with a name or logo too early can be dangerous if you haven't figured these things out, but if those visual cues can help you identify these and strengthen your idea, then they can prove to be an asset.

Your name tells a story.

Speaking of, your name and logo are an obvious evolution of visualization. Naming a thing makes it go from *not* real to real. When I named one of my vacation rentals Sunset Escape, we hadn't even closed on the property yet. But the name was so vivid in my mind that I hired a graphic artist to help me come up with the logo.

On the branding side of things, this is all about the space you want to own and how people can find you. It means picking a killer domain name—something that increases your SEO value, if possible, so that you can be more easily found by your potential customers. It can also help communicate what you want your brand to mean—that is, who you're for. Part of the reason why we picked the name Sunset Escape is that the home faces west over the Gulf of Mexico, so it has killer sunsets. We wanted to impart the benefit of the great view in the name.

In the last chapter, we talked about Bill Birgen's startup SAVRpak, but that wasn't the company's original name. At first he called it Soggy Salad Sucks. While that certainly tells a story, it wasn't a scalable story, since his product is good for more than just keeping a salad fresh—it could also apply to keeping other foods fresh for longer, like french fries being delivered.

On a practical level, there are some very simple actions you take to make sure the name you want is available for use. In the US, there's the free TESS database, and in Canada there's the NUANS database. Using either of these methods, it usually takes about five minutes to see if the name is available, putting you one step closer to bringing your idea to life.

Unfortunately, this can be a very expensive lesson. I was working with a startup that had launched a brand only to later discover that they had been using a trademark owned by a Fortune 500 company selling in their same category. Ouch!

We spent an afternoon coming up with a great new—and *available*—name, but this failure to check on the name first was really expensive to their startup, as they lost branding and "Google juice," had to make website changes, and so on. Take five minutes to check it out before you register that domain name.

Don't bring in investors too soon.

Sometimes new entrepreneurs think they need to jump straight to finding investors or venture capital before they can act upon their ideas. But it's more important to first figure out whether you can actually attract paying customers. Before you can ask people for money, you need to prove that your idea is investable.

To do this, you can create some prototypes, run a Kickstarter campaign, or even seek out government grants or other organizations that support startups. At the end of the day, the more you can do *without* getting investors, the better off you'll be in the long run and the happier you'll be. Bringing investors in at early stages can be highly dilutive.

Why? Because investors are nervous by nature. They would rather invest at a higher valuation for a more certain outcome. Seldom do you see professional investors making bets on early-stage startups. And if they do invest, they're looking for huge slices of the pie.

In order to attract investors, you need to prove your concept. And I don't mean just a minimum viable product; I'm also referring to proving that you can sell it. Most investors prefer to augment your growth rather than to jump-start it. Through these other methods, you not only can build your business by taking action on your idea but also you can gather the market research you need, build positive feedback, and establish good local PR, even if your long-term goals are national or global.

We'll talk about investors more throughout the book, especially when we get to Scale. I'm not anti-investor by any means. In fact, it's the opposite. You just have to understand that you're giving up a lot of ownership and control once you bring them in, since they're footing the bill. There will be a time and a place for outside investors, which we'll discuss in more detail later.

For many of us, our business is something we start and run for many years. Giving up 25 percent of your company for a small investment is basically the same as signing up to an additional 25 percent tax rate for the life of your company. Is that really something you're willing to do? For me, watching the show *Shark Tank* is heartbreaking. I won't deny that the media attention may help some of these companies become successful, and it may be worth the pill they swallow to get a deal done. However, it pains me to see how much equity these early-stage founders give up.

Sleep on it.

This is just a bit of good old-fashioned advice. One of the best practical actions you can take doesn't sound like an action at all—sleep on it. New ideas are exciting, but sometimes excitement can turn out to be a blind spot. You may learn some things in the first day or two that show it's not an idea worth pursuing. Or you may find that it's definitely worth pursuing. But there's simply no replacement for taking a moment to let your idea simmer. I wonder if Elon Musk should have considered this before throwing out a fifty-four-dollar per share takeover bid for Twitter.

Sleeping on it supports all these other action points: Do you still feel like sharing the idea with others? Can you visualize it? Do you have a name? Do you know what problem you're solving or who your target market is?

Maybe you're thinking, "Colin, these actions are so simple." Right. That's the point. One of the biggest reasons why people don't act on their ideas is because there's a big scary unknown of what needs to happen next. But by taking these very simple actions, you can remove that scary unknown and plot a way forward. After all, taking action on your idea is what

&& Taking action on your idea is what makes innovation happen. 77

makes innovation happen, and catching the next wave of innovation is critical to determine whether your startup has the legs to not only survive but also thrive in a less competitive environment.

CHAPTER 3:

Catching the Next Wave Is Critical

THERE'S SOMETHING TO BE SAID about the cliché of being in the right place at the right time. In entrepreneurship, it might be more accurate to say the right *idea* at the right time. Over the years, I've discovered a pattern in how new products and services emerge around new technology or regulatory/market changes. I've seen the advent of the World Wide Web—or at the time, it was called the information superhighway—followed by the advent of broadband in 2000, resulting in the emergence of cloud computing and social media, the rise of microbrand and e-commerce companies in the 2010s, how the pandemic changed the way we work and travel, and how AI is going to transform industries in the 2020s.

Around the year 2000, my colleague Jeff had a groundbreaking idea that he dubbed Barpoint.com. The idea was to provide a platform where consumers could scan a barcode for a product and instantly see reviews and price comparisons for it to make sure they were getting the best deal.

There was only one problem: the market wasn't ready for this groundbreaking idea. This was well before the era of smartphones and the ubiquity of QR codes, as online shopping was still in its infancy. In short, he'd built a great surfboard … but there was no wave to ride it.

Timing is essential.

A game-changing book in my own entrepreneurship journey has been *Crossing the Chasm*, by Geoffrey Moore. In it, Moore changed the conventional thinking around technology adoption by introducing his concept of the chasm, which is the space between the early adopters of a technology solution who are enthusiasts and excited about the tech simply for the sake of it and the risk-averse pragmatists who adopt the technology only once it has built a track record of verified reviews and references.

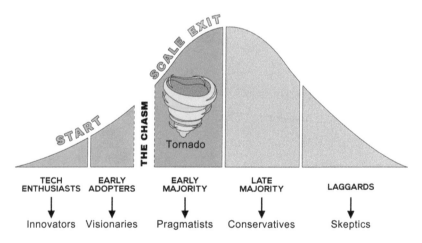

Adapted from Moore, Geoffrey, A. (2014). Crossing the Chasm: Marketing and Selling Disruptive Products to Mainstream Customers.

The chasm has to be crossed before the tech can become viable in the market, which means it can prove to be a dark, dark place for new tech. It's easy for new technology solutions to fall into the chasm and never find their way to the greater public. But once a new tech has crossed the chasm, it becomes ubiquitous. Here's a case in point: everyone has a smartphone today. Even my mother, who has somehow managed to live without a credit card her whole life, has a smartphone. That wasn't the case in 2000.

Some entrepreneurs are particularly good at figuring out what is coming next—people like Elon Musk, Steve Jobs, and Bill Gates. Fortunately, I have been able to see the way the wind is blowing and position my companies correctly. I do believe this is a skill that can be learned, and it simply means being more aware of your society, your surroundings, and your industry.

Not every technology can cross the chasm, or at least not as fast as the startup might like. Virtual reality is a good current example of this, as I believe it's still in the chasm and will be for a while. Mark Zuckerberg learned this in 2022 as the metaverse struggled to catch on with a wider audience. We'll see what Meta (Facebook) can deliver over the next few years, but given the stock price, investor confidence isn't quite there yet. If you want to build an Oculus application, by all means you're allowed to do so, but you might be heading down a dark and dangerous path, since the market isn't ready for your product. At least not yet.

Another example is Apple's original tablet, the Newton. It failed because it was released into a market that wasn't ready to embrace it, falling into the chasm and never finding its way to the pragmatists, where it could begin to scale. Likewise, with any startup, you want to make sure that you are neither too far ahead of the wave where no one cares about your product or service nor so far behind that the market share is already dominated by others. We don't know when the chasm will end, but we do know that if we position ourselves correctly, we can win the ultimate prize: leadership in our space and the spoils of war that come along with it.

Ideas live in the future.

I've always been an early adopter of the latest tech. It started when my father bought the family a 4K Sinclair computer in 1977, when I was seven years old. I also had one of the first HDTVs in Canada, I've always sought out the fastest available internet connection, and I bought one of the first Tesla Model Xs—number 984 to be exact. I believe that if you can live in the future with an entrepreneurial mindset, you can start to see opportunities that exist around emerging technology before the general population is using those services.

And it doesn't always require making expensive purchases. I recently bought an NFT for fifty dollars that was developed by a tenth-grade student. Although the NFT was intriguing, it wasn't the main motivator. I wanted to understand exactly what was involved by actually going through the NFT-buying process. In doing so, I learned quite a bit about what it takes to acquire NFTs, and I can say that it's *not* easy. It took me a couple of days to figure it all out. Opportunity knocks for those who can simplify processes and make technology easier to use. NFTs are by no means out of the chasm, but learning about how they work is an important step.

Bill Gates once said that the mission of Microsoft was to put "a computer on every desk and in every home," but after I bought a PalmPilot early on, I said that one day there would be "a computer in every hand." From using the PalmPilot in the beginning stages, I was able to think of ways that our company Tucows could capitalize on the new tech before the general population had adopted it. We launched application sites long before there was the App Store, because we could anticipate what kind of applications people would want on their PDAs once they became more commonplace.

So we were able to get ahead of the wave just enough to ride it, and subsequently we were able to position Tucows for a healthy sale price when it came time for us to exit and move on. This doesn't mean your idea has to be tech itself to thrive in a wave, but you can look at the tech to help you gauge whether your idea is going to be able to catch that wave at the right moment to be successful. The next step is having a computer in everything—what is termed IoT, the Internet of Things. Those who move the fastest in a Moore tornado win.

It's not the first person who wins but whoever can deliver the fastest.

At the end of the day, this was the biggest takeaway for me from Moore's writing. Timing isn't about being the first one in the market but about being in the position to deliver the quickest when the wave swells.

> Timing isn't about being the first one in the market but about being in the position to deliver the quickest when the wave swells.

It's what gave AOL the lead in the US. A few may remember the late 1990s when AOL was dropping their diskettes in every magazine—it became so pervasive that we started using them as coasters in our office. AOL dominated in the early years because no matter who you were, you were getting hit with their free diskettes to activate your internet account. At Internet Direct, we were able to beat out AOL in Canada because we established a broad distribution network before they arrived. Getting to the wave first doesn't mean much if your product isn't ready to effectively deliver when the demand swells.

In other words, rather than rushing a product out to a market that may not be ready for it, focus your time and energy on some initial exploratory projects and gauging interest in the market. This could include consulting others around your area of interest or expertise, which is something you can charge for even as you're collecting information about whether the timing is right.

Once you have the necessary data to judge that the timing is right, then you can move forward with production. If you've identified in the exploratory work that your product or service is needed and solves a problem, then you can have the confidence to move forward. Just because someone else is already in the space doesn't mean you can't also help—and you can possibly improve upon their solution.

Earlier I referred to the opportunity for some enterprising entrepreneurs to make purchasing NFTs easy. This is key for winning adoption from the early majority. Generally, new technology gains adoption among innovators and early adopters who tend to be tech savvy. I, on the other hand, am not a geek and only aspire to be one, so I see the challenges existing around the adoption of technologies like NFTs that the early adopters overlook.

On that note, one tactic we used was "Make It Easy" and "Market Easy." In 1994, we had a competitor in Toronto who did a great job appealing to computer geeks. They ran ads for their internet service provider featuring Jolt Colas dropping from the sky. What that has to do with internet access, I have no idea. I guess a lot of geeks were drinking Jolt Cola at the time.

We responded with pictures of a happy baby floating in the sky, excited to get on the internet. And although the other provider was the first to market in Toronto, we did a better job of appealing to the early *majority* adopters, not just the early adopters, which accelerated our growth and ultimately led to their bankruptcy in 1996. A similar story played out in the US with CompuServe and AOL, where the former led the market with the early adopters but the latter won the market with the early majority. Who will win in the NFT market? Will OpenSea become the next CompuServe, with Coinbase winning with a faster and easier network? Or will another startup come along to deliver a winning move? Or will NFTs simply die in the chasm?

We continued to work on "Making It Easy" on all of our subsequent companies, even naming our products EasySiteWizard, EasyHosting, EasyStoreMaker, etc. When the wave swells, the companies that deliver their solutions faster and easier than their competitors will likely be the winners, even if they have fewer bells and whistles in their offering.

Don't try to change customer behavior.

An easy rule of thumb to gauge whether the timing is right is to ask yourself, "Am I trying to change customer behavior?" If so, then that can be a red flag, and you may need to either kill the idea or pivot it in a way that doesn't demand disruptive behavior change—or plan to settle in for the long haul. With Barpoint.com, Jeff fell deep into the chasm because as forward-thinking as his idea was, it would be a success only if enough customers changed their buying behaviors— and it would be another decade or so before buyer preferences reached that point. For me, I'd rather position for evolutions versus revolutions. It's a lot easier to predict the former.

There's nothing wrong with being disruptive in the marketplace, but the more disruptive you are to the customer's behavior, the less chance of success. We were lucky enough to have Geoffrey Moore share examples of this insight during one of our Startup Club live shows during which he pointed out, "Uber and Airbnb leveraged the existing technology to benefit from the marketplace. Their disruption was in the industry, not in consumer behavior. People were already hailing cabs and staying in hotels."

For example, when I purchased that NFT, it was a change in the way I've typically purchased items on the internet. There was no one-click purchase on the OpenSea platform. Instead, it involved complicated techniques, including opening a digital wallet, transferring Ethereum to OpenSea, converting Ethereum to Polygon, and then approving it on my phone with an authenticator app. It wasn't easy. All that was combined with the fact that the image is only digital, which requires wrapping our brains around a new concept of art altogether.

If your idea requires a change in customer behavior, it's going to be very risky because you're banking on people changing just for you. More often than not, those discontinuous innovations can have the highest rewards, but just be careful to pick and choose the ones you believe will take off with the early majority. It may make more sense to hold off and wait for a market that is more receptive and more closely aligned to customer behavior than to pour a ton of time, money, and energy into an idea the world isn't ready for.

Strive for depth before breadth.

Often the best approach to ensure that you're not demanding a change in customer behavior is to focus on one problem at a time. Your service or product may be able to solve a host of problems for people, but sometimes it's best to use what Geoffrey Moore calls the bowling pin model, specializing in a fragment of your target market in the beginning while you're still small and then scaling up as you grow.

Striving for depth—or density—means having an extreme focus on your niche rather than trying to become a solution for everyone all at once. In order to cross the chasm, after winning the innovators, you've got to be able to attract the pragmatists. Pragmatic people know they aren't experts, so they rely on recommendations from friends, word of mouth, and so on.

In a 2010 study from McKinsey & Company, researchers found that as much as 50 percent of buying behavior was influenced by word of mouth, more than twice that of paid advertising.[3] Successful word of mouth can be accomplished only when there is a depth that inspires your early adopters to become evangelists to their pragmatic friends. That's how depth transforms into breadth, allowing you to then scale and even sell wider applications for your solution.

In a recent Startup Club session, I learned about two companies using the metaverse to target specific users, one in education, the other in hospitality. Clearly, the metaverse is in a deep chasm, and the companies best positioned to survive it are those that can find specific applications and can appeal to a specific set of users.

We can beat the big corporations— and then sell to them.

During my almost three years working at a Fortune 500 company, I learned that most corporations are risk-averse by nature and fearful of change. The fact is that people who are risk-takers at big companies

---

3   Jacques Bughin, Jonathan Doogan, and Ole Jørgen Vetvik, "A New Way to Measure Word-of-Mouth Marketing," McKinsey Quarterly (April 1, 2010): https://www.mckinsey.com/business-functions/marketing-and-sales/our-insights/a-new-way-to-measure-word-of-mouth-marketing.

will fail from time to time and then the knives come out. This often leads to an organization of political survivors who float to the top while the John Galts of the world find new homes.

Enter the entrepreneur.

We take the risks, we're good at figuring out what the customers really want, and we have the tenacity (or stupidity) to keep it going no matter the adversity. Ultimately this leads to a model where entrepreneurs start businesses and the large corporations acquire them. The vast majority of startup successes end with an exit.

Smart corporations acquire entrepreneurial companies, since they know we entrepreneurs thrive on innovation. They'll come to you begging to buy when you're riding the wave and have proof that you're winning in the market. This requires patience, since the big win comes from the valuation of the company after it sways the early majority.

Catching the new technology or regulatory waves isn't the only way to win. There are exceptions where startups can challenge the incumbents in mature industries. Take Allbirds, which was founded in 2014. I think we can all agree that footwear doesn't constitute an emerging technology, but they're a great example of another kind of wave: the social-conscious consumer. Climate change is a problem on the forefront of many consumers' minds, and by positioning themselves as an eco-friendly brand, Allbirds has been able to catch the wave at a critical moment and find success. Unfortunately, they were crushed in 2022 like most e-commerce companies, which is another reason to point out that when things are good, it may be better to exit than to continue to grow. More on that later in Exit.

If you're struggling to narrow down your ideas, it's worth looking at some of the current upcoming waves and technology trends that are already generating new problems ready for entrepreneurs to solve. Here a few that the members have talked about in Startup Club:

➤ Artificial intelligence

    ▫ ChatGPT, an natural language processing tool by OpenAI

    ▫ DALL-E, an image creator based on written descriptions by OpenAI

➤ E-commerce

➤ Cryptocurrency

➤ Blockchain

➤ NFTs

➤ Virtual reality

➤ Augmented reality

➤ Blockchain technology

➤ Energy storage

➤ Robotics

➤ Drone technology

➤ Metaverse

➤ Self-driving vehicles

➤ Tokenizing assets, including real estate

➤ Everything green

➤ Online teaching (think MasterClass, Udemy, video-based coaching)

➤ Online counseling

➤ Gene editing (CRISPR)

➤ Cloud computing

➤ Mobile app development

➜ Sharing economy (Airbnb, Vrbo, Turo, Boatsetter)

➜ Social audio chat and podcasting

➜ Creator economy

➜ Social influencers (YouTube channel, newsletter marketing)

Time and time again, we have launched businesses in new spaces, catching the next big wave, the latest being the rise of AI when ChatGPT 3.5 and DALL-E 2 launched in late 2022. The potential to transform existing industries and open opportunities for startups will be huge as AI continues to make great advances. The concept of looking at the waves and trends in the market is, I believe, a fairly simple but underutilized strategy for entrepreneurs to vet their idea and assess the next steps forward. Too often I see young business grads launch trendy T-shirts or cool bar apps only to find it a very difficult business to grow. But if you can get traction in a startup benefiting from the rise of a wave, you have less competition from the big companies. It's that simple.

> **The concept of looking at the waves and trends in the market is, I believe, a fairly simple but underutilized strategy for entrepreneurs to vet their idea and assess the next steps forward.**

CHAPTER 4

Focus on Something You (and Others) Love

REMEMBER IN CHAPTER 1 when I talked about how we shut down our thriving BBS company, ComputerLink, to start an ISP called Internet Direct? It was a bit controversial since ComputerLink was profitable, but ultimately we loved the idea of Internet Direct more. So we ditched a profit-producing company and used its assets to help us venture into the uncharted waters in the burgeoning internet industry.

Keep in mind that this was 1993, so the internet was still very much new. We were excited by its possibilities—for business, education, file sharing, commerce, and everything in between. While the story of Internet Direct didn't end the way I'd hoped it would (more on that later), I don't regret this decision at all. Despite the risk involved, it was the right choice—because we focused on something not only that we loved but that others loved too.

Don't fall in love with your business and go down with it.

There's a subtle difference between loving your idea and loving your business. Instead of falling in love with your business to the point that you go down with the ship, it's important to focus on the reason you started the business in the first place.

While running ComputerLink, I remember attending the BBS conventions in the early 1990s, where we would meet up with many other BBS operators who had created commercial success. Several years later, after they changed the name of the conference to ISP Con, several of the operators had failed to move on and still clung to the early days and successes from their BBS. They couldn't accept that the industry had been a moment in time and that the moment had passed.

A revolution greater than the Industrial Revolution was about to occur. The idea we loved about the BBS would live on through the internet, but the specific vehicle was being replaced. The opportunities were simply enormous, yet some hung on to their buggy whip.

Had we held on too, ComputerLink would have eventually been forced out of business like the rest of them. Don't get me wrong, we loved the idea of the BBS and reminisced for years over the good old days. If we had the money, we would have kept both businesses. We even attempted to launch our BBS on the internet but with no success. We missed the social aspect and local feel that the BBS brought about, but we had to move on.

Serial entrepreneurs must avoid being serial.

One of my biggest personal issues is that I want to launch a new company every other week. I get so excited about an idea, and it boosts something in my brain akin to a gambler winning a hand in blackjack. I am convinced that entrepreneurship should be classified as a drug.

Many serial entrepreneurs don't struggle with coming up with ideas—they struggle with picking one and sticking with it. Even within a company, entrepreneurs often make the mistake of launching too many initiatives when, in reality, they should launch fewer and be more focused. It's easy to want to jump on the bandwagon of whatever the new, shiny thing is, so sometimes the best thing you can do to cut through the noise is to ask yourself, "Which idea do I truly love?"

> **Many serial entrepreneurs don't struggle with coming up with ideas—they struggle with picking one and sticking with it.**

Not to beat a dead horse, but if you still feel stuck, that's why it's all the more important to share your idea with others and to see what they love as well. Excitement can be contagious, so if you feel your affections pulled between a couple of ideas, others may be able to help you pick the right love to follow.

Love will see you through the hard times.

Other than my family, there are two things I really love: dogs and how technology can help humanity. And it is for these reasons that I have stuck with our e-commerce pet product company, Paw.com, for the last six years, going from periods of high growth and high profits to periods of no growth and low profits. Or in other words, times when

I've partied like it's 1999 and times when I wanted to climb back into my cave and curl up into a ball. No one is immune to the ups and downs; we face them all the time as entrepreneurs.

Sometimes the biggest question you have to ask yourself is, "Do I love what my startup is doing? What is it achieving? How is it helping people? Or do I just love making money?"

I discussed the term *love* with my book coach. Does it really have to be such a strong word like *love*? The fact is that there just isn't another way to describe the massive commitment you will need to make on behalf of your startup for the next ten years or more.

There's nothing wrong with liking to make money. Everyone likes being able to pay their bills, go on vacation, send their kids to school, and all the other things you need money for. But startups tend to be a roller coaster, and when you have a bad month when sales dip (and so does your cash flow), then it's inevitable that your feelings and interest will dip too. But when you have a deep love for your company's purpose or what your company is accomplishing, then it will sustain you through those tough seasons.

> **There is an overlap between love and patience, and you'll be more patient with the idea you love the most.**

There is an overlap between love and patience, and you'll be more patient with the idea you love the most. Some ideas you come across may feel like a sure thing because it's what everyone else is doing, but loving your idea will give you the motivation to keep going when you need to get through those difficult days.

As long as it's an idea you love, you will be committed to see it through when you might otherwise be tempted to quit too soon. Furthermore, in my experience, loving your idea is key because it can often lead to helping others love your idea too. Enthusiasm is contagious, but *authentic* enthusiasm is even more contagious, which can come in very handy whenever you're pitching to a potential investor, recruiting a new business partner, or hiring that hard-to-get key employee.

Your idea should reflect your values.

The question, however, is, "How do I quantify the level of love for my ideas?" It's not as simple as writing a pros and cons list. But I still believe that you can write down what you like the most about each idea and what excites you about each idea and then assess how each idea aligns with your personal values.

For example, if you feel deeply about climate issues, ask, "How does this idea promote sustainability?" If you feel strongly about helping parents, ask, "How does this product help to destress parenting?"

With Paw.com, my partners and I wanted to find ways to help senior dogs. I had three King Charles spaniels at the time, and they were aging, so coming out with products that helped them feel more comfortable kept me going on a personal level. Sometimes a simple exercise like this, checking how your idea reflects your values, can really clarify which idea you truly love the most.

This is another area where seeing what others love can prove absolutely essential. If one of your ideas appears to incite more excitement in others to the point that they want to come alongside you and help you grow your idea, then it can really help you understand. When you find that you have an idea that reflects not only your values but also the values of others, *and* it solves a problem, then you might not need to look any further. Real love for an idea has a way of cutting through both the naysayers and the yea-sayers we discussed earlier and finding those who are genuine in their input.

Furthermore, you can love different things about your business in different ways. For example, you may not love the product or service per se, but maybe you love the impact you're able to make through it. If you have multiple businesses, you might even find that you love each of them for different reasons and in different ways. There's nothing wrong with that.

I know that this concept of loving your idea can feel a little too fluffy for a business book, but life is too short to focus your time, attention, and resources on chasing after ideas that you and others aren't really excited about. Once you've figured that out, there are two very foundational questions that will help the idea you love on the road to success:

First, can you scale it?

And second, can you defend it?

CHAPTER 5:

Pick an Idea That Can Scale

EVERY BUSINESS COMES with unique challenges, regardless of its size. In fact, I'd argue that it's just as hard to run a small business—and it's arguably even more difficult to run a small business than running a business that can scale. I know this probably sounds counterintuitive, which is why I always advise people, even in the startup phase, to pick a business idea that can scale.

For the past ten years, my wife and I have owned a Montessori school with a capacity of 110 students. The school building itself was a substantial investment, and as the classes started to fill up, we entertained the idea of buying some neighboring lots so that we could expand our capacity. However, doing so would have required municipal approval, which would have been very difficult to get, not to mention a significant financial investment to acquire the additional real estate.

Next, we looked at renovating the current building—could we expand capacity by adding an additional floor? But we soon learned that renovation costs would be just as much as constructing a brand-new building, so we decided not to move forward. No matter what, for us to scale the school from 110 students to 111 students, it would have required hundreds of thousands to potentially millions of dollars in infrastructure costs, not to mention the added expenses of equipment, hiring staff, and other expansion costs. And if 2022 taught us anything, it's that hiring has become much more difficult.

We learned the hard way that the school was a very, very difficult business to scale. And we had to learn to be okay with that. Most businesses have the capacity to scale, which can then generate significant revenue with higher profit margins, but some are significantly more difficult to scale than others.

For example, businesses limited to physical space like retail stores, gyms, and medical offices all will have limits to how much they can scale based not only on space limitations but also on the owner's time and ability to be in multiple places. I am an advocate for early entrepreneurs to explore franchises as part of a way to learn the trade of entrepreneurship, but be aware that it's difficult to scale a franchise beyond what's allowed in the agreement.

Pick an idea that can scale.

When selecting your startup idea, you need to determine your comfortability with scaling, specifically what will be involved for you to scale. Can you scale a restaurant or medical office by acquiring and launching more and more locations? Sure! But it's difficult, expensive, and time consuming to pull it off, so you need to understand the choice you're making when you start.

> **When selecting your startup idea, you need to determine your comfortability with scaling.**

This isn't to say that a small business can't be a great lifestyle business. Many entrepreneurs are content to run their own location and never scale beyond that. My wife is perfectly happy with how the school is doing today and has no desire to expand it. Even so, the choice *not* to scale is a lifestyle choice because you're deciding to limit your profit possibilities based on the type of lifestyle you want to live and how much time you want to give to it. This is why many people choose real estate—it's a great lifestyle business because you can generate considerable wealth over the long term. Even then, you're making the choice on how much to scale it, how many clients to take on, how much you want to diversify the properties, and so on.

Either way, scaling—or not scaling—is a choice. Most businesses don't simply stumble into scaling, at least not successfully. So while you may know what idea you really love, you have to decide what you're comfortable with in terms of scaling the idea—that is, how much of your time, energy, and resources are you willing to put into growing it? This can be a very difficult question for even an experienced serial entrepreneur to answer, which is where rating your idea's scalability can help you set proper expectations.

Rate your idea's scalability.

If you're in a position where you have a blank slate, then you absolutely must consider the scalability of your ideas based on what you're comfortable with. Personally, I use a 1 to 5 scale, where 1 represents the least scalable and 5 the most.

For example, one of the companies we started was called Brisk Mobile, a mobile development company with a time and materials model. It is frustratingly hard to scale profitably because doing so requires more space, more people, and more contract wins. I would give it a 2 out of 5 on my index because of these difficulties. On the flip side, .CLUB Domains has a worldwide marketplace with very high profit margins. I would rate it a 5 based on the fact that we signed up almost a million domains during the time we owned it.

Both companies are technology companies, both require great people to scale, and both require capital to start, so what's the difference between the two? Although I required great people to start .CLUB, I required far fewer people to support a much larger revenue base. Brisk, on the other hand, built revenue through consulting, which required both a heavy dose of people with the right skills and a heavy dose of time. Ultimately, we decided to pull out of Brisk and sold the company off, simply recovering our initial investment after running it for over ten years.

There's nothing wrong with moving forward with an idea that's harder to scale, but you must have a realistic expectation of the capital required to grow, how difficult it is to hire the people you'll need, and so on. If you choose one that can scale with fewer roadblocks, then you'll be in a better position to defend it and grow it.

To help you rate your ideas, here are some examples on the 1 to 5 scale I use:

SCALABILITY RATING	BUSINESS TYPE	BUSINESS TYPE EXAMPLES	GROWTH CHALLENGES
1	Brick-and-mortar based	School, restaurant, retail store, medical office	Limited scalability, high fixed costs, location-dependent
2	Time-and-materials	Consulting, marketing services, customer service provider	Limited scalability, labor dependent, competition
3	Product or service-based	E-commerce business, online training	Costly inventory, high interest costs, production constraints
4	Recurring revenue business	Subscription boxes, accounting software, cloud computing	High build and personnel costs, competition, customer retention
5	Digital businesses	AI content, domain name registry, SaaS	High growth costs, distribution, market saturation, global competition

Even if you've already picked your startup idea, this is a helpful exercise so that you know what to expect out of the scaling process when you reach that point.

The more scalable the idea, the higher the risk and reward.

There are obviously lots of potential rewards to scalability like generating more revenue and making yourself more appealing to investors or buyers. While we'll dive much deeper into what is required to successfully scale in the next section of the book, it's essential to understand now that along with the possibility of higher reward, there is also the possibility of higher risk.

While scalable concepts will open you up to a larger geographic marketplace (or even global marketplace), which results in greater opportunity, you will also face greater competition. If you're catching the wave at the right time, there may be others riding it too as they fight to gain market share and who will be happy to knock you off your board if given the chance.

So don't be surprised if you have a target on your back, whether this is a competitor trying to badmouth you or an overseas company trying to copy your designs. Because whether you're still starting or ready to scale, knowing how to defend your business will be key in its ability to succeed.

CHAPTER 6:

Can You Build a Moat around Your Idea?

IF HISTORY HAS TAUGHT us one thing, it's how to build a good castle. Build it high up on a hill, surround it with shark-infested waters, make the high walls difficult to climb, and fortify it with the best cannons.

We invest a large portion of our life building our dream company, and the more we succeed, the more our competitors hit us. We have to think about ways we can strengthen our moat and protect our investment.

An easy start to building a moat is creating or buying a great domain name.

As I said earlier, I am undeniably a dog person. So it was only a matter of time before I backed a startup inspired by my love for dogs. My business partner David Gimes built a company around making high-quality products for dogs, focusing on memory foam-style dog beds and blankets, christening the business as Treat-a-Dog.

Late in 2018, though, we had the opportunity to purchase a domain name—Paw.com—that we felt would be better for both branding and search engines. The transaction was not cheap or easy, and it required us to develop a relationship with the owner of the domain name. To say the least, purchasing the domain represented a significant investment of time, money, and energy.

But the name Paw.com allowed us to reinvent our whole business, giving us the credibility we needed to win in our category. In fact, in the year following the rebranding, our business more than doubled in sales and profitability. In short, the name Paw.com created a moat for the business by giving us the opportunity to sell products under a specific, easily recognizable brand name that helped us build credibility and strengthen our relationship with our customers—something no competitor could take away from us.

Building a moat is all about defensibility.

Perhaps you can scale your idea, but can you defend it long enough to allow it to scale? If not, then you may want to go back to the drawing board. Beyond scalability, the level of defensibility for your idea is another good way to add checks and balances to your vetting process. For me, these two are very linked because an idea that can't scale may not be worth the necessary resources to defend it, and an idea you can't defend will prove challenging to scale.

There are a number of moat-building activities you can do early on in the life of your startup that can make a huge difference down the road and help the business scale.

> **" Perhaps you can scale your idea, but can you defend it long enough to allow it to scale? "**

You may come up with ideas that aren't immediately defensible, but you can still launch them and build moats around them after the fact. That's exactly what we did with Paw.com. We were far from being the first in the dog beds space, but acquiring the domain name was a moat we were able to create to protect the brand.

In fact, every entrepreneur should factor the price of a strong domain name as part of their marketing funds. It can be tempting in the early days of your startup, especially when all the funding is coming from your own pocket, to do everything on the cheap and to use the free website address provided by your hosting site of choice, but in the long term, that won't help you build your brand or defend it.

Don't forget—or ignore—legal protections.

A very practical moat for your business is to pursue patents, trademarks, and copyrights for your products. With Paw.com, we obtained both design and utility patents wherever possible. This allowed us to scare off potential copycats to maximize our share of the market. Depending on how much of the market you want to control, you may need to look into the patenting process in multiple countries.

The same could be said for obtaining a registered trademark for your company's name or copyright for other intellectual property.

Build a moat through distribution.

With Hostopia, we were late to the game when we launched our web hosting service in 1999. In our first couple of years, we tried to sell directly to small businesses, but given our delayed entry into the market, the cost of acquisition per subscriber was just too high, and there was too much competition in trying to go head-to-head with the likes of GoDaddy and major telecoms. We had no moat to protect the castle we were trying to build.

We had a great platform—in my opinion, the best in the world. We had pioneered a concept called cluster server hosting, similar to the way Google ran thousands of Linux servers for search.

The Story we had was strong. But the company wasn't going to make it on Story alone.

Not long after 9/11, we slashed millions in expenses and focused our efforts on a new strategy of distribution: We reallocated our remaining resources, staff, and funding to support a 100 percent focus on *wholesale* distribution. Believe me, it wasn't easy giving up on our initial plan, but by distributing wholesale, we could build the moat we needed and face fewer competitors. In fact, we could now turn our competitors into customers.

In our new strategy, we began meeting with telecoms, cable companies, and other hosting companies in an effort to offer our platform as a service, which is now commonly referred to as cloud computing. Companies no longer had to hire dozens of employees, develop software, and run hundreds of servers. We would do all that for them on a completely private label brand.

Interestingly enough, the first deal we cut was with our former ISP, Internet Direct. During our time there, we knew that the costs of developing our own platform were escalating and that we needed to outsource the services. We just couldn't find anyone to outsource it to.

Next, we signed a venture capital deal with Telus Ventures, which gave us access to pitch these services to the second largest telecom in Canada. After some back and forth, we cut a deal where we would buy the data center services from Telus (which amounted to millions), they would outsource their business hosting and email to us (which amounted to millions), and they would fund us in the millions. Although I'm generally negative about venture capital, this was truly an example of how partnering with a strategic investor could work to benefit both sides.

After proving the concept by signing our first ten customers, we needed to scale the company to a hundred customers. All we had to do was sell more of the same thing to similar buyers, making the sales process very repeatable. In order to do this, we needed to expand our geography from Canada to the United States and then to Europe and South America.

Eventually the company sold for a huge premium, but what gave us that premium was not only the IP but also the distribution channel. Distribution allowed us to build Hostopia on the highest hill with the highest walls and the widest moat that our competitors simply couldn't rival. In fact, I believe that the premium valuation we sold for was mostly due to the distribution moat we had created, effectively making us the gold standard in the market—a position no other company has touched in over fifteen years since selling the company.

Build a moat through exclusivity and laser focus.

There's nothing like having a corner on a market early on. How exclusive is your product or service in terms of competition? Does your idea provide something no one else can offer? While you don't *have* to be the first one on the market to be successful, it also doesn't hurt to be first so long as you're prepared to capitalize on it and not get swept away in the wave.

A good example of this in my own journey was the .club domain extension we applied for when ICANN started to allow the creation of more unique domain extensions beyond the established likes of .com, .org, .edu, .gov, and so on.

As stated earlier, .CLUB was highly scalable, but it also checked the box of defensibility because we held the exclusive rights to the .club extension. No one could compete directly with us, no matter how much money they had—not Amazon or Google. No one could take it away from us.

We had a digital widget we could sell with infinite inventory, and it was defensible because it was the only domain extension with the word .club. If you were a club or a subscription service, or even if you wanted to promote the idea that your customers were members, .club could be the go-to extension in the same way that .org is the go-to extension for nonprofits.

Sometimes we focus on areas with huge addressable markets. Of course, venture capitalists often look at this particular aspect too. If we could get 1 percent of 1 percent of the total market, we could generate $1 billion. This methodology can be very flawed, though, because it's rare that such large industries don't have vicious competitors. Sometimes success can be found by being the largest fish in a small pond. Dominating a small industry through brand and distribution can provide more protection because larger companies often don't want to go into that space.

Richard Pollack, a business partner of mine who runs a number of e-commerce companies, found a strong niche in offering decorative concrete stains. His website, DirectColors.com, features a breadth and depth of product that no other company wants to compete with in a very niche industry. His exclusivity gives him the competitive edge.

In the same way we did with scalability, I'd encourage you to rate your idea's defensibility on a scale of 1 to 5. This can be challenging to do in the Start phase, since you don't yet know what the threats to your startup will be, so it's best to look at the rating here based on the actions you can take or have already taken.

DEFENSIBILITY RATING	STAGE
1	I don't know of any ways to build a moat.
2	I have an idea of how to build a moat but haven't taken action yet.
3	I know an idea of how to build a moat and have taken at least one action.
4	I have multiple ways to protect my idea. (Ex: received a patent, exclusive distribution agreement, etc.)
5	I have an ironclad moat with supporting defenses in place. (Ex: owning multiple patents, distribution agreements, and dominating search engine results)

At the end of the day, building a moat is about taking actions in the present that can protect your idea long enough to survive the rocky Start days and begin to Scale. While success will look different for each entrepreneur, it's essential to always be looking ahead by defining for yourself—and your potential investors—what success will look like through establishing Stage Gates.

> 66 Building a moat is about taking actions in the present that can protect your idea long enough to survive the rocky Start days and begin to Scale. 99

CHAPTER 7:

Stage Gates

HAVE YOU EVER PLAYED a racing video game where you have to hit a certain checkpoint before the time runs out? Then once you hit it, you get your time extended to keep racing forward to the next checkpoint. This is the same basic idea behind the concept of Stage Gates for your startup, the milestones you have to reach to either keep moving forward (or if you don't, pivot in some way) or bring it to an end.

When we launched our company GeeksForLess, the idea was for it to be an offshore development center to provide IT human resources and professional services. Our first Stage Gate was to break even by a certain date. Once we achieved that, we then set our next Stage Gate: $1 million in profit. And then after that, a third Stage Gate: all debt paid off. These Stage Gates not only propelled us forward after achieving each extended time checkpoint but also provided a guidepost of compensation for our partner and CEO.

Stage Gates define when to keep going—and when to stop.

I promised early on not only to share my successes but also to share what I've learned from my failures. One such nonsuccess was my company Shareholder Blockchain. Our first Stage Gate for it was to have an established minimum viable product within four months. But when our programmers went rogue on us and we failed to meet that Stage Gate, I decided to shut the company down altogether.

For me, Stage Gates go beyond the typical goal setting you do within a company. Stage Gates happen on a more macro level and are a more do-or-die situation, whereas regular goals exist to support the plan to achieve the Stage Gate. In this way, it's entirely possible for your company to miss some goals and yet still hit the necessary Stage Gates to continue.

For example, you may have a goal to increase sales by 25 percent during Q3, but your Stage Gate might be—like my earlier example— to get ten clients. Then the end of Q3 comes and you find that you increased sales by only 15 percent, but because you created some greater efficiencies and cost cutting, you were still able to get the clients, earning you extended time to continue your business. In this way, the Stage Gates help you maintain perspective.

But when you fail to hit a Stage Gate, it serves as a warning bell that you need to weigh your options to minimize damage. Do you need to shut down the company? Reorganize it to focus on a specific product or service? No matter what you decide, the Stage Gate is there to help you know when to make those tough decisions, because doing the same thing over and over again without seeing different results is not only the definition of insanity; it's simply not an option for a startup.

Stage Gates create momentum.

In his book *Good to Great*, Jim Collins introduces a concept called the flywheel effect. Essentially, the idea is that if you had a massive flywheel set up, it's tough to get it moving in the beginning. It's resistant, it's hard, and it requires a lot of pushing to get it to even budge an inch. But eventually, with persistent effort, it gains momentum and accelerates and becomes easier to push until it almost feels like it has a life of its own.

Whether you share your Stage Gates with the entire company is very much a case-by-case decision. If you're a very small startup where it's just you and a business partner, that's not a problem. If you're a bit further along and have some employees, it may be prudent for them not to know all the details of the Stage Gates, as it's not fair for them to have that pressure hanging over their heads alongside the regular goals you've laid out for them. Certainly, they need to understand their expectations, and as long as you've set their goals within the scope of the Stage Gate, that could be sufficient.

Stage Gates create a window of opportunity to breathe.

Just like in the racing game analogy, when you meet your Stage Gates, they give you a window of time to get your business to a point of viability without feeling the stress of the startup all at once. For example, when you first launch your business, there may be a lot of negativity from people around you, who are saying, "It can't happen, you're making a mistake, others are already doing this, you're going to lose all your money," and so on.

This happened to me in college when all my friends said, "Why would you ever start a business when you could make so much money being a lawyer?" The negativity around me when I first began my entrepreneurship journey was *everywhere*.

A lot of the negativity you experience may come from a good place—people think they're being helpful, but deep down you probably already know what you're getting yourself into. You already know there's a chance of failure looming over you, and that prospect is stressful enough without adding in the extra negativity from others.

Setting your Stage Gate allows you to concentrate on just reaching that point and narrowing your focus so that you don't have to worry about all the long-term challenges from day one. In other words, you get to compartmentalize the stress and tackle each piece one at a time. We've all heard the saying that it's easier to climb a hill than a mountain, but if we climb enough hills, we will eventually conquer the mountain. Let's start by climbing the first hill.

> **Distractions will come along to pull you off course; the Stage Gate keeps you centered and moving in the right direction.**

Also, I believe that having a Stage Gate to focus on can stop you from deviating from your plan. Distractions will come along to pull you off course; the Stage Gate keeps you centered and moving in the right direction.

Stage Gates are SMART.

But how do you define a Stage Gate? Simply put, a good Stage Gate must be SMART:

If it doesn't check off all these boxes, then it's not truly a Stage Gate. And if you're having trouble thinking of your first Stage Gate, then turn these items into questions you can answer:

➔ "What is a specific goal I can set for my company to succeed?"

➔ "What kind of measurement will show whether we're succeeding or not?"

➔ "What is a goal we can achieve that contributes to our success?"

➔ "What is a goal relevant to this stage of the company's life?"

➔ "What is a realistic time frame we need to achieve this goal so that the company can continue?"

Let's start with a bad example like "We want to have a global customer base." That sounds great, and I'm sure you want your company to have a global impact, but this would not qualify as a Stage Gate for the following reasons:

➔ It's not *specific*. What do you mean by global? Every country? More than one country?

➔ It's not *measurable*. How many customers do you think you need to have to be considered global? A thousand? A million? A billion? Are you measuring recurring customers or simply one-time purchasers?

➔ It's not *achievable*. Where are the connections and partnerships that enable and empower a global consumer base?

➔ It's not *relevant*. How long has your company been going? Have you built a healthy local or domestic customer base first?

➔ It's not *time-bound*. When do you want to achieve this? A year? Ten years? A hundred?

I think you get the point. In contrast, a healthy Stage Gate example could be something like "We need to have recurring monthly revenue of $10,000 a month by the end of Q4 in order to meet costs with sales in Miami." In this, we have the following:

→ It has *specific* goal. $10,000 a month in recurring revenue.

→ It's *measurable*. You have a set dollar amount that can be tracked through transactions documented by the CFO or accountant.

→ It's *achievable*. You can look at your data to establish where you need to be based on your KPIs.

→ It's *relevant*. By tying the goal "$10,000 a month" to a purpose "in order to meet costs," it reflects the point in the life cycle of your startup and is directly linked to a desired outcome.

→ It's *time-bound*. It has a deadline of "the end of Q4," so there's a sense of urgency to do the necessary work to meet the Stage Gate, and you're setting clear expectations of when new decisions need to be made.

> ❝ The failure to establish solid Stage Gates is a major contributing factor to why many startups don't succeed. ❞

On this last point, a Stage Gate clearly defines a time in which you must make a decision, whether that's to close it down and cut your losses, to pivot resources based on the results, or to recruit more investors by showing them the results you've generated.

The failure to establish solid Stage Gates is a major contributing factor to why many startups don't succeed. There's nothing wrong with being excited by your idea and taking action on it, especially if others are also excited. But without a clear picture of what you need to accomplish not only to remain viable but also to grow, then you could easily get stuck in the Start phase and fail to Scale.

There's good news, though. Not everything is solely dependent on your Story. Having the right People around you could very well make the difference between hitting that Stage Gate and extending your time or having *Game Over* flash in front of your face.

PEOPLE

CHAPTER 8:

First Hires: Pay Your People with Love, Ownership, and Freedom

LET'S FACE IT, we entrepreneurs really are just a Jack or a Jill with a couple of beans that we believe can grow into a beanstalk. We know that these idea beans are going to change the world, but we need to convince others to join us on our quest.

The unfortunate side of being a startup is that you have no money—or even negative money if you took out a business loan. This means that in the job marketplace, you can't compete with the Fortune 500s or even the Fortune 5000s for that matter. You're not going to be able to pay a competitive salary right out of the company coffers. Which begs the question: How are you going to hire A players when you simply cannot compete in terms of salary and benefits?

We need to rewrite the rules of employee engagement. It's not all about money but about employee happiness and development. If you can provide people something they value that they cannot get at a Fortune 5000 company, then you'll create an opportunity to attract people who have a growth mindset.

> ❝ It's not all about money but about employee happiness and development. ❞

Create transparency from the beginning.

To attract those with a startup and growth mindset, you need to be able to lay out for them the vision of growth you have for the company. In other words, they need to possess a sense of ownership and have some stake in the success of the company. They also need to be flexible enough to truly understand what they're walking into with a startup—that there are no guarantees of success but that they will need to take ownership of helping create success.

One way to achieve this sense of ownership is to develop a level of transparency where your people are aware of the exact financial state of the company, warts and all. With all of our companies, the executive leadership team knows the KPIs and understands the trajectory of the company. Transparency on these matters creates a higher level of ownership because they realize that success is dependent upon each of them.

Obviously, the level of transparency depends on the size of the team, and I'm not saying that you should pull out your balance sheet during an interview with an applicant. Create transparency even before the interview by being frank in the job post. You can let prospects know that you'll be paying lower than market value and may not have all the benefits of a larger company, but you can also lay out the potential and the opportunities available. I tend to be very direct about what the goals for the startup are and what that looks like for their role so that they understand exactly what will be expected of them.

This will naturally weed out a lot of people—those who don't want to take a risk with a startup and those who realize they'll be overwhelmed by the expectations. And that's okay. But it will also attract people with a healthy startup mindset who are excited about the prospect of getting in on something on the ground floor and helping to build it.

Pay your people with love.

Startups have an advantage here because you have an opportunity from the very beginning to build quality relationships with the people you hire and to give them the kind of love they're looking for in a workplace: appreciation and respect.

I have found three very simple ways to do this in my own startups:

➼ *Recognize greatness.* When people are recognized for their hard work, they feel truly cared for and seen.

➼ *Learn who they are and who they want to become.* Simply put, know something about your people beyond the skills and experience on their résumé. What are their hobbies and interests? What gets them excited? And, most importantly, what are they looking for? Where do they want to take their career, and how does the startup fit into that?

➼ *Focus on their continuous development.* When you know who people are and where they want to be, then you can look for ways to develop them in that direction. For example, let's say that you hired a part-time bookkeeper, but you learn they really want to be a CFO one day. You can look for a project to delegate to them and say, "Would you be open to developing a budget for this?" In that way, you're helping them gain the skills they'll need as a CFO.

In fact, one study showed that over 52 percent of survey respondents reported that they left a job because "employers didn't care about employees."[4] Imagine the opportunity that startups have to change this and to build a team that knows they're cared for. And guess what? It costs absolutely nothing!

Pay your people with ownership.

Since my first venture in 1993, I have believed that everyone should have ownership in the company. By the time we started Hostopia, we'd learned a thing or two about hiring people for a startup, especially in finding ways to make people feel like they were a part of the company, not just a part *in* the company.

We did this by giving ownership in the company as a benefit of working there. The first group of employees of Internet Direct, Hostopia, .CLUB, and Paw.com were all given options so that we could attract top talent. The fact was that we could not afford market rates, and our salaries were 30 to 40 percent below market value. We wanted people who would work not only for a salary but also for an opportunity they could own—people who would bring an entrepreneurial mindset.

From a financial perspective, there are some very practical ways that you can pay people with ownership:

➔ *Annual bonuses based on company performance:* This is a very tangible way to show appreciation while also helping employees feel more ownership in the actual results of the company. You might even consider monthly bonuses, quarterly

---

4   Andrew Greenberg, "The Pros and Cons of a Salary Range in Your Job Description," ContractRecruiter.com, August 1, 2020, https://www.contractrecruiter.com/salary-range-job-description.

bonuses, or even guaranteed raises when you add investors or hit a certain Stage Gate—whatever works best for your team.

➜ *Stock options or phantom options:* These can be especially attractive for those who already have an ownership mindset, and they can be truly life-changing if the company ever goes public or is sold. On the one hand, they're sharing in the ups and downs of the company; therefore, it increases the desire to see everyone succeed. And on the other hand, you want them to succeed so that the option will be worth something to them someday.

➜ *Outright gifting of shares:* This is also an option, though I caution that you use great care with this one because you don't want to trigger a tax problem for the employee. To avoid this, the shares must be worth less than the annual gift allowance stipulated by the IRS in the US—and to be clear, it works only with friends who you can legitimately give money to. You can't give money in lieu of income to avoid paying taxes.

As I mentioned before, all our first hires at Hostopia had some kind of ownership in the company, which helped set them up for success later on. When we decided to take the company public, there were those who sold some of their stock, generating life-changing wealth for them and their families. The early days of being underpaid ended up working out well for them, but it required that sense of ownership to help them stick it out. I would argue that they made far more with us than taking a gig with a Fortune 5000 company—and they probably had a lot more fun.

Now certainly you have to be cautious with the level of financial ownership because you need to make sure that you and your business partners retain primary ownership. The number of shares you set can vary depending on what industry you're in. For example, with a tech company, you could go as high as dedicating 20 percent of the ownership for employees. But with other companies, you may want to be more conservative. With Paw.com, we dedicated 10 percent to offer up for ownership options. With .CLUB it was 7.5 percent. But I suggest that 10 to 15 percent is a good general range to stay within. Stepping outside the norm is not good down the road when you need to raise additional capital.

Speaking of ownership, giving options rather than shares can be an advantage because you still retain ownership of the company until the employee chooses to exercise those options. This can prove to be a benefit if you have an LLC set up from a tax perspective because you can take the losses individually until the company makes a profit.

Plus, when they do exercise their options, you're not actually losing parts of the company like you would with shares but rather you're getting paid back for the original investment you made or even a modest profit. It can be an advantage for the employees too, since giving away shares to employees can be deemed a taxable event for them, whereas options are not. In my opinion, employees should never execute their options unless there is a liquidity event.

No matter what method you land on, it's important that you write it down on paper and have both parties sign to document the agreement. This will save you from conflict, heartache, and even financial loss down the road, plus it helps create the transparency essential to developing a sense of ownership. Ambiguity is the enemy here. Everyone wants to know exactly what they will get in different outcomes.

Pay your people with freedom.

In the beginning, you're not going to be able to wow applicants with the best benefits. Maybe all of your employees are contractors and you're not even providing healthcare for them. This doesn't mean that you can't offer other benefits to show your appreciation and build trust. There are plenty of ways to get creative by giving them freedoms they wouldn't have at a corporate job.

For starters, allow people to wrap their work around the life they want to live rather than having to conform to a predetermined, rigid work schedule. This can include things like the following:

➤ Allowing people to bring their dogs or kids to work

➤ Allowing fully remote work

➤ Allowing customized work hours

➤ Allowing them to work from wherever and whenever in the world they want to

Obviously, you don't have to do all of these, but the point is to be creative and to figure out what kind of freedoms attract the people you want. You'll be surprised by how often these freedoms—or benefits—can make a big difference for applicants and how it can build trust and loyalty early on in the life of the company. Then, as the company grows and you can offer traditional benefits like a healthcare plan or a 401(k), you'll be deepening the trust and loyalty that's already been established. I will say that this startup flexibility advantage has diminished a bit, as even the largest of companies have begun to set up a work environment focused on employee needs post pandemic, but this is all the more reason to find unique ways to build in flexibility.

Pay your people with love.

There's that word again: *love*. But its importance really can't be understated in this process, especially during the Start phase. In the same way that love can help direct you to the best idea, it can help direct you to the best people. If you're interviewing two applicants, one who has slightly better qualifications but seems less excited about the mission of the startup, and one who has decent qualifications but is excited about the position, you're better off going with the latter.

> " In the same way that love can help direct you to the best idea, it can help direct you to the best people. "

Simon Sinek's take on this is that "you don't hire for skills, you hire for attitude. You can always teach skills." And I agree. People can gain skills and experience and people can be taught, but you can't *make* someone have an entrepreneurial attitude. That has to come from love of the idea and the pursuit itself.

Love for an idea or mission is an advantage for many reasons. It helps reduce turnover during those early startup days where consistency is key because people aren't there for a paycheck per se. Instead, you want people who have a desire to contribute to the success of the company and who are united around that shared love of purpose. This love of mission also becomes its own driver and motivator to encourage people to hit goals and drive you toward your Stage Gates without having to micromanage or threaten them.

Lastly, recognize greatness. We talked about it earlier, but in a startup we need to take it to another level. We need to recognize the contributions of each and every one of our team members. And again, it costs us nothing!

Make it easy for your employees to work for you.

There's no shortage of jobs or choices for people to pursue in their careers, so it's important to create a path of least resistance for those who want to work for you, especially when you don't have all the bells-and-whistles benefits to offer. A Gallup study found that half of those polled left jobs to get away from a bad manager.[5]

Turnover costs are bad for any business, but they're especially bad for a small business, where the loss of even one good worker can put a significant dent in productivity or even kill the startup. By being flexible with your team and easy to work for, you may not eliminate all turnover, but you can certainly limit it—and the costs associated with it. Plus, you're more likely to see higher engagement when employees find you easy to work for.

This isn't to say that you have to be a pushover who never sets goals or never has hard conversations when warranted. The same Gallup study found that the most highly regarded managers were also the ones who checked in frequently with their staff through a combination of face-to-face, phone, and electronic communications.

My colleague Michele has a unique take on this: "You shouldn't only ask whether the candidate is a good fit for the company but also whether the company is a good fit for them." Will they be happy there? Will the position and startup be good for them as a person? Do they have staying power where they can grow with the company because it's good for them?

---

5   Jim Harter and Amy Adkins, "Employees Want a Lot More from Their Managers," Gallup, April 8, 2015, https://www.gallup.com/workplace/236570/employees-lot-managers.aspx.

At the end of the day, it comes back to love. Do you love your employees' talents, and do they love working for you? After all, it's a two-way street. Yes, you get to choose who will work for you, but they also get to choose if they will work for you. It takes a special—and different—kind of person to join a startup, so appreciating them can go a long way in whether your startup is a success—or not.

CHAPTER 9:

Hire People Who Are "Different"

PROBABLY ONE OF THE MOST classic examples of business partnership is that of Steve Jobs and Steve Wozniak. The two Apple founders complemented each other in so many ways, and it was their differences that strengthened the business in its early days and built the foundation for what is one of the best-known companies today.

With Wozniak, you had the technical knowledge and practical know-how to design and build a top-line product. And while Jobs certainly wasn't a novice with technical design, his strengths were more in the department of business building and understanding the importance of how human behavior relates to getting a product to market, attracting investors, and so on. Take one without the other, and I don't think there would be an Apple today.

But where their disparate talents overlapped was in their love of the technology itself and the desire to bring a powerful and user-friendly personal computer into the public space at a time when computers were still thought of primarily as a business tool—and certainly not for every business. They both were self-aware enough to realize what areas they needed to take ownership of and how to have the flexibility to bounce ideas off and defer to each other's expertise.

That's not to say there wasn't conflict along the way. That's just human nature, and sometimes, especially where love of an idea is strong, then emotions will also be strong. It can be tempting to want to avoid conflict and try to do everything on your own, but I hope to save you some time, pain, and money by cautioning that you could be setting yourself up for failure by not involving others.

Look for complements, not clones.

Company culture is a buzzword at the moment and not just for massive corporations. More and more, entrepreneurs are seeing the importance of establishing a healthy and clear company culture early on in the life of a business. But sometimes there can be a temptation to believe that building a consistent company culture means hiring people who are exactly like yourself.

> " A truly strong company culture thrives not when there is just one type of personality present but when there is diversity. "

But a truly strong company culture thrives not when there is just one type of personality present but when there is diversity. Instead of looking for clones of yourself who have essentially the same skill set and outlook, you need to find people who complement you. It's okay to have weaknesses—every person and business in the world has them—so look for people whose strengths can complement your weaknesses and make the company stronger as a whole.

A common mistake I see among green entrepreneurs is that they go into business with their buddies or family members. Just because someone is a good friend doesn't mean they'll make a good business partner—especially if they don't have a complementary personality and skills profile to yours. I invested in my nephew's company, a jewelry business he was starting up with four of his friends. They ended up generating millions of dollars of sales, but two years in they had to file for bankruptcy. What went wrong?

Well, for starters, they were a bit out of control because they didn't organize themselves or the company thoughtfully. They behaved more than a bit like rock stars, and they each did whatever job they wanted to do without thinking about their strengths, profiles, or how they could complement one another. To their credit, after dissolving the company, they've all gone their separate ways into other businesses that have each proved very successful, so the bright side is that they all seemed to have learned from the experience.

Before you can be proficient at hiring complements, though, you have to understand yourself so that you don't accidentally hire clones or your bestie. If your best friend has complementary skills, that's great. But you still have to know what to look for first.

Also, consider the benefits of people from different backgrounds, education, geography, and sex. By doing so, you get a far greater representation of your customer base. Strength through diversity.

Being self-aware in this manner isn't just good for your emotional intelligence or your personal life; it's good for business. While I doubt Jobs and Wozniak did a personality profile, their combination of complementary skills can be duplicated through knowing your personality profile and recognizing which one to go after. If you're on your second, third, or fourth startup, you may not require the same business partner as before—the skills and personality needed will change depending on the type of venture you're starting.

Don't be a one-person show.

When I spoke about the importance of personality profiles at MIT, I was approached afterward by a woman who was teary-eyed and said, "I never thought of myself as an entrepreneur because I don't have a personality for sales, and I thought that's what you had to be." It was touching to see how validated she felt that being "different" meant she could still be a bona fide entrepreneur, without possessing all the stereotypical personality traits.

It's true that many entrepreneurs are dominant and influential types, but it doesn't mean *you* have to be that way. It can be tempting to think that you have to change your personality profile to be successful, when really you just need to find the person who complements you.

Failure to do so can lead to your organization being a bit of a one-person show, so to speak. A startup may thrive and grow fast in the beginning thanks to a charismatic leader, but if they're the only one driving sales and drawing people in, or if they're trying to put their hand into every project and task, the success could prove to be short lived and fail to scale.

One classic example is an entrepreneur we've probably all heard of: Walt Disney. The two Disney brothers, Walt and Roy, were about as different in personality as you could ask for, with Walt being the dominant, social, and influential type and Roy being the more analytical and steady of the two. He could have made it all about himself and been a one-man show, but as their company grew, Walt had the foresight to set in place the people and structure necessary so that the company could live on without his force of personality.

This meant hiring people with complementary skill sets for all of his teams, especially the skills he knew he was lacking in. While he loved animating, he quickly realized that there were others who were far more gifted at animation than himself, so he stepped out of that role early on and directed his attention to his strengths of influence. Whether he knew what he was doing or not, it was this mindfulness to *not* be a one-man show that enabled the company to grow from a startup founded by two brothers to the largest entertainment conglomerate in the world today.

Nothing motivates more than success.

Success is the law of attraction for startups. People want to be part of something bigger than themselves, and they also want to feel like they're winning in life. If you can authentically share your vision of your startup and what it can achieve, this will help you hire new people, retain talent, get new customers, drive PR, and secure investors.

> **" Success is the law of attraction for startups. People want to be part of something bigger than themselves, and they also want to feel like they're winning in life. "**

When we started .CLUB, we were launching a micro global brand on par with domain extensions like .org, .net, or .info. As the entrepreneur, it was my job to lay out a vision for what this domain extension could become.

Maybe I went too far when I was invited on an industry podcast before our launch and made the claim that .CLUB could register five million names in five years. After all, I'm human and suffer from the entrepreneurial disease of optimism. Although we hit only one million names in that time frame, it was still extremely successful for a new domain extension.

But the statement created some buzz in the industry through forums and blogs, and we topped that off with a launch party in New

York with rap artist 50 Cent—"In Da Club" being one of his more prominent songs at the time—and, boom, we managed to kick-start what would become a successful domain name extension. In its first twenty-four hours of existence, .CLUB registered over thirty thousand names, making it one of the most—if not the most—successful first twenty-four hours of any domain extension at that time. The perception of .CLUB continued to build on itself, improving our access to better search placement on registrars, hiring some great people, and raising additional funding, which ultimately led to a very successful exit sale to GoDaddy Registry.

A small caveat here: There is a fine line between selling the future and fraud. On one extreme, Elizabeth Holmes went too far with Theranos, leading to fraud charges. Elon Musk, on the other hand, has made bold statements that have failed to come to fruition—we're still waiting for the fully self-driving vehicle—but that's not fraud; it's just being overly optimistic. Earlier I used the word *authentic* when describing your success. This must be something that you believe your startup can actually deliver, not a manipulation of how you want to be perceived. If the evidence is clear that you can't deliver on your vision, then it's time to come clean and pivot to a different vision.

CHAPTER 10:

Hire Do-It-Yourself Employees

THE GROWTH AT HOSTOPIA reached a point where I became accustomed to having people do certain things for me. If I wanted to scan a document, then I could ask someone to do that for me and keep working on whatever project was in front of me that day. It's kind of a nice thing to have—and easy to take for granted.

After I exited Hostopia and moved on to my next startup, all of a sudden it hit me—I had to do my own scanning. I had to run errands. I had to go to Office Depot to pick up brochures. I had to put on many more hats.

Sure, I'd done it many years before, but it had been a while, and it took me some time to go back to being a DIY entrepreneur because—not to be too obvious here—it turns out that there's a huge difference between being CEO at a five-hundred-person company and a CEO at a ten-person company!

Large corporations thrive on consistency, which can be very appealing for many people who like having a routine to follow and a comfortable level of predictability. Startups, on the other hand, are the business equivalent of a roller coaster. They go through a ton of change in a short amount of time. Not everyone is built for enduring that type of constant change, so this becomes a make-it or break-it quality when adding people to the team.

DIY is a mindset, not a skill.

When you're adding your first few employees, ask: Who among your applicants has a DIY mindset? Do-it-yourself is more of an attitude than it is a skill set. This isn't to say that someone can't learn how to have a DIY attitude, but it takes a lot more time and energy to change someone's mindset than it does to teach a skill. So for a startup, where time and resources are limited, you need to look for people who already have a DIY mindset.

> **66 For a startup, where time and resources are limited, you need to look for people who already have a DIY mindset. 99**

This can be tricky if you're hiring—or partnering—with highly talented people. There's no place for arrogance in a startup. We're looking for skilled employees who will fit the culture of the organization.

So early on you'll want to be transparent with people about the level of change at the company and ask, "Are you comfortable with change? How would it make you feel to have your job description tweaked once a quarter—or more?" That doesn't mean you *will* change job descriptions once a quarter, but you should at least pitch the concept to an applicant to see what they think about it.

There are lots of people who want very clearly defined job descriptions from which they never have to deviate, and that's fine. But they probably won't be the ideal fit for you, no matter what their skill or experience level. Having people who are flexible with doing tasks outside of their job description when a deadline is looming or when a new product launch runs into a speed bump is key.

Hiring DIY employees starts with you.

Chances are that as an entrepreneur, you're already accustomed to the DIY mindset and have been doing most things—or everything—on your own. But as revenue grows and you're able to either outsource duties or hire new positions to take over certain responsibilities, it's important that you maintain the DIY mindset.

This doesn't mean stepping in and doing other people's jobs for them or interfering in their work. But it means showing your team in your actions that you're willing to be the one to go on the coffee run for *them* or to deal with the delivery person so that they can stay focused on their tasks.

To go back to the example of Walt Disney, there is a famous picture of him picking up trash at Disneyland. In fact, to this day the second rule of new employee orientation for Disney park employees is that "everyone picks up trash."[6] Likewise, when we launched .CLUB, we ordered dozens and dozens of pizzas for the GoDaddy staff, since they were our top distributor. That day, the CEO of .CLUB could be found pushing a cart full of pizza boxes through the GoDaddy offices on his way to the lunchroom. In other words, whether you're an executive or a sanitation worker, it's your job to "keep the park clean" by continuing to serve your staff and customers.

---

6   Jeff Kober, "At Disney, Everyone Picks Up Trash!," MousePlanet.com, August 30, 2007, https://www.mouse-planet.com/6971/At_Disney_Everyone_Picks_Up_Trash.

Again, it's not about doing someone's job *for* them but about showing your willingness to do a job you don't *have* to do. You can't ask others to go beyond their role if you're not willing to do it yourself.

DIY is about adaptability.

Startups by nature are always in a state of change, which can make them a very stressful environment. But there are some people who are energized by change and embrace it. So when you're hiring a DIY employee, it's not simply about being willing to do more than the job description or having know-how to scale—it's ultimately about their adaptability.

Not everyone has the personality to adapt to change, and in a startup, if they can't adapt, then they won't survive. I know that sounds very Darwinian, but it's the truth. For those who do have that spirit of adaptability, though, it can serve a few different purposes.

First, it encourages individual excellence in the job because there is more ownership of the job.

Second, it encourages teamwork because a DIY mindset not only makes you adaptable but also promotes a desire to help others adjust to changes and survive as a team.

And finally, it encourages innovation, which is the lifeblood of startups and one of the greatest contributions a startup can make to society as a whole. When you're willing to do it yourself, you begin looking for ways to work smarter instead of harder and finding new ways to get the work done that improves the experience for everyone.

So far, our Start discussion has focused on the Story and the People needed to launch your idea into a successful startup. The two are inextricably linked because stories need people and people need stories. These are foundational for success and should take up a lot of your initial energy and thought. They cannot bring success on their own—instead, they help to set the stage for the second two key areas required for success: the Money you raise and the Systems you set up to get this startup off the ground.

MONEY

CHAPTER 11:

Proving Your Concept

BACK IN STORY, we touched on the importance of proving your concept by discussing it with others, getting honest feedback, and, if possible, taking it through an incubator program. But now it's time to prove that your concept can generate money— both in terms of bringing along investors and in sales. To do that, we're no longer looking at whether people like the idea and whether it solves a problem but whether there is a formula that can scale.

> ❝ Proving your concept isn't a one-and-done activity; instead, it's all about proving that it will scale through a repeatable formula. ❞

Proving your concept isn't a one-and-done activity; instead, it's all about proving that it will scale through a repeatable formula. Specifically, can you prove to investors that it will scale? Investors don't want to invest in businesses that aren't scalable, so providing the proof that your company is scalable helps them assess the risk. The more clarity you can offer them, the greater the chance of closing the investment and at a higher valuation.

Believe it or not, most investors fear loss more than they desire gain. If an investor knows they can quadruple their investment through a company with a proven track record, they will be happier with that investment even at a higher valuation versus the startup still in launch mode.

When we were building Hostopia, which we started in 1999, the idea of a cloud-based website and email software was still very novel at the time. So we needed a way that we could both sharpen our skills and show proof that we knew what we were doing.

We decided to launch another company that acted and behaved like our first customer—BlueGenesis. Hostopia was a wholesale provider of services, and BlueGenesis was our retail brand set to be the first guinea pig. This gave us the chance to practice, tweak our process, improve it, and then create a solution to show other potential clients. When selling B2B, especially regarding the larger resellers, your solution has to be flawless for them, or else they will choose your competitor.

Once we had our retail division humming, we reached out to some smaller resellers in our marketplace—ones willing to take a risk with a brand-new company like us. That gave us more proof of our work to turn around and show bigger companies, and so on, until we eventually were able to approach the top ten telecom companies in Canada, nine of which ended up signing with us over time.

The key was to start with the smaller companies. There were two primary benefits to this. First, they were faster to onboard, which meant that they could start generating revenue early on. Second, they had more ability to handle (and forgive) the early-stage bumps and bruises that come along with launching a new platform.

We had proved ourselves with a retail business, signed up small providers, and started to win telecommunication companies in Canada. We had made it!

Or had we?

Many companies have tried to expand from countries like Canada to the US, with a large percentage failing. Even US-based companies have trouble doing the reverse—expanding to Canada. We had only sold in Canada at this point, so it was time to cross the border to see if we could also be successful in the US. And then South America. And then Europe. By the time we exited the company, we had been successful in all of those markets, proving our concept at each level and raising tens of millions of dollars along the way.

Ideas are tough to fund.

If you're running a platform company, it doesn't matter what your market is, and it doesn't matter what your idea is—before you do much of anything else, you have to pour some money into developing a minimum viable product (MVP), something that takes the idea from being a concept to being tangible. Maybe you're wondering where exactly this money comes from, but I promise we'll cover that in the next chapter.

In many ways, developing your MVP goes back to chapter 2, where we discussed the power of visualization. Having something visual that you can show to potential customers—and then, later on, to potential investors—drastically increases your chance of success. After all, it's really difficult to sell an idea on its own merits,

> **Having something visual that you can show to potential customers—and then, later on, to potential investors—drastically increases your chance of success.**

which is why we had to create a separate company to become our own customer.

Developing an MVP is rooted in the *Field of Dreams* mentality: "If you build it, they will come." Even if it's just a prototype, that's okay—so long as you have something to show to others. This also helps you identify and present the costs behind producing the product in comparison to the value it can provide.

You might say, "Colin, I'm not selling a product, though—I provide a service." Even so, you can still develop something visual. Photographers have portfolios to show potential clients, and remodeling companies can show before-and-after pictures. Consultants show graphs detailing the impact of their services. The point is to provide some kind of visual to prove the value. Will it take some money and time to develop this? Of course. But you won't get far without them.

Your first sale does not prove your concept.

That first sale or first client can be a real rush and a great motivator—but it doesn't prove viability. Not by a long shot. Your first hundred or even a million in sales doesn't necessarily prove your concept. Instead, what proves your concept is showing your ability to grow your business from investments in the company.

Simply look at how much it costs you to acquire additional customers, what profit is coming in from each sale, and then whether you can repeat that on a mass scale. Once you can show sustainable growth, it will help attract the kind of investment capital we'll discuss further in Scale.

With Paw.com, we invent new products all the time, including the memory foam dog rug. We also pioneered the waterproof blanket protector and the memory foam car seat for your pooch. So whenever we come out with a new product, we first test the concept by seeing if we can sell it to our existing customers directly from our website. If that proves successful, we sell the product using ads on Facebook, Google, or other media. This helps us figure out our costs to acquire a new customer, or our return on ad spend (ROAS), which we want to keep below a certain percentage.

If the product passes this second test of ROAS, which is specific to e-commerce, then we can scale to infinity, meaning we know that we can sustain sales so long as we invest in having the additional inventory. Now, eventually in every ad market, you'll experience diminishing marginal returns because you don't necessarily get the same return on every single ad campaign. So you'll continue to test and prove the concept to see how far you can take it.

Distribution and partnerships are key.

I can't overstate how important distribution is not only to proving your concept but also to helping you scale quickly and efficiently. You might be able to demonstrate that you can sell to one retailer, but what about ten? Maybe you've shown that you can sell in your city, but what about the region? At this level, it's all about growing the distribution of where you can sell.

Going back to Hostopia, this is why we didn't stop with conquering Canada and continued to take it to the next level. Being able to show that you can have success across multiple markets only makes you more appealing to potential investors, increasing the value of your company. Again, investors are more likely to take a risk on a concept that's been proven in multiple distribution channels; they're willing and eager to add fuel to the fire, even if it means getting a lower rate of return.

I know this may sound like we're already talking about Scale, but I promise that these are the things you have to be doing during your Start phase to ensure that you'll be able to scale successfully. You can think of proving your concept as practice in scaling, because the lessons you learn here will carry over to help you be successful when you scale the business, especially in terms of finding investors. It'll also help set you up for a successful exit when your concept has been proven so effectively that buyers are knocking on your door to talk.

CHAPTER 12:

Paying for Your Idea

IN 1992, I WAS a broke college kid. I wasn't able to pay the residential fees, but since I had been voted vice president of the student council, I had an office I could use, so I'd sleep there, then get up and go shower in the school gym each day. I will say it was no picnic, as the lights ran twenty-four hours a day, and I slept on couches made for your local airport. I got away with this for several months before the administration found out and offered me free residence—so long as I paid it back after graduating.

During my fourth year, I moved back home to work on the farm, hoeing the fields for days on end while listening to my Sony Walkman, then going to various markets to buy vegetables and then reselling those veggies at a stand I set up on the street. That summer, I was able to make about $7,000 that I put aside for a business idea I had.

I then went back to college, took the first month of courses, dropped out in my fourth year, took the tuition money back, maxed out my credit cards, took the vegetable money I had raised, a $12,800 loan from my mom, and used all that to plow into my first company—a software rental business called Megachoice.

Needless to say, I don't recommend this strategy for everyone. But for me, I knew it was going to push me to give it everything, because in the back of my mind, I told myself, "If I fail at this, no matter what, I'm going to pay my mom back. I'll get a regular job and do whatever I have to do." Paying her back was so important to me, it became part of my driving force. Not to mention the credit card debt looming over me, plus the fact that the tuition money I'd gotten back was actually a government-backed student loan, so I still had to repay that too.

> ❝ Raising money for a startup is daunting, whether you've done it before or not. ❞

Raising money for a startup is daunting, whether you've done it before or not. And this piece of the process can be so difficult, especially if you don't have a lot of collateral to show the bank to get approved for a traditional business loan. But the good news is that there are other options available to help you pay for your idea and turn it into a reality.

Funding starts with you.

This first bit of advice feels painfully obvious, but you might be surprised how often it gets overlooked and how often new entrepreneurs just skip right over the notion of funding their idea themselves through hard work and saving money—both skills that can come in handy at every stage of a business.

For many entrepreneurs, early funding to prove your concept has to come from yourself—maybe you set aside a portion of your regular paycheck to go right into developing your business, or maybe you decide to liquidate part of a retirement account or take out a personal loan.

I know some might hesitate at the idea of asking their friends and family to give money to help their startup, which is why I think it's important to treat it as a loan and not as a handout, like I did when I borrowed money from my mom. This can even be a good way to vet your idea—if you're not willing to go to your closest friends and family with it, do you really believe in it yourself? If they're not willing to loan you money, then does that tell you something about the viability of the idea?

However, when scaling, I have an entirely different mentality around family investment, but we'll cover that when we get there.

I know I keep going back to this, but that's why you need to be in an incubator or innovation center. Not only will they help you improve your idea but also they will surround you with a group of trusted advisors who can help you find ways to raise the money you need—without having to forfeit control to a group of investors at an early stage. They might let you know about community programs that support small businesses, or many college business programs even have funding that you can take advantage of—all without investors.

Banks aren't the only organizations with money.

Banks are ruthless and difficult to deal with. That doesn't mean you shouldn't ever try to secure a business loan, but don't fall into the trap of thinking they're the only organizations to tap for startup funding, especially when they're probably even more risk-averse than your average investor.

Instead, there are other organizations that have money they are willing to give to startups. For example, Google and Facebook have had programs for funding startups. Procter & Gamble has a program called P&G Ventures that gives entrepreneurs a chance to pitch their idea and receive funding.

Incubators not only will help you improve your idea but also will surround you with a group of trusted advisors who can help you find additional ways to raise the money you need—without having to forfeit control to a group of investors. They might let you know about community programs supporting small businesses or even point you to some college business programs with funding that you can access. There might even be connections with local angel investors with whom you can build relationships or pitch to once you're ready. Some of these programs even include pitch competitions or at least have partnerships with such competitions.

Microfinance has also been growing in popularity, especially since they often don't require collateral and can be acted upon quickly, though they do carry a higher interest rate than your standard bank-backed loan. But another great benefit is that many microlenders also offer mentoring and training to startups and small business owners, since this reduces the risk involved in the loan.

Also, don't forget about the government. I'm amazed by how often I see new startups never even look at government funding. There are lots of government funding options available such as grants at the federal level, the state/provincial level, or even local city government.

For example, when we were working on a building in Fort Lauderdale, we reached out to the local government, and they gave us $350,000 because we were supporting the local community by launching an incubator. Sometimes all you have to do is ask, or at the very least look for those opportunities, especially through a local incubator.

Paying for your idea is a concept that's never going to go away for as long as you have your business, so it's important to get creative with funding early on and to use those lessons to help you grow. Too many would-be entrepreneurs never get going with their idea because they don't realize that all these options are available to them if they would just take a second to look. And even better, what if you can get customers to fund your business?

> **" Paying for your idea is a concept that's never going to go away for as long as you have your business. "**

CHAPTER 13

Becoming a Customer- Funded Startup

EARLY FUNDING IS EXPENSIVE. It astounds me how small businesses often sell 10, 20, even 30 percent of their company early on to obtain funding. If I asked you if you would accept an additional tax rate of 30 percent for the life of your company, would this make you think a little differently? Don't get me wrong, raising money is critical in any startup, but you can mitigate how much you need by running the business efficiently and by considering using other methods.

> **You can mitigate how much you need by running the business efficiently and by considering using other methods.**

One of those approaches is to use your customers' or suppliers' money to fund your business.

When we discussed the concept of a customer-funded startup on a *Serial Entrepreneur: Secrets Revealed!* session, guest Verne Harnish told us about Dave Rogenmoser's Austin-based startup company Proof, which provides tools to help companies boost their sales conversion rates through social proof. A year out from having an actual product available, Dave invited a group of two hundred potential customers—not investors—to demonstrate what they were working on.

And then, as bold as this sounds, he made a pitch that if they paid that day for the service—which didn't even exist yet—they would get a 50 percent discount for the rest of their life as a customer. And guess what? It worked! With the funds raised from the customers who prepaid, they were able to generate the capital they needed to finish building the service, provide it to a now-existing customer base, and then build from there.

Put the customer at the center of the business.

In this same session, John Mullins, author of *The Customer-Funded Business*, shared his insight into this, mentioning how if you look at the *Inc.* 5000 list of fastest-growing businesses, fewer than 10 percent of them have actually raised outside capital. Instead, they're getting their money from customers.

That sounds crazy to some entrepreneurs, but John's reasoning behind this is incredibly basic in terms of business-building. "If you put the customer at the center of the business," he said, "that's likely to take you a long way."

While he admits that this isn't an easy thing to do, it's often preferable to trying to get investors involved, especially given that many businesses need to adjust their plans during the startup phase. "If you've raised money on a pitch for plan A, what is the investor going to ask you to do? Flawlessly execute plan A," John says.

And he makes a good point. Because what if you don't flawlessly execute plan A? What if you discover a plan B that's better than plan A? It's going to be a much more difficult conversation with an investor to ask for money to switch to plan B when they were initially sold on plan A.

On the contrary, your plan B is probably going to be much more in line with the customers' needs and therefore more likely to get you some traction to build off, which is why John says, "You're much better off spending time with customers, getting to understand them deeply, find a real compelling problem they have, and get them to pay you for it." Solving those real problems proves your concept and gives you better footing for seeking out investors when you scale.

Get customers to pay in advance.

This sounds ridiculous, I know. But this is exactly what Dave Rogenmoser did with Proof, and it's also what Michael Dell did when he started Dell Computers while he was still a student at the University of Texas. He went to local businesses and told them he could design a computer built for exactly what they needed and have it for them in seven to ten days instead of them having to deal with technobabble from the standard computer salesperson of the day.

Many of them loved the sound of that and gladly paid him up front before they had the product in hand, which is what Mullins calls the pay in advance model of customer funding. This isn't a new concept at all. Most service businesses are actually pay in advance, but we don't take the time to consider this.

This was huge for us when we launched Internet Direct because we used an annual pricing model, and this gave us the capital we needed to operate. In the early to mid-1990s, if you approached a bank for a loan for an internet company, they considered you crazy, so we didn't have much choice but to be customer-funded. Mullins points to Costco as the master of this model and the fact that their membership dues add up to two-thirds of their operating profit, which enables them to run a retail business on very low margins.

This model also includes now-accepted practices like crowd-funding campaigns where you might give something to supporters in exchange for the funding. And unlike investors, this can be incredibly advantageous because they don't have any say in the day-to-day decision-making of the business and can also serve as your first pool of positive reviews.

Kickstarter is one of the more popular platforms, but I'd caution you that I see a lot of copycats on successful Kickstarter campaigns. There is a risk in running a successful campaign and then failing to get to market. The whole purpose is to get to market—period. When crowdfunding, it's essential to get to market as soon as possible after the campaign is over. It's better to first get your product patent pending and to place your initial order to the manufacturer *before* doing your campaign. That way, you can use the campaign money to pay the manufacturer and actually launch.

Create a subscription for your business.

I'm a huge fan of the subscription model because it means guaranteed income. Your mind probably immediately goes to digital content businesses like Netflix, but subscriptions don't have to be limited to a digital service. Almost any company can launch a subscription component of their business. Think of companies like Stitch Fix, BoxyCharm, or BarkBox, where customers pay a monthly subscription whether or not they keep any of the products recommended for them.

Even if you're a small e-commerce business, Mullins provides a great tip to figure out what you might be able to offer as a subscription: "What have I got that customers would like to have on a regular basis?" This could be some kind of regular built-in discount as part of the subscription or a top-tier service that might typically be inaccessible to your regular customers. This question can also help you weed out bad ideas for a subscription because the key words here are *on a regular basis*. If it's something your customer won't need again for six months, then why would they keep the subscription?

Amazon caught on to this idea when they created Prime. They realized that people hate paying for shipping and capitalized on it. As of the writing of this book, Amazon now has two hundred million Prime customers. Multiply this by the annual Prime membership fee and that's nearly $3 billion worth of guaranteed revenue for the company *before* any product is ever added to a cart and shipped. Not to mention that they discovered their customers were willing to buy more when they didn't have to pay for shipping.

It doesn't have to be anything big either. Some businesses create a low-cost paid newsletter of content for subscribing customers. Independent podcasts have monetized this strategy, allowing subscribers to pitch topics for the show or reading their names aloud on the show itself. Never underestimate the value of vanity! The key is that whatever perk you provide through the subscription, it creates a base of recurring revenue you can then build upon.

Train your customers to buy right away.

Train your customers to buy right away. This is what Mullins calls the scarcity model, and one of the best examples is the apparel company ZARA. Because they turn over their inventory more times than other clothing chains, they've trained their customers to buy items right away instead of waiting to see if it goes on discount. Their customers understand that the next time they walk in, it may not be there anymore.

In this way, they've discovered a proven way to capitalize on FOMO (fear of missing out) and reduce the impact of abandoned carts and casual shopping. Your business might be able to do the same thing by holding inventory for a limited time or by bringing in new styles of popular products on a regular basis. Certainly this requires more work in terms of product management, so you have to determine whether the increase in your sales close rate is worth it.

Transition your service to a product.

In the course of providing your service, you may discover that you actually have a product to sell to your customers. This is where noticing your customers' problems comes in especially handy.

This is exactly what Microsoft founders Bill Gates and Paul Allen did when they were still a startup. In the beginning, they were providing software design services and began to notice that a lot of their clients had very similar needs. This resulted in them building the MS-DOS program to address those core pain points and then sell it to customers, including IBM when they licensed MS-DOS for their first personal computer in 1981.

Start to take note of your customer's pain points and what recurring needs they have and ask yourself, "Can I make a product to meet their needs?" This increases your offerings to your existing customer base and grows revenue among that customer base, and it can provide an alternative way to attract new customers.

Become the middleman.

A lot of times we think of the middleman as a problem, but Mullins suggests that you look for the opportunity to connect a service to the customer. This is what might be thought of as the matchmaker or marketplace platform model, and it includes the likes of eBay, Uber, Airbnb—any service that brings buyers and sellers together.

One of the pluses of this model is that you can start it with little capital because you don't actually own anything except the means for the connection to be made. Airbnb doesn't own any of the properties off which it's making money; rather, it's providing a simple way for guests to find the hosts. Meanwhile, when Zillow tried to copy this model but wanted to own the properties themselves, they ended up having to shut it down because of the cost.

Another example is services like Angie's List (now simply called Angi), where companies are literally paying for the privilege to be on the list because it can connect them with savvy customers looking for their service. It helps reduce the marketing costs for the business and decrease the time customers spend vetting a good provider—a win-win-win scenario if there ever was one!

> **If you can develop a way to become a customer-funded business, you stand a much better chance of success.**

While you can fund a business yourself like we talked about in the last chapter, if you can develop a way to become a customer-funded business, you stand a much better chance of success. A problem that entrepreneurs face is that they start raising money before they figure out their business model or how they're going to monetize. This results in wasted time and, even worse, wasted equity that's left on the table.

By utilizing one or more of John Mullins's customer-funding models, it forces you to build your company on the very idea of having customers to serve, which is both foundational and pivotal for long-term success. Because while it's love for the idea that helps you weather the hard times in the life cycle of your business, you need customers to generate money, and it's money that keeps the business alive.

CHAPTER 14:

Cash Is the Oxygen That Keeps Your Business Alive

WHAT HAPPENS WHEN you start to run out of oxygen? Breathing becomes more difficult. You begin to gasp for air. You start to focus on your next breath over everything else. That is exactly what happens when you begin to run out of cash.

Your stress goes through the roof!

You're about to default on payroll, so you do whatever it takes to keep breathing: maxing out credit cards or signing high-interest loans, slowing down supplier payments, cutting key staff, personal guarantees—whatever it takes to survive.

> **You need a great story, the people to execute it, and the systems to scale it—but if you don't have the money, all of that falls apart.**

But death can be expensive, and when this happens, the founder is neither focusing on the customer nor the employees. Instead, they're digging a bigger and deeper grave.

I can't tell you how many successful companies that have great ideas and great people working in them simply run out of money. See, it's a simple equation: you need a great story, the people to execute it, and the systems to scale it—but if you don't have the money, all of that falls apart.

Focus on the Stage Gate.

So many entrepreneurs practice ready, fire, aim instead of ready, aim, fire. It really doesn't take a lot of time to figure out what your first Stage Gate is and how much money you need to get there.

This is where your established Stage Gates can be a real asset to help you focus your funding efforts. When you first start your business, you should identify what the actual funding amount is going to be for you to hit that Stage Gate. For example, if your first Stage Gate is to develop a minimum viable product, then what is that number? If it's reaching your first $10,000 in sales, then how much is it going to cost to hit that? Or if you're trying to get distribution in ten stores, how much will that take? Figure out that Stage Gate and stick with it.

Here is a unique problem: the faster you grow, the less cash you'll have because you'll be spending more on making more products and hiring new people—all good but expensive problems you'll have to solve. When your business is no longer just a concept but a reality, then identifying the realistic amount of money you need to hit the next Stage Gate is key.

A common problem facing many startups is that they simply do not have enough funding to achieve a level of success where they have proven the business model, unlocking the key to the next Stage Gate. I know it might be tempting to kick off the business and raise money as needed, but without lining up that initial funding, you're risking a lot.

How much money will we need to get to our first Stage Gate? Let's find it on day one. And let's build in some buffers for when things inevitably become more expensive than we thought. If we have extra left over before hitting the Stage Gate, we can celebrate and then reallocate.

Hold on as long as possible.

While I stick by my previous tip, you don't need to run out and get investors right away. In fact, if we have enough funding to hit our first Stage Gate, it may be better to delay fundraising to avoid excessive dilution. It's a bit of a reverse equation: The more we need to raise early on, the greater we lose our ownership. And the longer we delay, the greater the ownership.

Next, in the startup phase, you must be focused on building your case for *why* investors should choose to give you their money. When focusing on your Stage Gates, you can build a track record of milestones backed up by data to show potential investors what the cost of acquiring new business is and therefore what you're able to realistically accomplish through additional funding. The sooner you can show the company's potential for success with a high degree of probability, the better.

Not all investors are going to be comfortable with investing in a business that loses money for multiple years, so building your case is key not only for getting the investors but also for being able to educate your investor group on the story behind any losses and show what you're building toward so that they don't give up on you. In addition, they will be more receptive to fund your subsequent rounds, if needed.

Finally, you'll want to target investors who can stomach the roller-coaster startup ride. The fact is that most don't, so you have to be careful that you don't spend all of your efforts pitching to the wrong investors. Instead, focus on the ones interested in early-stage companies.

The cheapest way to fund your business is by running it lean.

If you take away nothing else from this chapter, remember this: cash is the oxygen you need to survive. What do I mean by that? I mean making sure that you're always liquid enough to take action and cover your essential costs to stay alive. If money is the oxygen that keeps your business alive, then cash represents having enough air in the room to keep breathing.

The best way to keep cash available is to run an efficient startup. Let's hold off on those lavish offices and jump into an incubator for advice on how to launch and scale.

> **If money is the oxygen that keeps your business alive, then cash represents having enough air in the room to keep breathing.**

Remember, instead of offering huge salaries to attract talent, you can use alternate currency: your stock. You can offer employee options in the company, which gives them the right to buy our stock at a predetermined price. However, unless they're sophisticated employees, options may not be as effective in motivating them due to the fact that they might not receive a payout for years—or in their minds, maybe never. Instead, consider the alternative of offering bonuses for hitting Stage Gates or certain profit or revenue targets.

Negotiate everything as a startup.

There's also something to be said for the art of negotiation, no matter what stage of your business you're in. Most people want to help the startup. Back in my broke days of college, I would flog vegetables at the local markets and our family food stand. Although we grew a lot of our own vegetables, we would also supplement by buying in bulk from other farmers.

When visiting the food terminal in Toronto, I'd often wear my university jacket while negotiating prices with supplies to communicate, "Hey, I'm a student just starting out in life and want to pay for my way through college. Can you give me a break?" They would hem and haw but ultimately give in.

A startup is no different—negotiate everything! Trade shows are a perfect example, where you can tell vendors that you're just a startup and need a startup rate, followed by, "If it works out well, we'll be back next year to pay the posted rate."

It doesn't have to be complicated either. It can be as easy as asking your supplier and sharing with them your story, your challenges, and your potential to help them when you succeed. Chances are that they've been there before too.

The point is, the fewer expenses you have, then the more cash you have. The more cash you have on hand, the better you can weather the startup roller coaster. You've got to always make sure that you have oxygen in the tank so that you're not gasping for air. Money is the oxygen keeping your lungs pumping, led by your brain to find the right Story, with your People providing the heartbeat, then they all link together around the Systems that form the skeleton holding it all together to deliver success.

SYSTEMS

CHAPTER 15:

The Four Sticky Note Business Plan

YOU'VE PROBABLY HEARD of a traditional MBA business plan—ones with a fancy SWOT analysis and market share potential with aggressive targets that happen to be only 0.01 percent of an addressable market generating millions or even billions over the next few years. I'm not saying you don't want to put that plan together when raising money to scale, but at this stage we can have a greater impact by figuring out our strategy in a more simplified way.

So why use sticky notes for your business plan? For one, they're sticky! You can post them on your board to stay on track. Second, they're small, and less is more when it comes to developing a simple strategy. You want to boil down your concepts to very simple points that you and everyone around you can relate to.

Lastly, you can do it in under an hour. I run an exercise with my incubator cohorts

> **❝ You want to boil down your concepts to very simple points that you and everyone around you can relate to. ❞**

asking each person in the group to assemble a business plan, and even with everyone presenting, we can do this in under two hours. The actual work involved is no more than thirty minutes, yet it can have such a profound impact on your future.

You'll notice that this chapter is filled with a lot of topics we've already addressed. The Four Sticky Note Business Plan forces you to translate those topics and ideas into actual systems you can implement. But before we get into it, one of the biggest things you need to accept is that you don't have to know all the answers yet.

You don't have to know everything right away.

This is great news! It's impossible to know everything right away. The Start phase is filled with discovery, learning, and making adjustments. You may have stumbled across business plan templates online and felt stumped by certain blanks that needed to be filled in, but I'm here to let you know that not every blank has to be completed. Having a spirit of flexibility and curiosity can be a strength during the Start phase, which is all the more reason to keep things simple.

That being said, each individual sticky note pertains directly to the things you need for Story, People, Money, and Systems:

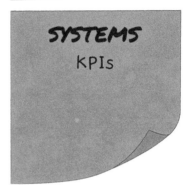

What is your story?

I like to start off by thinking of the purpose behind the startup: Why does the startup need to exist? What problem is it solving?

To fill out your Story sticky note, consider the following questions:

- ➤ What is the big idea? What is your Story? Make that the heading of your first sticky note, with a focus on solving a problem.

- ➤ Underneath you'll want to state your Purpose—your big *why*. Why are you doing this? Who are you helping? How are you changing the world?

- ➤ Next, you want to identify the space you want to own in no more than five or six words. It helps to think about what people would type in a search engine to find your business and what will land you on the front page of Google. As a side note, you can use these five to six words to set your title tags on your website. Remember what we discussed in chapter 2: this one trick costs nothing to do and takes only a few minutes.

- Can you then identify who the customer is? What is the persona of the customer you're targeting? It's okay to try to come up with someone who is a likely buyer, such as the head of the household who makes the design decisions, aged between twenty-five and forty-five.

- What is your X factor? I debated putting this in the Start business plan—it's one of the keys for scaling your business and can sometimes take *years* to truly figure out—but it makes sense to begin thinking about it now. This will be the most challenging of all the asks. The earlier you can identify an X factor, the better. What bottleneck in your industry are you solving? What do you have that none of your competitors have? What is your competitive advantage?

- Lastly, set the first SMART Stage Gate. Minimum viable product, revenue target, sales target? If you want to be really aggressive, write out a second or third Stage Gate.

Again, you don't necessarily need an answer for each of these. The questions serve as a guide to help you figure out your Story and how to launch your idea successfully.

Who are the people you need?

I like to say that you can't hire or outsource the entrepreneur. That's your job! But you *can* increase your chances of success by surrounding yourself with the right people. During the Start phase, this is most likely going to be a very small group of people, which frees you up to get really specific and to recruit those who are the most excited about your idea, whether they're coming along as a business partner, a coach, an employee, an advisor, or even a contractor you are outsourcing specific aspects to. Don't just think about employees—think about anyone who can add value and insight to help you along to your Stage Gates.

Business is like a puzzle. We're assembling it to create a work of art, so all your people need to connect together, and diversity matters. In fact, you need diversity in many ways: age, sex, ethnicity, knowledge, and, most importantly, personality profile.

Remember, we want to hire people who complement us. If we're not good at sales, we need someone who is. If you're a process person, then you also need someone who is a people person. We'll talk about this more in Scale, but to fill out the People sticky note in Start, you need to ask yourself the following questions:

- ➤ Who do you need on your team at launch?

- ➤ Who will you need to hit your first Stage Gate? Second Stage Gate? Third?

Obviously, you may not know the exact names of who you need at all these milestones, especially beyond launch, but the point is that you know at least the *roles* that will help you move past Start and into Scale. Do you need a CFO, or will a bookkeeper do for now? Do you need a product designer? A marketing person? Which of these roles can be outsourced, and which ones need to remain internal?

A note on outsourcing: Too many entrepreneurs burn out because they can't give up control over certain aspects of the business and they're trying to do everything themselves. There are lower-cost ways of hiring out tasks by using platforms like 99designs, Upwork, or Fiverr. Also, consider using offshore labor right out of the gate. We've had a lot of success with Eastern Europe and India for coding and with the Philippines for customer service and other business processes.

What money do you need?

As we discussed in the last chapter, money is the oxygen for the business—too many startups fail because they don't have the money piece figured out. The Money sticky note simply helps you break down that big question into smaller chunks:

- ➡ What money do you need at launch?

- ➡ How much money will you need to hit your first Stage Gate? And if you want to be aggressive, the second and third Stage Gate as well.

Again, you may not have all the answers yet, but having some idea of where your money is going to come from can really make it or break it in terms of hitting your Stage Gates so that you can move out of Start and begin to Scale.

What systems do you need?

During the Start phase, the startup relies heavily on your instinct as an entrepreneur.

On this sticky note, you should focus on tracking leading indicators, also known as KPIs—key performance indicators. These leading indicators are simply the reference points that allow you to connect your KPIs to your Stage Gates. This could be knowing that you can generate a hundred sales from a thousand phone calls, or if you book a hundred meetings, it will result in thirty proposals and then you'll get ten deals out of those proposals.

In other words, you need to be systematically tracking these leading indicators so that you understand the health of your startup and can hit your first SMART Stage Gate. For example, a subscription business will track several KPIs:

→ Cost of acquisition of new customers (spending on ads, new deals, etc.)

→ Monthly recurring revenue (how much revenue are you bringing in each month)

→ Churn rate (how many customers do you lose each month)

→ Lifetime value of a customer

Using those numbers generates the leading indicators necessary to make adjustments rapidly. With Paw.com, we track daily our return on ad spend, because we know that if it goes higher than a certain percentage, then we need to make changes to our advertising strategy immediately.

Having data alone is not enough—you need to know specifically which KPIs are connected to your health and growth and which ones contribute to hitting your Stage Gates.

Check, double-check, and triple-check.

Having a Four Sticky Note Business Plan is all about drowning out the noise that comes along with the chaotic roller coaster of the startup phase of your business. There are going to be a million distractions that could pull you off course, which is why it needs to be right in front of you, reminding you of your purpose and what you're trying to accomplish. It's there to help you check, double-check, and triple-check yourself every day.

> 66 Having a Four Sticky Note Business Plan is all about drowning out the noise that comes along with the chaotic roller coaster of the startup phase of your business. 99

With that said, I would encourage you to first go back through this list, revisit everything you've learned so far, and make sure that you have a clear understanding of each concept—and then let's write that business plan! I've found that this plan will increase your chances of success and help avoid failure.

CHAPTER 16:

Why Startups Fail

THIS ISN'T EXACTLY a pleasant topic, but it's a necessary one. So far, we've focused on what you need to succeed, and that's going to continue to be the case as we move forward. However, some of the greatest lessons I've learned in my own entrepreneurship journey have come about not from my successes but from my failures. Over time, I've not only noticed the patterns leading to a startup's success but also the patterns leading to its failure. In the same way that it's not luck that creates success, it's not necessarily bad luck that creates failure.

To put my own cards on the table, I want to revisit one of my failed startups—Shareholder Blockchain. I mentioned in chapter 7 how when one of our programmers went rogue, we failed to hit our first Stage Gate, and we were left in a position where we had to decide whether to pivot, do something different, or shut things down. We chose to shut things down.

That was a really hard decision personally because I had invested $50,000 in the company, and my colleagues and I really believed in the concept. In fact, I still love and am obsessed with the idea to this day. And as easy as it would be for me to blame the programmer who went rogue and say, "That's why we failed," at the end of the day, I had to accept responsibility as the entrepreneur for not having all the right ingredients in place to be successful: the Story, the People, the Money, and the Systems.

We had a good Story for the company, and we had the Money in place, but obviously we didn't have the right People. Looking back, I think I'd caught a case of Silicon Valley Disease and moved too fast. My colleague Michele watched that train wreck happen, and her take on it was that in the hiring process, we failed to "Look for Mr. or Ms. Right rather than Mr. and Ms. Right Now." We simply hired too hastily and, in her words, "We ended up putting the wrong people in place." But *we* were the ones who put them in place, so we have to own that.

Furthermore, we didn't have the right Systems in place to protect the company and prevent people from going rogue. Jeff Sass, who was also witness to that disaster, puts it this way: "You have to inspect what you expect." But we had not taken the time to put a system in place to make sure the work was on track.

And this is why I focus so much on having the Four Sticky Note Business Plan as part of your Systems for your startup—because had I followed my own advice, maybe we could've prevented the shutdown of the company and it could've been another success story instead. That's why you need to check, double-check, and triple-check your Story, People, Money, and Systems to be successful.

No one's perfect, and no business is ever perfect. Chances are that you've already failed at some point with a prior business, and the whole reason you're reading this book is to prevent it from happening again. If so, that's fine—and you're in very good company.

You'll make more mistakes, and you'll learn from them. But that being the case, why is it that so many startups fail? According to the Bureau of Labor Statistics, 50 percent of businesses close up shop within five years.[7] Why is that? And what can we learn about those reasons to avoid them?

The company doesn't solve a problem.

The saga of the company MoviePass, Inc. is an interesting one. On paper, the concept seems like a slam dunk. For a small subscription fee of ten dollars per month, users could buy up to three tickets to any theater for any movie they chose. Originally started in 2011 and operating based off printed vouchers, they eventually released a mobile app for a more user-friendly experience. So why did it fail?

There are a lot of things you can point to: hostility from major theater chains, the problematic math of paying full price for tickets while offering users a premium discount, and the usual behind-the-scenes corporate drama that comes along with Silicon Valley Disease. Their long-term strategy was volume—gain enough subscribers at the discounted rate, then scale pricing up after people were committed to the service.

But ultimately I think the main issue was that they weren't solving a big enough problem for enough people. They needed volume to stay afloat, but there just weren't as many people as they expected who would want to spend ten dollars per month for three tickets. In the era of streaming, people just don't go to the theater as much as they used to—and this was *before* the COVID-19 pandemic.

---

7   Sean Bryant, "How Many Startups Fail and Why?," Investopedia.com, November 26, 2022, https://www.investopedia.com/articles/personal-finance/040915/how-many-startups-fail-and-why.asp#citation-1.

Those who did use the service were drawn in by the price point, but once the company announced they would increase pricing, those discount-hunting subscribers dropped out. Plus, many potential subscribers were lured away by competing programs offered directly by the theater chains, which provided loyalty rewards and discounts on snacks that MoviePass couldn't offer.

By late 2019, the company had essentially ceased to operate, and in early 2020, they filed for bankruptcy. As of the writing of this book, it's attempting a resurrection by revisiting what problems the service *can* solve.

Stacy Spikes, one of the original cofounders, was ousted in 2018 and later reclaimed possession of the company. He stated in an interview, "We contacted studios, we contacted theaters, we contacted members and we started having a conversation … We took everything that they were saying and put it in a box and said, 'What does everybody want? What did they not have from the first MoviePass and what do they want from the new MoviePass?'" In other words, he's having a conversation to figure out what problem they can actually solve, because only then can they prove viability.

The wrong people are running the company.

I'll say it again: You can't outsource the entrepreneur! My colleague Jeffery Wolf had an incredible company set up in the early 2000s, right in the dot-com boom. You could think of them almost like an online Radio Shack (if you remember Radio Shack), as they could get you any piece of audiovisual equipment you needed for any appliance in your home, and they partnered with every retailer in the country. Times were good, business was booming—over three years in, they had three hundred employees, were generating nearly $80 million in revenue, and had an office in New York, looking for a buyer.

Unlike many startups, they were incredibly well funded, not lacking in oxygen. But the board—including Jeffery—felt like things were moving too slow and thought it would be good to bring in some fresh blood. Specifically, they wanted to find a new CEO—a star CEO—who could take the company to the next level. So they began the hunt, researching and vetting candidates, and found their star CEO. But within four months of him being in the job, they were completely out of business. Just like that.

How did they go from being—in his words—"the darling of the industry" to another victim of the dot-com crash? As Jeffery shared in one of our Startup Club sessions, the new CEO got into a conflict with their biggest retail partner—who accounted for 60 percent of their business—and the retailer decided they were done and pulled out, which was devastating for the company.

"That was our Achilles' heel," Jeffery lamented. "Everything in startups and business is about relationships ... and this guy came in like a bull in a China shop ... there was no flexibility in his approach ... and how he managed the key relationships with the business completely killed the company."

And that's why I always say you can't outsource the entrepreneur. While there were others like Jeffery who were trying to offer counsel and to communicate the delicacy of the conflict with the retail partner, they also wanted their new star CEO to be front and center and to establish himself by managing this conflict and proving that they had made the right choice. So this should serve as a cautionary tale. You can make it to the big time like they did and still lose your way by trying to replace the entrepreneurial soul of the company with a corporate soul.

Often this is a confidence issue. You start to grow and do really well, have some early success, and a bit of imposter syndrome sneaks in and you start to think, "Well, maybe someone can do this even better than me." And while it's important to find the right people with the right skills who will help you scale the business and who complement you, there's simply no replacement for the entrepreneur's mindset and spirit.

A time may come to find a new CEO—that's not a problem. Later on in Repeat, I'll share how we can hire or partner with entrepreneurs. I have successfully replaced myself with another entrepreneurial-minded CEO on several occasions.

Red flags are ignored.

Another key takeaway Jeffery shared about the collapse of the company was that they ignored the red flags they saw before selecting the new CEO. He discussed how their board was filled with intelligent people and how their research and vetting was really thorough—it wasn't a rush job by any means. "When we interviewed him," he recalled, "there were concerns about him … but he had an impressive résumé."

The impressive résumé and their own smarts got in the way, blinding them to those red flags. "He never should have been hired, obviously," Jeffery stated, but he learned a lot from "how all these smart people can make the wrong decision." This critical takeaway—to never ignore the red flags—has since helped set Jeffery up for multiple successes.

Perhaps things would've gone differently if they had vetted further or had gone in another direction. But since entrepreneurs generally tend to be optimists, that means we're also susceptible to optimism bias, the belief that "It won't happen to me," even in the face of red flags.

So whether the red flag is a financial issue, a personnel issue, or something else, it's important to sometimes slow down and make sure to address them before they become bigger problems for the company. Entrepreneurs can also be guilty of being all go and wanting things to go faster and farther so that we end up flying by the red flags without even seeing them for the warnings they are. Sometimes the hardest thing to do is to slow down and stop, especially when you've reached a point of momentum, but as Jeffery's story proves, there can be a very thin line between success and failure, and paying attention to the red flags might just make the difference on which side of the line you fall.

> " There can be a very thin line between success and failure, and paying attention to the red flags might just make the difference on which side of the line you fall. "

They raise too little money— or too much money.

If money is the oxygen for your business, then, quite frankly, not having enough of it is likely the number one reason companies fail. In fact, according to a study by US Bank, 82 percent of small businesses that fail do so because of poor cash flow management.[8]

On the flip side, *too much* money can be just as dangerous. There's so much Silicon Valley carnage on the startup highway, it's sad. I have worked with companies that have just simply raised too much venture capital, diluting the founders' ownership and authority. Nothing beats

---

8   Brandon Metcalf, "82% of Small Businesses Fail Because of Cash Flow Problems. Here Are 3 Ways to Fix That," Minutes.co, accessed November 22, 2022, https://minutes.co/82-of-small-businesses-fail-because-of-cash-flow-problems-here-are-3-ways-to-fix-that/.

a lean or efficient startup, and although venture capital can play an important role in scaling, the vast majority of startups can do without it.

There's a good chance that you often can't survive on sales revenue alone in the beginning, because as your sales increase, so will your production costs, your personnel costs, and your shipping costs. Put simply: the more you grow, the more it costs.

If you don't have the money, it doesn't matter how good your company is. That sounds harsh, but it's true. And that's why it's absolutely essential to know your first Stage Gate early on so that you can have the right money in place to reach it.

There are too many cooks in the kitchen.

Partnerships can be beneficial in many ways, but the wrong ones can be destructive to a startup. I shared previously about when I invested in a family member's business that failed. That company hit $12 million in e-commerce sales and within a year went bankrupt.

Some of that was the accounting and the inexperience of the partners, but ultimately the problem I saw was they had too many cooks in the kitchen, where no one person was really in charge. While they had early successes and had good cash flow at first, this lack of a plan, lack of direction, and lack of systems ultimately led to failure.

At the end of the day, the buck has to stop somewhere, and you have to decide what that's going to look like. Are you going to be a democratic organization where all the partners get a vote and a say? If so, then you must be willing to go along with the decisions, even when you get outvoted.

Otherwise, you need to have a single CEO or an executive who sets the purpose and vision and is the final decision maker—or else chaos rules. This comes with a cost, though, because when setting one person in charge, if it's you, then you need to be ready to make some very difficult decisions and stick with them. And if it's someone else, then you have to be willing to accept those decisions and let the person truly be in charge. Micromanagement doesn't work—there has to be clarity at the management level or else it turns into an anarchy.

Companies can fail even when they do everything right.

I'm going to end both this chapter and our discussion of Start with my biggest failure of all, though we'll get into more of the nitty-gritty details later in Exit. Internet Direct, the ISP I cofounded in Canada, ended up being worth about $80 million. My business partners and I decided to merge with a large wireless cable company in Canada, applied for licenses from the government, and as a result, saw our stock shoot up to over a billion dollars. Things were looking great, especially for me personally, since I owned 13 percent of the stock.

So what went wrong? Unlike some of the other examples we've included where internal issues led to the failure, this time it was an external event—the dot-com crash.

These types of external events are going to happen from time to time and affect companies, whether they're startups or major corporations. And it didn't help that the company was being too free with spending, which made it impossible to survive the fallout. The company ended up filing for bankruptcy protection in 2001, and I found myself selling for a measly six cents a share compared to what had been a high of nineteen dollars a share. Even worse, all our employees lost the value in their shares.

This might sound obvious, but the biggest factor in success and failure is *human failure* as well as the fact that as entrepreneurs, we can often get in our own way of success and be our own worst enemy. All of these failures can be traced back to a human choice that impacted the outcome. Because, regardless of the external circumstances, had we not given up control of the company during the merger, perhaps we could've had more say in the overspending I saw happening or set up some systems to minimize the impact of the dot-com crash.

Companies fail for many reasons, but most of those reasons can fall into at least one of the categories mentioned earlier. The good news is that we can reframe failure—we can learn from it and do better. I've learned from these failures, my colleagues have learned from them, and now I hope that you can learn from them too. You can have failures and mistakes in your Start phase and still find a way to get back on track or, if worse comes to worst, start a new company.

Walking away from a business you were hoping to scale can be terribly difficult because, as entrepreneurs, we look at our businesses kind of like they're our children. We don't want to walk away from them! It's especially difficult when you have early successes and then an unexpected external force comes along to derail all your hard work.

Because we can never fully predict every change, this means we have to redefine our view of failure. By launching something, building it, and then failing, you have an opportunity to learn what you *don't* want to do next. I know it's a cliché, but every failure you have is really a learning event.

Viewed in this light, I truly believe that failure can help strengthen your chances of succeeding in any subsequent efforts. You might fail ten times and then hit your success on the eleventh try.

And you would be in good company! In 1923, Walt Disney produced a short film that was intended to be the first in a series but ran out of money and had to declare bankruptcy—but we all know how that worked out in the end. Soichiro Honda's automotive parts designs were rejected by Toyota in 1936, but when a terrible gas shortage hit Japan after World War II, he released the first Honda motorized bike as a solution. Milton Hershey had two candy shops shut down before he struck success by focusing on selling only caramels—*not* chocolate, as you might expect. He then sold that business for $1 million, which allowed him to open the first Hershey Company chocolate factory.

All these are examples of entrepreneurs who were trying to scale their business in one way and failed to do so. Instead of giving up, they took what they learned from those failures, made their own changes, and found a new way to scale. I have learned so much from every one of my own failures. Startup failures are the scars of our past that guide us forward in our new ventures.

> **" Startup failures are the scars of our past that guide us forward in our new ventures. "**

START.
SCALE.
EXIT.
REPEAT.

I hate startups.

Believe me, as a serial entrepreneur, I know that sounds ridiculous. For me, the startup phase is a necessary evil so that I can get to my favorite part of the process—scaling! The reason I hate startups is that they grow very slowly. Remember the flywheel effect described by Jim Collins in his book *Good to Great*? At the beginning it's difficult to turn that flywheel, and anyone who has launched a startup can attest to how slow things can be in the early days.

Scaling, on the other hand, is where it gets fun!

As we established in Start, a successful startup doesn't happen by accident—it's never dumb luck. Nor is it just hard work. Some of the failures I just discussed happened despite a ton of hard work.

So before we get into it, I want you to sit back, close your eyes, and imagine your company right now at ten times its current size. Visualize it ten times larger. If you're doing $10,000 a month in sales, I want you to add a zero and make it $100,000. How has the story changed? What about the management team? Did you bring in new leadership? What kind of sales team do you have in place? How much cash flow? How much money did you raise to 10X your current size? What about the annual company parties? What car would you be driving to the office?

Okay, I may be going a little too far with the last one, but you get the point.

Over the next few chapters, we're going to talk about your Story and how we need to change it to scale. We're going to figure out who we need driving this bus to get us out of the startup wilderness and into the promised land. We're going to understand how much money will be required and the key systems we need to put in place to hit our 10X goal.

As you'll see, scaling can be complicated. But if you're willing to endure the pain, there is a formula for you to successfully scale your business . My partners and I have done it over and over again by following the principles we'll cover.

Change will still reign and continue during this phase—that's not really different from Start. Be prepared for chaos to be the norm, maybe even extreme, on a day-to-day basis. Brace for growth. It's time to Scale.

STORY

CHAPTER 17:

Scale Quickly, Kill Quickly

YOUR STORY HERE is at a pivot point. A fork in the road. Do you continue on? Or do you let it go?

As I've said before, scaling isn't something that happens by accident—you have to choose to scale. You make the conscious decision for your company to grow and you implement People and Money and Systems for it to grow. But how does that factor into your Story?

> **"Scaling isn't something that happens by accident—you have to choose to scale."**

In the later years of Internet Direct (the internet service provider we started in the nineties), we had built a first-generation web hosting and email platform. Not only were we providing internet access for hundreds of thousands of Canadians, but we were also supplying small businesses with the tools to build a website and run their email. Although we had considerable success with this and sold over one hundred thousand domains, we had to keep investing heavily in coders and were beginning to fall behind. Building and developing a commercially viable platform was not cheap in those days—arguably, it's still not cheap.

SaskTel, technically one of our competitors at the time, reached out and asked if we'd be interested in licensing our hosting platform to them. When that happened, the bells started to go off for us and we thought, "If we're doing this for ourselves already, could we provide this service to other telecoms? Instead of competing with them, what if we took the platform we've already built and made it available to customers similar to us?"

These questions helped us realize that we could make it available to a dozen, a hundred, maybe even scale it to thousands of different companies with similar needs to ours. And to do it not only in Canada but also the United States, South America, and Europe.

We decided to launch a new company (with authorization from the board of directors) called Hostopia.com LLC. The company would endeavor to create a new, more advanced platform to which we could outsource current services. But to do so, a few standards had to be met, including building a platform that could be independently verified as the best solution in the world for Internet Direct. My brother and I partnered with another entrepreneur, raised the initial working capital from our prior exit, and hired dozens of people, including a lot of coders to get things going.

In 2001, I wrapped up my duties at my prior company and joined Hostopia full time, which was racking up big losses at the time. At one point, I calculated that we were burning about $500,000 per month. This was days after 9/11 hit us and businesses had put a stop to any major buying decisions. In response, we had to also pull back, cutting a third of our staff. We focused on a clear strategy of building the best platform in the world to sell to service providers, including telecoms, cable providers, and web hosting companies.

We were pioneering our platforms in an early version of cloud computing that at the time was referred to as an application service provider (ASP) and later as a software as a service (SaaS) provider, but this was in opposition to what many of the telecoms were doing at the time, believing they needed to host all their systems locally rather than across thousands of servers in a cloud-like environment. We decided early on that we wanted Hostopia's platform to be web based rather than downloadable like most software at the time. This was our second big lesson as a startup trying to scale—surviving the technology chasm.

In 2003, we ran into a complicated issue where if half of our customers upgraded their browser, our software would no longer work. So we had to make a choice: Do we upgrade our software? Because if we did, then half of our users would no longer be able to operate it.

We decided to stick with the SaaS plan and remain web-based— even though this meant a potentially negative impact for at least half of our customers. But ultimately this was the move that allowed us to scale and provided a huge advantage over our competitors. Prices of data dropped, and the complexities of managing these services increased, which eventually persuaded the telecoms to simply outsource these services to us.

I'll save the story of how we scaled outside of Canada for later on, but you'll notice that a lot of these decisions happened very quickly— and in the midst of us facing losses and an economic crisis resulting from the 9/11 attacks and then subsequently surviving a multiyear tech chasm. If your head is starting to hurt a bit at the thought, then you've got a small taste of what we were going through!

If it's not growing, it's dying.

Again, sometimes we as entrepreneurs can be our own worst enemy. Sometimes we love an idea so much, we won't walk away from it when we should—or sometimes we're so afraid of the risk involved in growing, we walk away too soon and never challenge ourselves. Knowing when to take each action is a little bit like trying to read a crystal ball.

But the key differentiator is this—if it's not growing, then it's dying. Though we were losing $500,000 each month, we were still growing and we were still seeing interest in what we were providing. Had we flatlined—or lost customers—it would've been a different story.

When we made the choice to stick with our cloud-based strategy, resulting in tepid demand at the beginning, Telecom believed they had to run their own infrastructure. We dithered in what Geoffrey Moore refers to as the chasm. We stuck with the original vision and trusted that the technology would catch up to us. Eventually it did, and we greatly benefited by entering a very high-growth period with huge demand again, what Moore refers to as the tornado. Here is the truth: the chasm is kind of a hard slog, but the tornado can be a lot of fun.

Sometimes sales and revenue are going to flatline, and when they do, you have to ask, "Why? Do we need to tweak our ad strategy? Is there a problem with our product that we don't know about?" Because if you determine the answer to those questions, then you can either pivot to make the necessary changes and get over the plateau, or you can be made aware that you've taken the business as far as it can go and start working on your exit strategy. On that note, we have to admit defeat or break the mold.

Admit defeat or break the mold.

It just happens. Sometimes your idea ends up being a lot harder to scale than you predicted or a new variable comes along to disrupt things. There are two approaches when you get to that point, and the first one is to admit defeat, find a way to package that puppy, and get the hell out of dodge!

There are a number of strategies you can implement to do so, which we'll talk about in Exit, but the key thing is to not wait until it's too late. You need to do it as quickly as possible once you've made the decision to walk away, or else you'll run out of oxygen and suffocate instead of being able to sell.

Too many times, entrepreneurs don't want to admit defeat. I sometimes wish I'd followed my own advice here instead of letting ego get in the way. But sometimes the best thing you can do for your business is to kill it before it kills you—or before it dies a slow, agonizing, and painful death. The faster you can move on, the faster you can get to your next success.

The other approach here is to break the mold. This is where you realize that maybe things aren't going quite the way you thought they would, but you discover a way that you can pivot the business. Sometimes this means revisiting your purpose itself, because the purpose you had in Start may not be the one to carry you through Scale.

> **❝ The faster you can move on, the faster you can get to your next success. ❞**

For example, let's talk about Android for a moment. When it originally launched in 2003, it was designed to be a cloud-based platform for photo storing and interfacing between digital cameras and computers. After all, digital cameras were established in the mainstream at this point, so it made sense for them to try to ride that particular wave.

But in 2004, when its founders realized this would be hard to scale and they would eventually flatline after a certain point of market share, they decided to break the mold by changing the purpose itself from photo storage to being an operating system for smartphones—three years before smartphones became a household word with the launch of the iPhone.

Seeing the potential of the smartphone market, Google acquired Android in 2005, and the rest is history.[9] While the iPhone may have popularized the smartphone in the US, Android's OS enjoys an 87 percent market share globally.[10] I think it's fair to say that they would have never scaled to that point if they had stuck with their original plan instead of breaking the mold.

Sometimes this can be a challenge because when we love an idea, it can be difficult to see beyond the original intended purpose we came up with. But there are times when it's appropriate to ask, "Is there a bigger and better purpose for my idea than what I'm seeing?" And sometimes we get so blinded by a narrow view of our idea that we miss out on opportunities that present themselves.

That's why when SaskTel approached Hostopia about licensing our platform, I'm glad we didn't say, "Sorry, but you're our competitor; it's not our job to sell you a platform." By pivoting our initial concept, we broke the mold of our plan and were able to launch a company that could scale in ways we couldn't have imagined at the time.

---

9   Brittanica.com, "Android Operating System," accessed May 24, 2022, https://www.britannica.com/technology/Android-operating-system.

10   Jason Cohen, "iOS More Popular in Japan and US, Android Dominates in China and India," PCmag.com, September 4, 2020, https://www.pcmag.com/news/ios-more-popular-in-japan-and-us-android-dominates-in-china-and-india.

This all goes back to the Story of your business and seeing where it might be tweaked in order to effectively scale. After all, even the greatest stories need some editing to be their best, or they need a cover redesign to be more appealing to the customer walking through the bookstore. Why would we think it would be any different with our businesses?

CHAPTER 18:

Scale in Zeros

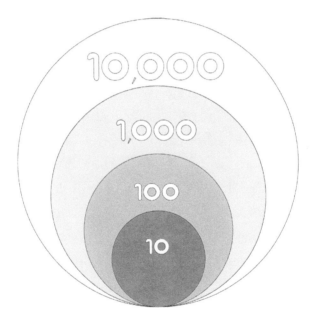

AT THE VERY BEGINNING of this section of the book, I asked you to visualize your company ten times larger. In Start, we created Stage Gates that were based on hitting certain milestones, but Stage Gates are focused on keeping oxygen in the tank—keeping the company alive. In Scale, you're no longer worried so much about survival but about thriving and growing.

This is what I refer to as scaling in zeros. I originally learned this term from my mentor, Lance Tracey, a fellow serial entrepreneur who has also been an investor in my companies. He was using the term well before 10X became a popular concept and has made it a practice to back companies that are highly scalable and in a position to scale in zeros. It's the idea of taking actions that will move you from ten customers to a hundred, from $10,000 in monthly revenue to $100,000, and so on. Doing so starts with the way you *think* about the decisions you make, because the same things that made you successful in Start won't necessarily work in Scale.

Think in zeros.

This concept touches on all elements of our Four Sticky Note Business Plan—to scale in zeros, you need the right Story, the right People, the right Money, and the right Systems. Like you did with your Stage Gates in Start, your growth goals need to be SMART—that is, you have to start asking, "If we do this, will it get us to 10X?" Thinking this way can save you from pursuing the wrong actions.

One of the biggest problems I see with other entrepreneurs is that they fail to make a shift in mindset to start thinking in zeros. They wonder why they're flatlining because they're doing the same things with the same people that made them successful in the beginning—but *that's* exactly why they're flatlining, because they're doing the same things!

> **If you *think* in zeros, you can begin to *grow* in zeros.**

A key principle of scaling is to start thinking of scaling even when you're still in Start mode, because it's a lot harder to make this shift in mindset than you realize. To go back to the school example I mentioned previously, my wife and I were obviously not thinking in zeros when we bought the school because once we wanted to scale, we realized that the cost of doing so was far too much. If you *think* in zeros, you can begin to *grow* in zeros.

Plan to scale in zeros.

Before you can act in a way to scale in zeros, you have to plan for it first. With the success Hostopia had achieved in Canada, we knew it was time to scale, but breaking out of Canada was going to be an issue. We couldn't do it without a plan.

We turned our eyes south of the border to the US, where our first step was to set up an office operation. But where exactly?

In our planning, we learned that Miami had built a network access point called NAP of the Americas, and it was one of the largest in the world. Before we could scale in zeros, we knew it was key for us to have access to the bandwidth we would need to exponentially grow across the US. With that, we began the move to Fort Lauderdale, Florida.

You know the phrase about being in the right place at the right time, but you have a better shot of being in the right place at the right time if you plan it out.

Act to scale in zeros.

From mindset, you build a plan. From a plan, you take action. After moving Hostopia to Fort Lauderdale, the real work began. Early on, we were doing all right—we won a few telecoms by implementing a similar strategy to what had worked in Canada. But we knew over the long term that it wasn't going to give us anywhere near the kind of growth we envisioned for the company.

So we made a few key moves very different from what we had done during our Start phase. One of the biggest was that we hired the top salespeople from our competitors. Unlike before when we had to operate at discount salaries, now we were willing to pay top dollar to get top people. And we did. We hired the best, most expensive people in the industry and brought them over to Hostopia.

This is where we were able to start scaling in zeros as deal after deal came through. But this happened only because we recognized the actions necessary to scale and then executed them.

In terms of Story, this relates most to *who* you want to be serving. With Hostopia, we knew that meant breaking into the US. For you, it means asking, "Who do I want to serve next? What market do I need to break into? Where do I need to focus my attention?" You may have a long-term vision to be a global company and that's great—but answering these questions is the start to your scaling strategy.

In the same way that we discussed the power of visualization for your Story in Start, the same is true here. You have to be able to visualize 10X and what that means for your company. You'll need to build your human resources, your funding—*everything* around the 10X mindset and create SMART growth goals. But to do so also means finding that one thing about your company's story that sets you apart from the competition—your X factor.

> " You have to be able to visualize 10X and what that means for your company. "

CHAPTER 19

Find Your X Factor

FINDING YOUR X FACTOR is tough. There's no denying that. Frankly, a lot of entrepreneurs end up stumbling upon it through experimentation. But the earlier you can figure out what sets you apart from your competition, the better for transforming your Story into one that scales.

The term *X factor* dates back to at least the 1930s and simply refers to "a circumstance, quality, or person that has a strong but unpredictable influence."[11] Author and speaker Jim Collins has frequently used this in terms of leadership and identifying what sets you apart to be truly great, so it's not exactly a new concept.

> **The earlier you can figure out what sets you apart from your competition, the better for transforming your Story into one that scales.**

My CEO coach, Patrick Thean, once put his own spin on the X factor, saying, "It's actually not something special about you—it's you creating something special." He goes even further to say that doing so "gives you a 10X advantage over competitors in your industry." I'm biased toward his advice, obviously, but I like his take on

---

11   Merriam-Webster.com, "X Factor," accessed October 19, 2022, https://www.merriam-webster.com/dictionary/X%20factor.

it because it means the X factor is less about you and more about what you can do for others. In other words, your X factor isn't what makes you the hero of the story—it's what you do to make your customer the hero.

Don't panic if you don't have your X factor worked out yet. As we were establishing Hostopia in the US, we were several years in and still hadn't figured out our X factor. In Canada, I probably would've told you our platform itself was our X factor because very few others could provide multi-language services to the Canadian market to the extent that we did. But it was a different story in the US, and we were no longer unique in our offering. So what were we going to do to really set ourselves apart?

Connect your Story to your Nearly Unbearable Brand Promise.

We talked briefly in Start about how your X factor can relate to your Nearly Unbearable Brand Promise (NUBP). While they are not always the same thing, it's not uncommon for them to be linked or for one to lead to the other in the same way that many still identify Domino's Pizza with the "30 minutes or free" promise, whether they mention it in their advertising or not. That's the power of the NUBP!

Our opportunity to define this for ourselves at Hostopia happened when we met with EarthLink, who was running a request for proposal about potentially becoming one of our customers. It was the mid-2000s, and they knew they needed to get off their old hosting architecture—they needed a new provider to manage both the web hosting and the email hosting for their customers. In total, this would require migrating seventy-five thousand websites and hundreds of thousands of emails. This represented the largest deal to come to market in our space at the time, so we *had* to win this one!

After being told we were going to lose the deal, we went for the Hail Mary. Dirk Bhagat, my CTO, and I flew to Atlanta to meet with the buyer, and we did something very risky and very uncomfortable—we made a Nearly Unbearable Brand Promise to them. We said, "We'll guarantee one hundred percent migration of all these websites. If we lose even one of your customer's sites, then we'll pay fair market value for each one lost."

See, in the world of large companies, middle managers who make a mistake can get fired. Migrations are notoriously complex and dangerous for one's career. Our NUBP was a matter of de-risking the decision to go with us for that middle manager.

Fair market value for a website at the time was around $350, so if we were to lose ten thousand sites during the migration, we would end up paying EarthLink $3.5 million, which obviously would've been a huge hit to us. But this was great for the middle manager to be able to report to their boss and say, "I'm going to get them to pay for any mistakes they make."

That being said, they took us up on it, and I'm proud to say that we didn't lose a single website in the migration. By fulfilling this NUBP to them in such a major way, this made their guy look like a hero to the company, securing his job—and for us, we discovered the X factor for scaling our Story in the US and the rest of the world. We could now approach each new conversation with our 100 percent migration guarantee and continue to scale.

Now let me be very clear—this was *not* easy. And it completely transformed our company, especially in how we interacted with the customers. We vetoed any request that might risk a migration. We developed the best migration software in the world and had a team of administrators checking every single site. It wasn't easy. But it was truly the move that began our dominance in the industry.

Look for your X factor in your failures.

Coming up with Hostopia's X factor wasn't exactly happenstance—and it wasn't rooted in a success story. It actually came from one of the biggest mistakes we made when we were trying to scale in the US. It was so bad, it hit CNN.

We had a telecom that needed to migrate millions of email addresses, but this meant the individual users had to change their email settings on their own computers when they logged in following the migration.

You can imagine what happened. Hundreds of thousands of people couldn't get their email to work. This was a nightmare for the employees, a nightmare for the company, and a nightmare for us.

But we took a very valuable lesson out of it, saying, "We're going to put policies in place to ensure that we never have an outage like this again." We reengineered the entire organization and process, testing our systems until we became the best in the world at migrating websites. This led us down the path to figure out our X factor.

Look for the bottlenecks.

Back to EarthLink for a second—they were at a crossroads with their customers. They knew that their infrastructure was archaic and that they were going to start losing business if they didn't upgrade things. Their story at that moment was that they were facing an ugly dragon breathing fire right at their face, and they needed a way to fight it.

Verne Harnish has pointed out that a great way to discover your X factor is to look for the bottlenecks being faced by others—whether it's your competitors or your customers. What setbacks are they facing? Where are things slowing down in their work? What's causing friction or frustration?

Tiff's Treats, an Austin-based cookie bakery, figured this out when they realized people love to bring cookies to work for special occasions like birthdays, work anniversaries, or hitting a milestone, but by the time they would drive to the bakery and back to the office, the cookies would get cold, not to mention the lost time and energy.

So what did they do? They said, "Hey, don't worry about it—we'll bring you the cookies hot and fresh from the oven." They established themselves as a cookie delivery service, allowing them to bypass the bottleneck faced by other bakeries in their area. This allowed them to then scale from one location run by the two founders (a married couple—Tiff and Leon) to over seventy locations and more than seventeen hundred employees. Also, they have a really killer domain name of cookiedelivery.com, instead of their company name, which zeroes in on their X factor and is key in owning their space.

Other bakeries could've had the same idea, but Tiff and Leon saw the bottleneck from the customer's perspective and capitalized on it. When the pandemic hit in 2020 and businesses had to shut down or had to limit customer numbers, their X factor allowed them to continue with business as usual and keep growing.

A great example my CEO coach Patrick likes to use is Tesla—not because of their technology but because of their sales process. He points out that one of Tesla's distinguishing factors is that they noticed the bottleneck caused by dealerships and how they actually created friction and constraints in the car-buying process. Over time, this had simply become standard practice for dealerships, but by identifying this bottleneck, Tesla removed the friction by allowing customers to buy directly from them, giving them a competitive advantage. Uber did the same by noticing the bottleneck of a lack of taxi drivers in their backyard of San Francisco. Why can't you do the same thing? Answer—you probably can!

But why do we as entrepreneurs so often miss this concept of the bottleneck? As Patrick puts it, "Because we're so excited by our own ideas, we jump quickly to sell and make some money. This works for the first few sales … but to scale your company, you must sell beyond your first hundred customers. As you begin to scale, you realize there is friction and you begin to see these bottlenecks."

To notice bottlenecks, he gives three very practical, easy tips:

➤ First, check out similar businesses in your industry. Ask yourself, "Where do things slow down? Where is the friction?"

➤ Next, see what older companies in your field are doing. Are there illogical things happening because that's just the way it has always been for that company and the industry? Often these accepted practices are a bottleneck that no one else is noticing—just like the car dealerships.

➤ Finally, if you're entering a completely new industry, that's a good thing. Make a list of the way things should work and then a list of the difficulties people are having. By approaching things with fresh eyes, you can find the bottleneck that the "old-timers" in your industry have in their blind spots.

Consider adding an X-factor-specific brainstorming session to your annual strategic plan. For my vacation rental business, Escape Club, we had a session to brainstorm how we could make the business more successful. It yielded modest results. A few days later, I called the team back and asked a different question: "What is something Escape Club can provide that no one else on the island is doing?"

The results were amazing. Within thirty minutes we had come up with really powerful ideas, including exclusive access to services like a miniature golf course and renting the company's pontoon—something no one else had on the island. We also decided to offer luxury services like Westin Heavenly beds and to develop a consistent feel between properties. Lastly, we realized that we could link up the properties for weddings and other events. The results of all this? We were able to cross-promote our properties and get a higher return rate of customers.

At this stage of the process, your X factor isn't optional. It's a must-have in order to really scale. Companies that can't figure out their X factor may experience early success but then eventually flatline, and as we've already established, if you're not growing, you're dying.

> **At this stage of the process, your X factor isn't optional. It's a must-have in order to really scale.**

What are you already doing for others that is special to them? What *can* you start doing that would be special for them? At the end of the day, it's about making your customer the hero of the story, and your X factor is the sword that allows them to slay the dragon.

CHAPTER 20

Prove It

YOU ALWAYS NEED to be proving your business model—it's not something that's one and done. If we sold to a hundred customers, can we sell to a thousand? And then ten thousand? If we have sold into ten distributors, can we target a hundred?

Going back to the story of Facebook, they proved their concept by selling first at Harvard, then launching into other colleges, then into other cities, then into other countries, every step of the way proving they could grow in those markets.

Proving yourself in a new market is easier said than done, but it's also one of the fun challenges of scaling. Too often, entrepreneurs reach this stage of growth and think they can go into a new market and just do the same things they did before, assuming customers are the same everywhere.

To scale to a new market, you'll have to prove you've developed a keen understanding

> 66 To scale to a new market, you'll have to prove you've developed a keen understanding of who is in your new market—their needs, their preferences—and shape your decisions to those cultural nuances. 99

of who is in your new market—their needs, their preferences—and shape your decisions to those cultural nuances.

Not all markets are the same.

Every market has its own culture, and you have to really do the work to understand the needs of the new market culture you're hoping to enter. When Hostopia came to the US, one of the differentiators between us and our competitors was that we were already set up as a dual-language platform because in Canada, the law (and the market) required us to be able to serve both English and French speakers. So when potential customers in the US asked if we could add Spanish, it was a pretty easy adjustment, so we could answer, "Yes, we can." This multilanguage ability became almost like a mini X factor for us, since our biggest competitor was only a single language platform at the time. This may sound simple, but designing a platform to be multilanguage after it's already been built and launched is anything but easy, so it was going to take some time for them to catch up to us in that arena.

Speaking of other cultures, this also allowed us to tweak the platform to go into Brazil by adding in Portuguese. In the end, we included more than ten languages as we scaled to new markets, proving ourselves each time, which eventually set us up for our IPO.

Understand the culture of your new markets.

It's easy for your market research to look only at bottom-line issues like projected costs to acquire new customers, overhead, distribution, and so on. While all those are important, it's more important to understand the cultural preferences of your market: "How do they like to pay for things? What language are they most comfortable in? What are their expectations for communicating problems?"

For instance, let's say you run an e-commerce clothing store and you want to scale to a new country or even a new city. You've already lined up distribution and employees, and you've already registered all the legal documentation needed to do business there. But do you have payment methods set up that are popular or available in that country? Do you have designs that will appeal to those customers? Do they expect a full refund if they're unhappy with a purchase, or would they be just as satisfied with store credit? Do they prefer to receive communications via email? WhatsApp? Facebook? Having good distribution and employees won't mean anything if customers don't feel understood. In fact, they won't be your customers—they'll be someone else's customers!

As we discussed in Start, you don't want to go into a new market expecting a change in the human behavior there. Instead, you need to adapt and mold your business practices to meet the preferences of that market. The more you can culturize your product to your new market, the better success you'll have at scaling.

For example, when we set up Paw.com, we originally designed it as a US-based business, even though the founder and I are Canadian. When it came time to scale, it was only natural for us to look north to our homeland. But simply buying up ads in Canada or adding Canadian distribution was not going to be enough to make it successful there in the same way that it was in the US.

After all, there are plenty of examples of US brands that have failed when trying to move into Canada and Canadian brands that have failed when moving into the US. Being a Canadian, I understood some of the cultural nuances of my own people. We can be really sensitive when seeing a US flag on a website and seeing prices listed in $USD. Americans are no different when a product price is listed in euros or pounds. It can be a real killer in terms of converting someone from a *browser* to a *customer*.

So when scaling into Canada, we took a few key steps to prove that we could serve Canadians as well as our US customers. For one thing, we bought up the domain extension paw.ca to ensure that we would get Canadian web traffic and that no one could steal our traffic. We also added the red maple leaf flag in the corner of the website so that people would know it was a Canadian-owned business—even if it was still technically based in the US.

But because we understood the differences in both preferences and needs between US and Canadian customers, we were able to soon see the proof, as 10 percent of our sales were coming from Canada— which is a big deal when you consider the population of the US is nearly nine times that of Canada!

Sometimes this need to prove your concept again and again in new markets is the reason entrepreneurs stop scaling and get comfortable. They simply don't want to do the work that's involved and they're comfortable with the market they have. Launching into a new market and proving it can be as stressful as launching the company itself.

> **If you're not growing, you're dying.**

If that's a lifestyle choice, again, that's fine, and I don't hold anything against that choice. But comfortability can be deceptive—because once again, if you're not growing, you're dying. And a big plus to needing to prove yourself over and over is that even if you fail sometimes, you learn valuable lessons that can help you be prepared for the unexpected.

CHAPTER 21:

Promote It

AFTER PROVING YOUR CONCEPT, the next step is to get out there and tell everyone about it. I know that sounds painfully obvious, but you'd be surprised by the number of entrepreneurs I meet who are nervous about pitching their product. Believe me, I get that pitching can be nerve-racking—it's never been my strong suit either. That's why we'll talk about how to perfect your pitch later on.

> **" There is a danger to doing this in the wrong order—promoting a product you haven't yet proved. "**

For now, though, learn from my mistakes in this area. There is a danger to doing this in the wrong order—promoting a product you haven't yet proved. In the early days of Hostopia, we were not ready to be selling our product, yet we were spending tons of money on marketing and advertising. Let me correct myself here—we weren't *spending* tons of money—we were *wasting* tons of money. Spending implies that we were actually getting something out of the expense.

What we should have done instead was focus our resources and efforts on creating a really great product and then start selling it on a limited basis to get feedback and make improvements, scaling our marketing as the product improved. Eventually we got there, and I believe we had the best platform in our industry, but we wasted a lot of money early on telling everyone about it before it was really ready. This only hurt us and gave us new roadblocks to overcome later on, costing us more time and money.

Many times, this mistake is the result of our own excitement over our product and an urgency to make money as quickly as possible. On the other hand, it's equally a mistake to have a great product and then develop cold feet about letting people know—or assuming people will simply find your product on their own because of how great it is.

Build it, then promote it—in that order.

This is where the movie *Field of Dreams* does a disservice to the entrepreneur—the message of "If you build it, they will come" doesn't apply here. In fact, the movie industry has proved this over and over.

I know I'm dating myself a bit here, but let's talk for a second about the Kevin Costner film *Waterworld*. Universal marketed the heck out of that film, even though, let's be honest, it was a terrible movie. Despite all the money they spent on promoting it, the word of the critics proved stronger and the film flopped. And it wasn't just the critics who hated it—the few people who went to see it hated it too. In fact, on Rotten Tomatoes, the critics' score is slightly more generous than the audience score.

In short, they had a terrible product and then went out and told everybody about it. And now it's here in this book as a bad example of marketing. Probably not what the producers were going for!

While writing this book, Warner Brothers decided to shut down the movie *Batgirl*, even though it was nearly finished. Though they haven't said why exactly they chose to do this, one thing is clear: they decided it made more business sense to eat $90 million in losses than to spend millions more to finish and promote a product they saw as a bad gamble.

Now let's talk about another flop—the Martin Scorsese film *Hugo*, a movie that I loved. On Rotten Tomatoes, it scored 93 percent with critics. The movie also went on to win five Academy Awards, so it wasn't exactly a shoddy product. It's reported that the film cost around $156 million to make—plus an estimated $40 million advertising budget—and yet it only grossed shy of $74 million at the North American box office. Ouch.

There are a number of reasons why it probably flopped. First, even though it was based on a number one *New York Times* best-selling book—*The Invention of Hugo Cabret*—shortening the title simply to *Hugo* meant that a lot of people didn't make the connection between the film and the book. So they didn't go see it.

For another thing, the marketing focused heavily on the fact that the movie was directed by Martin Scorsese, who is typically known for grittier R-rated films like *Goodfellas*, *Raging Bull*, and *The Departed*—not family-friendly flicks like *Hugo*. The intention of emphasizing Scorsese's name ended up having the opposite effect: the target audience—families with children—stayed far away.

This goes back to what we discussed in the last chapter about understanding your target market. Had the makers of *Hugo* truly done so, their marketing strategy would have been totally different. They would have made the book connection clearer, underplayed Scorsese's name, and highlighted more about the family-friendly story line. They had a great product, but they sold it to the wrong people. They simply did not market it well.

So now let's look at how this is done the right way with the 2022 film *Top Gun: Maverick*. Not only did it score high with critics at 93 percent, it also scored high with audiences at a whopping 99 percent. The producers did an incredible job of promoting the film ahead of time as well as capitalizing on positive word of mouth, and the movie earned over $700 million at the North American box office and nearly $1.5 billion at the global box office, despite its price tag of $170 million.

There are four scenarios we can learn from here:

A. You have a crap product but don't promote it. No harm, no foul. Example: Unreleased *Batgirl* film.

B. You have a product that's poor quality and then promote the heck out of it. This hurts your reputation and wastes resources. Example: *Waterworld*.

C. You have a great-quality product but don't promote it properly. This kills your growth because no one knows about your product or what makes it great. Example: *Hugo*.

D. Finally, you have a great product and great promotion. This is the magic that allows scaling to happen. Example: *Top Gun: Maverick*.

The reasons for avoiding B and C are obvious. With A, at least you have the chance to recognize that the product is bad, kill it quickly, and pivot accordingly. It may even be crucial in helping you create a better product. You go back to the drawing board and figure out what you need to fix and then try again. The key, though, is to make sure you do it in the right order.

Doing it in the right order helps you achieve the perfect nexus of a great product with great promotion—increasing the chance that you can scale. You want to make sure you that have a great Rotten Tomatoes score—loved by critics and audiences alike to enjoy the *Top Gun: Maverick* effect rather than end up like *Hugo*—and at all costs, avoid becoming *Waterworld*.

Although we have simplified this concept by using movie launches as an example, it applies to every business. With the launch of .CLUB, we knew from day one that we had a great top-level domain, so we raised $12 million just to acquire and promote the name. Once you know you've got a good product and the market for it, there's no reason not to go ahead and promote it to scale.

> **" Once you know you've got a good product and the market for it, there's no reason not to go ahead and promote it to scale. "**

CHAPTER 22:

Finding the Right Distribution/ Sales Channel

ONE OF THE MOST compelling lessons learned from my Hostopia days was the power of distribution to scale a business. At the time we launched Hostopia, we also launched BlueGenesis, our retail web hosting platform. As I mentioned earlier, we were late to the market at this point, and the cost of acquisition for new subscribers was extremely high. Other web hosting giants like GoDaddy and large telecoms already had a foot in the door, and we were losing $450,000 a month. If we continued down this path, the company would go bankrupt.

There were two things we did to adjust our strategy. First, we came up with a private label wholesale strategy for telecoms. Second, we created a virtual managed server concept that we could sell to web developers. We changed the definition of our customers. Instead of going after individual end users, we realized that it made more sense to go after big telecoms and the web designing firms.

Pay attention here—we changed very little about BlueGenesis as a product. The software was the same, and its purpose and use were the same. The only thing that had changed was *how* we were going to distribute it, or more specifically, *who* we would distribute it to.

By doing so, we dramatically drove down the cost of new customer acquisition. Think about it this way: the cost of acquiring one million individual subscribers would have been astronomical. Instead, we could sign one deal with a Canadian telecom that would then get our platform in front of *their* millions of customers. Our customers became our method of distribution for our product.

Even though we weren't the first to market, our web hosting was the easiest on the market, and by changing our distribution, we were able to get in front of more users and really make an impact, both on the market itself and on our revenue. It was a great value for them too because they didn't have to build the platform themselves, but now they had a new offering to give value to their existing customers and to attract new ones.

> **❝ To scale, you'll have to be innovative in your approach to how you get to market, how you define who your customer is, what value can be provided, and your distribution channel. ❞**

That's the real power of finding the right distribution or sales channel for scaling your company. You can have the greatest product in the world—which I believe we did with Hostopia—but it does no good if it's not reaching anyone. To scale, you'll have to be innovative in your approach to how you get to market, how you define who your customer is, what value can be provided, and your distribution channel.

Build strategic partnerships with others to acquire new customers.

One of the fastest and lowest-cost ways that you can scale your company is by expanding your distribution through strategic partnerships with other companies. If you have a physical product like we do with Paw.com, then there's no reason you can't use third-party distributors to reach more customers.

Some entrepreneurs are averse to this because they falsely believe that they have to do everything themselves, so they continue to pour tons of money into advertising as sales level off. But by building a strategic partnership with a like-minded company, you're essentially using someone else's customer base to drive sales.

In chapter 1 we talked about Marcia Reece, who invented sidewalk chalk. Remember how she scaled her small business? She partnered with Walmart, who began to distribute her product in a couple of stores and then eventually expanded to all their stores at the time. This allowed Marcia to reach customers she would have otherwise had no access to—there was no internet yet for parents to Google "fun and cheap outdoor activities for kids." But while browsing the kids art and activity section, they stumbled upon her product, which allowed her to successfully scale.

Going back to Hostopia, I mentioned how we eventually joined forces with Telus Ventures while we were still focused on Canada. While I'm typically pretty negative about venture capital (more on that later), they became a true strategic partner by allowing us to buy the data center services we needed from them, and they in turn outsourced their business hosting email to us, which was funding us in the millions. This is exactly the sort of partnership that allowed us to reach far more customers faster than we could have on our own.

Building these kinds of partnerships is especially advantageous since it keeps your cost of customer acquisition very low and creates a win-win opportunity for both you and the partner company that is distributing your product. When you approach a potential strategic partner, you'll need to be able to prove why it will be worthwhile for them to take up space on their store shelves, so remember to have your proof handy because you'll need to sell them on the idea before they sell your product to their customers.

Start researching and build a wish list of your potential strategic partners. Are there managed service providers you can approach? Businesses with large customer bases that could sell your product as a value-add service? If you can crack that code, then you can scale your company very quickly at a very low cost. So many SaaS businesses have been built by using their distribution partners.

Figure out who your real buyer is and build everything around them.

To develop effective sales channels, you have to know who your buyer really is and then build your systems around them. It's no use having a great Story if you don't know who you need to tell it to and where they are.

As I mentioned in the introduction, it was a major breakthrough for us at Hostopia when we realized that we were selling to the wrong people. We had assumed that individual website owners were the target market for BlueGenesis, but—wow—were we wrong! By white labeling our services, we made customers out of our "competitors." But even then, we discovered that the telecoms were also *not* our buyers. So who was?

Simply put, our buyers were the midlevel executives who cared about one thing—not losing their jobs! Because they knew if they made the wrong decision, then they would lose their cozy lifestyle and have to start all over. Discovering this, it changed how we could approach them on our services and how to package it to them.

For example, let's say that you create a nontoxic, plant-based cleaning solution. You have to ask yourself who your buyer is: Is it the homeowner (B2C sales)? Or is it the organic grocery store (B2B)? Or is it a purchasing agent for a nontoxic-based cleaning company?

Once you've determined who your buyer is, you start the process of getting connected with them. Where can you network with them? What conventions, conferences, or trade shows do they attend?

Next, it's about building rapport with those people. Even if they're looking for a product like yours, few people like a hard sales pitch. And just because you have a booth at the conference doesn't mean they'll come to you—you have to figure out how to position yourself correctly to get to them. You'd be amazed how many deals get made sitting at the bar of the conference rather than at the sales booth. I'm not saying you shouldn't have a sales booth, of course, but you have to be willing to go beyond.

Furthermore, you have to look at each of these as opportunities to prove yourself. Chances are that you're not going to land Walmart or Target on the first try. Even when Marcia got in with Walmart, it was because they were a lot smaller back then—and they came to her! It can be next to impossible to sell to a big company, which is why they are *not* your buyer early on in your company.

When you're still in the early stages of your company, you're going to have issues that need to be ironed out. Not all customers appreciate being the guinea pig. Generally, the larger the company, the less forgiving they are when you make a mistake. Once you have a track record, then you can approach a buyer for Costco or Walmart or whoever your big dream distributor is.

When you know who your buyer is and where they are, you can streamline a lot of things. You can better target your advertising and be more selective about which trade shows or conventions to attend. It's always better to have a target in front of you rather than a blank canvas. Even if you occasionally miss the target, you know where to make your next move.

All this is part of scaling in zeros as you turn ten small deals into a hundred. Too many companies fail to scale because they spin their tires trying to do everything on their own or going after the wrong buyers. If you can catch yourself early on and redirect, looking for both your strategic partners and your buyer, then you've got a better chance to successfully scale.

> **❝ Scaling won't happen overnight, but continuous long-term growth is better than meteoric growth. ❞**

Scaling won't happen overnight, but continuous long-term growth is better than meteoric growth that could plummet because you didn't invest the time in building good relationships. People often refer to meteoric growth like it's a good thing, but remember—meteors fall to the ground and vaporize. Is that really what you want?

Near the end of this section, I've included a chapter on growth hacks—or minor majors—that you can implement once you've identified who your real buyer is. All of them are strategies we have effectively utilized to successfully scale. But no matter what you do, what channel or buyer you identify, remember that you can't do everything on your own.

PEOPLE

CHAPTER 23:

Profile Everyone, Especially Yourself

I LIKE STAR TREK. One of the things that makes the show work so well is the variety of personalities on the crew. You've got Captain James T. Kirk, the dominant let's-get-it-done personality; Scotty, who's the life of the party; Dr. Leonard "Bones" McCoy, who brings a spirit of calm steadiness; and then, of course, Spock, who is highly analytical and wants to make sure that things get done right.

There are a lot of lessons that we can learn from the crew and the way they balance each other and accomplish big things as a result of their mix of personalities. We talked a lot in chapter 9 about the importance of finding complements instead of clones when you're building a team, and that's even more true when scaling.

In building your team during Scale, you're still going to use some of those same concepts, but it's going to look a bit different because what made you and your team successful then can't be exactly duplicated to grow. And that starts with *you*.

Check your dominance at the door.

The number one enemy of every small business is the entrepreneur. And yes, I know how oxymoronic that sounds. But too often what gets an entrepreneur to start a business successfully is what ends up undermining them when they try to scale. Obviously, there are plenty of exceptions, but entrepreneurs tend to have dominant personalities—and they are not always the nicest people.

> **Too often what gets an entrepreneur to start a business successfully is what ends up undermining them when they try to scale.**

I can say this because I'm one of those myself. I know I'm speaking in generalizations here, but we tend to be a little too tough on the people around us. What worked with Start can backfire when it comes time to scale.

During Scale, you have to learn your proper place on the team. You can't do everything anymore and be effective—and you're more likely to hurt things rather than help by dominating others on the team. While dominant go-getter skills come in handy to help you incubate the company, that same skill can make you lousy at scaling unless you learn how to control it.

Checking your dominance at the door is critical to scaling, and it's usually one of the hardest things at this stage because every entrepreneur wants to control every decision. Instead, you have to learn to rely on *other leaders* to make the decisions without you weighing in every time. It's that kind of micromanaging that ultimately leads to a failure to scale, all because of the inability to trust and allow others to help lead the organization.

So recognize that your dominance might be your greatest strength, but it's also your greatest weakness and can impair your ability to scale the company if you're not aware of it. If you can get over this hurdle and begin to trust others, it's magical—because then you've got others out driving the business and wealth for you without you having to think about every component.

Delegate responsibilities, not tasks.

In Start, you *are* delegating tasks, since you're still involved in all the decision-making. But here in Scale, you've got to stop delegating tasks and instead move entire responsibilities to members of your team so that you're not having to think about every item every day.

When Hostopia grew to six hundred employees, we had five key executives, and I spent 80 percent of my time with them, working on the issues they brought to me. But otherwise, they were making the decisions that fell under their responsibilities.

To effectively delegate those responsibilities, you've first got to know your own strengths and keep only the responsibilities that most closely align with your strengths. Then you delegate the other responsibilities that match the strengths of others based on their profiles.

The reverse is also a nightmare—literally. The larger and more complex your company becomes, the greater the propensity for things to go wrong. If you have your hand in every aspect of the company, you will eventually burn out, and the wheels will begin to come off the bus.

Here's the thing: entrepreneurs take on the responsibility of running their company during the day, but it doesn't stop when we get home. The stress comes home with us and rears its head during the night. I have spent too many nights up at 3:00 a.m. worrying about issues at my startups. That's when I realize I need to start delegating more responsibilities. I'm not saying that you can completely get rid of those 3:00 a.m. stress moments, but I am saying that you can minimize them.

Delegating responsibilities—and not just tasks—can remove entire areas of concern for you. Eventually, someone will mess up and you'll have to jump in to fix it, but that occurs a lot less frequently than you might think. If you hire the right people and you let go, magic will happen to the company. You and your family will be the beneficiaries of your newfound freedom—and your company can accelerate faster.

Profile yourself.

One of the biggest areas of success for me has been using profiling to identify individuals and correctly match them to a job and delegate responsibilities based on their profiles.

The two systems commonly used are Meyers-Briggs and DiSC. Personally, I like the simplicity of DiSC. It takes only minutes for candidates to complete, and it can have a huge impact. I've filtered candidates and made my best hires this way. Over the years, I've done this so much that I can often profile candidates without even testing them!

But first you have to start with profiling yourself. There are many free or low-cost sites where you can take the test, but the following is my "Colin's Notes" version for DiSC:

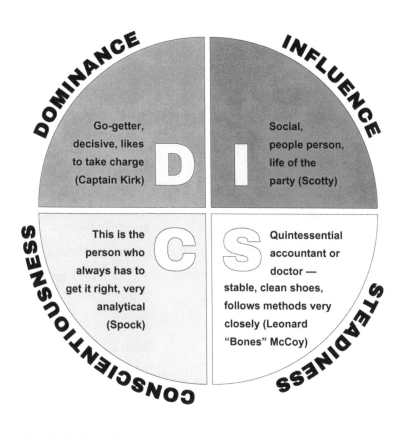

D — DOMINANCE: Go-getter, decisive, likes to take charge (Captain Kirk).

I — INFLUENCE: Social, people person, life of the party (Scotty).

S — STEADINESS: Think of the quintessential accountant or doctor— stable, clean shoes, follows methods very closely (Leonard "Bones" McCoy).

C — CONSCIENTIOUSNESS: This is the person who always has to get it right, very analytical (Spock).

Obviously, people are complex, so most individuals have two personality traits that dominate who they are. From these four components, you can build twelve personality types. For example, I happen to be High D and C—Dominance and Conscientiousness—which is not that typical for most entrepreneurs.

Most entrepreneurs I know tend to be High D and I—Dominance and Influential—and they're really good at sales. With this combination, they're better at starting companies because they don't need to hire the salesperson right away. Along with his dominance (High D), Kirk is also a social animal (High I), and the analytical (High C) Spock is also the steady force behind the ship (High S).

No matter your profile, the key is to hire people around you who can fill the gaps. I'm not a social person who can spend hours talking with others to try to make a sale. I'm direct and to the point, which can work well in certain sales environments—especially on closing—but I tend to send in the Influencers on my team before hitting the deal myself. I know they can lay the groundwork a lot better without me getting in the way.

A word of warning for those who are DIs (Dominance and Influential). Yes, you may be able to win the deals, but you need to recognize your weaknesses and then hire those out. DIs have a particularly difficult time with scaling their companies due to the fact that they often become the bottleneck, as sales continue to rely purely on the force of their personality.

Profile everyone.

Once you've got your own profile settled, fill in the gaps. Those people may already be on your team from hiring them during Start, but now you have the tools to make sure you put the right people in the right places. And if you realize that you're missing a skill set you need, now you can go out and find them.

During the second or third year at Hostopia, we started hiring people for leadership positions. We hired a CTO who was DC (Dominance and Conscientious) and a chief marketing officer who was DI (Dominance and Influential), and a CFO who was SC (Steadiness and Conscientious).

One thing you've got to be aware of and ready for with all these different personality types is conflict—especially when everyone else is Dominant too. You're going to butt heads and argue, but that's not a bad thing. That's how you come up with the best solutions—and it's a lot better than having a bunch of yes-people who won't call you out when you might have a bad idea. You need to be challenged—and sometimes put in check.

For example, Elliot Noss, who has been the CEO of Tucows since we sold it in 1998, was partially responsible for helping me generate a good chunk of my wealth. He is also one of the guys I've argued with the most. He drove me nuts! We would go round and round for hours on different items because we are both Dominant—and I'd often lose because he was an ex-lawyer and he simply wore me out. Yet he grew the Tucows division from zero to $6 million in ad revenue in the 1990s, and now the company's worth over $500 million. Was he argumentative? Yes. Was he easy to deal with? No. And I'll always be grateful to him for that!

Learn to lead leaders.

Don't get me wrong—I'm not saying you don't ever get involved and never use your voice or make the final decision. That's not leadership either. There are times when everyone needs support, even your best leaders. What stops a company from scaling is the entrepreneur who tries to control every aspect of the business because it's what worked for them in the past.

Managing personality types is a skill you have to develop for scaling—leading leaders is a different ball game from leading a startup team. But it starts with understanding your profile and understanding the profiles of others. Otherwise, you could unintentionally create a team of clones or place people in the wrong positions.

> **❝ What stops a company from scaling is the entrepreneur who tries to control every aspect of the business because it's what worked for them in the past. ❞**

And finally, to bring this back full circle, all this truly does require checking your dominance at the door and being open to being challenged by other leaders, trusting their strengths, and delegating responsibilities to the right people with the right skills. Now let me warn you—great leaders are also going to be more expensive. Every single one of them has many different life opportunities. We just have to find a way to convince them that our opportunity is the best.

CHAPTER 24:

Hiring Great Leaders

SCALING IN ZEROS doesn't happen by accident—you've got to have the right leaders in place , but knowing what profile to look for certainly helps. Sometimes it can even help you notice people who can grow with the company, not just fit in a role.

When Hostopia was growing, there came a time when we needed to find someone new to run our call center. It's not the most glamorous job, but someone has to do it. Because we believe in profiling so much, we had the practice of sending DiSC assessments to all candidates.

This was new to some people and had the potential to offend, so we let them know that it was just part of our hiring process, that there were no right or wrong answers, and that it was designed to help us figure out how to best work with people.

Eventually, my VP of operations sent over several profiles for me to look through, and one in particular really stood out. The candidate's name was Peter Kostandenou, and his Dominance and Influence measures were off the charts. I could see how that would make him good in a sales environment like a call center, but it was to the degree that I said, "This guy can run more than our call center—he could lead the whole sales team!"

So knowing his potential, that's exactly what happened—he led the call center, and then, only six months later, he moved into the COO position, and then he became the president of the company after I left. And now he's working as president of another company because he's proven to be effective in helping businesses transition into being sales-driven companies.

Hire with scaling in mind.

As Jack Welch once said, "Hire people with runway," meaning that you want to hire people who not only fit the role you're filling but also people like Peter, who can also scale in their abilities. You want people who have done this before so that they can do it again for you.

> **Start was all about you and what you could do— but in Scale, it's about leveraging the talents of other leaders.**

In a lot of ways, Start was all about you and what you could do—but in Scale, it's about leveraging the talents of other leaders. Peter had built a $10 million company by himself, sold it, and then traveled the world for a year before he had applied for the role of call center manager—that fact on top of his DiSC assessment told me he had runway, could help us scale, and could scale with us.

In other words, you're looking for them to have those skills to scale in zeroes. So if you want your startup to grow to $1 million, you really need to look at hiring someone who's done that before and can prove it. If you're doing $1 million in revenue, then you want to hire people who have worked for a $10 million company because then they're coming to you with the built-in know-how of scaling.

These are the type of people who can help you scale because they either have the right *experience* (runway) to do so or they have the right *mindset* to do so. Either way, it means they have taken risks in their past and are not afraid to stick their neck out to make things happen.

Lastly, watch out for those corporate wonks who look good on paper but who know only how to play office politics to get ahead. If budget is an issue, look to hire young entrepreneurs who have failed in the past but who, with your guidance, can thrive.

Hire leaders who reflect your core values.

Later on in Systems, we'll talk about the importance of establishing core values for your company. For now, though, it's essential to realize that scaling requires you to hire people who can live by those core values not because they have to but because they *want* to—it's already in their nature.

At Hostopia, I had a sales manager who was one of the best I'd ever seen, but we had to fire him when we found out that some of the tactics he used to obtain those sales didn't reflect the kind of company we wanted to be. One of my values is integrity over money, so he couldn't stay once we learned he was practicing otherwise—despite his ability to make us a lot of money.

I promise you, following this simple best practice will save you a lot of headaches—not to mention money—in the long run. It also helps you retain the right people longer because they care about the same values.

In review, here are my top best practices for hiring great leaders:

- ➤ *Know everyone's profile.* Whether you use DiSC, Meyers-Briggs, or something else, I can't emphasize enough how important it is to find great leaders who fill in your gaps and get them into the right roles.

- ➤ *Look at past experience.* Do they have what it takes–experience and mindset–to 10X your business?

- ➤ *No ambiguity allowed.* Put everything on paper. Don't rely on verbal agreements or trust your memory. Build SMART goals into the expectations for their role and connect those with rewards.

- ➤ *Keep away from the yea-sayers.* You need people who can challenge you and push things to find the best direction.

- ➤ *Hire leaders with similar core values.* While personalities, strengths, and skills should be complementary, core values must be in alignment as the glue to hold things together.

CHAPTER 25:

Hiring a Great Sales Team

PART OF WHY PAW.COM did so well in the Start phase is that, as dog lovers, we were able to come up with a lot of product ideas that we knew other dog people would love. Dave, my business partner in Paw.com, is excellent at product development, so he was able to effectively bring those ideas to life. Even though these strengths got us on the *Inc.* 5000 list three years in a row, we fundamentally relied on direct marketing via social media.

However, if we were going to scale from $40 million to $400 million, we couldn't bank on doing things the same way that took us from $4 million to $40 million. Dramatically expanding distribution was key, but to do that, we first needed to hire and manage great salespeople.

As a DC, I'm not good at rejection, nor am I the life of the party, so I knew that was something I couldn't do on my own. We were great at product but not so great at sales and distribution. So we knew we needed to find someone to plug in to that gaping hole if we were going to scale.

In the end, we brought back Jeff Sass, who I've mentioned a few times, to be our CMO and head up our sales and marketing efforts. Jeff spent seven years in filmmaking, which I believe has helped him approach marketing and distribution with a level of creativity that Dave and I would never have had.

> " To scale effectively, you have to shift to being a sales-driven organization. "

To scale effectively, you have to shift to being a sales-driven organization. There's a good chance that *you* are no longer going to be the one driving all the deals and sales like in Start, which means developing a really great sales leader and sales team you can trust to grow the company.

Know which profiles to match up.

First, it's very important to understand your sales manager's profile and to match them up with the prospective employees working under them. It's crucial for the sales manager to have a High D score, and your sales team should be made up of DIs, ISs, or ICs. But if you have ISs or ICs doing most of your selling, then be prepared to be the closer yourself. Without the dominant trait, it's nearly impossible for someone to close deals on their own.

Sure, it would be nice if all salespeople were DIs, but I'd like to add a little caution here, as DIs can sometimes offend ISs and ICs. Pushy salespeople selling to an accountant most likely won't work, which is why it's key to also understand your team's profile and then match those salespeople with the personality types of your target customers. Nothing gets deals done more than establishing trust between two parties, and if you match up the wrong personality types, then you could be making a big mistake. In addition, DIs typically lead divisions of companies, or even run their own companies, which makes them harder to find *and* more expensive.

All your employees need clear expectations, which I believe should be written down. With salespeople in particular, you should document *everything* that is expected of them in their offer letter. Salespeople can burn profits like no other division, so it is imperative that you manage this group very closely. When hiring, you must set out the exact goals you need them to hit in the first thirty, sixty, and ninety days. Even if you have a long sales cycle, you can set up goals that can translate to sales, such as number of phone calls per day, number of proposals sent, number of in-person meetings, and so on.

My experience is that employees, especially in sales, love this because it spells out what they must do to succeed. They have very clear guidelines and targets for what they need to hit, and if they do so, then it gives everyone something to celebrate—which you should!

Ambiguity and verbal promises are your enemy.

Furthermore, document the rewards connected with your salespeople achieving those goals because verbal promises are also your enemy. By providing increased visibility about what they get out of their hard work, they'll know you're not making empty promises, thus establishing trust and creating motivation.

This needs to go beyond their commission payments too. It could include offering them shares in the company tied to their sales numbers, stock options, bonuses, earning extra time off—whatever you discover will motivate them. But the key is to document both the expectations and the rewards so that everyone's on the same page, moving in the same direction, driven to succeed. I've found that this advice works if you want to motivate *anyone* in your organization, sales or otherwise. Document everything—and eliminate ambiguity.

Over and over again, by following these practices I've learned the hard way, I've been able to find the right People to drive the Story to scale. But just like in Start, it's not enough to have only Story and People—Money will play a major role in whether you can successfully implement the Systems you need to Scale.

" Document everything— and eliminate ambiguity. "

MONEY

CHAPTER 26

Proof Sells

WHEN YOU'RE IN STARTUP MODE, money is the oxygen that keeps your business alive. But when scaling, your view of money should transform from being oxygen to being the gasoline you throw on the fire to accelerate your growth.

Unless you've been sleeping under a rock somewhere for the past ten years, you've probably noticed that it seems like everything is becoming cloud-based and that AI is the newest form of automation. From storing your favorite photos and videos of family vacations to whatever sales software you use, the cloud is becoming increasingly indispensable. So why not move bookkeeping to the cloud and combine human interactions with AI?

This was the idea that Lil Roberts had when she founded Xendoo, an online bookkeeping, accounting, and tax business specifically geared toward small business owners. One of the unique things about Xendoo is that it's subscription-based but priced on the monthly expenses of the small business rather than on a one-size-fits-all approach.

We've had Lil on Startup Club via Clubhouse to share her insights and experience—one of them being the surprising truth that you don't need profit to keep your business going; you just need growth. That sounds contradictory, but she explained how Xendoo has actually lost money in each of its five years of existence, yet it continues to grow. How?

> **" You don't need profit to keep your business going; you just need growth. "**

Adjust your Stage Gates for scaling in zeros.

Back in Start, your Stage Gates were connected to proving your concept: developing a minimum viable product or reaching your first thousand sales. But when you're looking at Scale, now it's about accelerating the growth rate. So it's no longer just about proving that you have a useful product or service or that you can gain customers. Now it's about proving that you can go from a thousand customers to ten thousand customers, one region to ten regions, ten products to a hundred products, and so on.

Think back to how Facebook grew. In the beginning, there was an exclusivity to Facebook in the same way that there is with any small local business bound by its geography. Starting out at Harvard, they grew by going college to college, the same way a small business might open new branches in surrounding cities. Along the way, the Facebook team proved that if they could take on five colleges, they could take on fifty. And after that, they asked, "What other sectors could we take on?"

These sectors included marketing, gaming, reducing the gap in communication for businesses to customers, and, of course, advertising. These strategic moves each provided proof that Facebook was a highly investable asset, which is why investors flocked to them and why at the time of their IPO, the company was valued at $104 billion. Keep in mind—this was a company founded in a college dorm room and with a CEO who dropped out of college, completely upending the idea of what a "successful" entrepreneur looks like. How?

Because they created proof and proof sells.

We'll get into this more in a later chapter, but a great example is to look at how venture capital investment operates. Investors don't like risk. To be fair, who does? They would rather have assurance that you don't need their money to keep your company afloat but that the money they give you is going to purely accelerate growth.

This means that your Stage Gates here need to be proof-driven and proof-based because the more you can prove that you can scale your company, the higher the valuation your company will be and the better chance you'll have of securing the money you need. This is true not only from a product standpoint but also in terms of distribution, geography, and so on. For example, the Stage Gate might change to "ten distributors to a hundred distributors," or "We need to go from ten cities to a hundred cities by the end of the year."

Follow the Rule of 40 for subscription businesses.

This brings us to the gold standard for subscription businesses like Xendoo: the Rule of 40. It means that if you have a net zero profit margin, you need to be able to show 40 percent growth. If you have a 10 percent profit margin, then you must be able to show 30 percent growth. If you have a negative 10 percent profit margin, then you need to be able to show 50 percent growth. You get the idea.

It all boils down to the concept that it's okay to lose money so long as you're growing—meaning that money is still coming in. Being able to show that data to investors helps them have confidence to invest in you when you're ready to scale. As long as you can educate an investor group about why you're losing money and what your goals are, then it can bolster their confidence.

We experienced the same thing with .CLUB, where we actually lost money for the first five years despite having a huge profit margin. When we first started out, we were losing roughly $2.5 million per year. The next year, $2 million. The following year, $1.25 million. The year after that, $750,000. And *finally*, the year after that, we broke even. And then something wonderful happened: the profits began to grow, going to $1 million the next year, and $2 million the year after that. We want to show our investors a continuous improvement in growth and, since the tech wreck of 2022, now also a path to profitability.

It's a lot easier than you think to raise money in Scale.

In Scale, raising money is a lot easier than you think. No joke, it really is. If you've proven your concepts, then it's a lot easier to raise money, no matter how you're raising it. It's difficult to convince somebody to fund something that doesn't exist. But when something does exist and you say, "I want to expand from ten distributors to one hundred," or "I want to go from ten cities to a hundred," the difference is that you have some numbers to back up your plan. Moreover, you can carry out that plan a lot faster with additional funding.

This is part of why I love scaling so much more, because in startup mode, it's a grind to generate that proof—here we get to show that proof off! And it's even easier if you can connect the proof to your X factor: What makes you unique? How are you different from your competitors? Those are the type of questions an investor is going to ask, and if you have an answer, it gets a lot easier.

Going back to People for a moment, this is part of why you need to have a great leadership team in place, because they will help you generate and document the proof you need. Too many entrepreneurs fail to scale because they think that the product is all they need to attract investors, but it's really never about the product—it's about the proof.

> 66 Too many entrepreneurs fail to scale because they think that the product is all they need to attract investors, but it's really never about the product—it's about the proof. 99

CHAPTER 27:

Perfecting the Pitch

NEVER BEFORE IN your life have you had to rely on others so much for your success as you do when you have to put your hat in hand to pitch your company to potential investors. It kinda sucks. I don't know about you, but it makes me feel a bit nauseous to know that my success relies on others' judgment of my company and me.

If you want to scale your company, you must figure out what the triggers of growth are and what fuel will supply expansion. This means reaching out—putting everything you've got out there and winning over skeptical investors. For me, this is tough. As I've already mentioned, I am not a natural sales-person. I hate rejection and being publicly humiliated. Pitching is not my core strength, but it is something that every entrepreneur needs to learn how to do. And not only learn it but also become a master at it.

> **If you want to scale your company, you must figure out what the triggers of growth are and what fuel will supply expansion.**

When it comes to perfecting your pitch, I've had to learn from others. In the last chapter, I mentioned Lil Roberts, the CEO and founder of Xendoo. As a serial entrepreneur herself, she's started multiple businesses in a variety of industries, and a big part of her success is that she is excellent at pitching, even winning multiple pitch competitions.

In 2018, she found herself competing in that year's eMerge America Startup Showcase. The stakes were especially high for this pitch competition, given her need to raise money. In that particular competition, the expectation was for her to take the stage, clicker in hand, with her pitch deck slides showing on a big screen behind her. Each participant would have exactly three minutes to pitch—that's it.

The three minute time limit was incredibly important because, for the investors who were judging the competition, going over time would come across as a lack of preparation. "They'll think you're not prepared, that you didn't do the work," she shared with us, "and that flows into how they think you'll run your company and that you're not going to execute."

She was the first to go onstage. She'd made it through only the first slide when, suddenly, the clicker stopped working and she couldn't advance to the next slide. Later, she found out that this was because the organizers had failed to do a rehearsal—but that didn't help her at that moment. She had no choice but to soldier on, slides or no slides. She didn't miss a beat and continued pitching. About twenty seconds later, the tech team got the clicker working again, and she managed to catch up on the slides and finish in under three minutes.

She ended up winning that competition, which comes as no surprise to any of us who know her.

It also should come as no surprise that pitching is one of the scariest parts of scaling for entrepreneurs. Pitching your idea to early investors like friends and family can be a nerve-racking experience, but it's a whole other ball game when you're pitching to investors you've never met before.

The key components of delivering a good pitch are the Three Cs:

➤ Calm

➤ Confident

➤ Credible

But how do you achieve the Three Cs? What actions do you take to develop those qualities?

Find the emotion in your business.

Lil defines pitching as "being able to deliver a story in a way that people understand, that's succinct, that's empowering and inspiring, and that you yourself are very comfortable as you do it." She also adds, "No matter what you're doing, there is an emotion to your business." It's this emotional core that truly captures the attention of investors more than any grandiose guarantees of how much money you're going to make for them.

It's this emotional core that also helps you keep the investor's attention. "The minute you lose their attention, you're never going to get it back in your pitch," Lil says. "If they glance at their phone, they're gone, and you're not getting them back." Emotion is a key ingredient in both sustaining their interest and making your pitch stand out.

There is a balancing act here because while it's important that your love for your business comes through in your presentation, you also can't be overzealous. I've been told that one of my pitching weaknesses is that I get a bit too animated and enthusiastic to the point that it can feel fake or intimidating to the investor, even though my personal feelings are authentic.

Connect to solving a problem.

Often the key to expressing the emotion of your business can be found in clearly communicating the problem you're solving. This should be something you've already established long ago, so bringing it up in a pitch should be second nature. Doing so also keeps you from just pitching another product but instead sharing a solution that can help people.

This is why having proof is so important. Having the numbers that show you can solve a problem places confidence and credibility in your delivery.

Who you pitch to is as important as what you pitch.

When we did the roadshow for Hostopia's IPO, we pitched to thirty-four institutional investors—twenty-eight were based in Canada and six were from the US. Being a Canadian myself, I understood that a lot of Canadian investors tend to be generalists—open to whatever comes their way and grabs their attention.

Meanwhile, the US institutions tend to be more focused on specific industries and markets, so we made sure in the US to pitch to investors who focused on SaaS companies. In the end, we closed three from Canada and three from the US, giving us a 50 percent close rate in the US and 11 percent in Canada. Simply knowing these kinds of distinctions can save you from pitching to the wrong crowd.

Not every pitch is going to be the same—sometimes it's on a stage like Lil's story, and sometimes it's in a boardroom, which can be *very* different. I've had pitches in boardrooms where I was met straightaway with questions before I could show a single slide. Either way, you're not always going to be able to research who is in the room, so you'll have to match the energy of whoever you're talking to and follow their lead. If it's clear that they want a very formal pitch, keep it formal. If they want to be more conversational, then embrace the informality.

At the end of the day, whether you're talking to a small group or a crowded room, size doesn't matter. You never completely know who's going to be in that audience that could lead to your big break. If that one investor is in there who loves what you're doing, that's what really matters. So always go into the pitch assuming that that one person is in there somewhere.

On that note, with so many pitches being recorded these days, that's something you have to consider. There may be only six people with you live, but your pitch could be seen by six thousand investors later on—so be hyperaware of who might see your pitch afterward.

Build a killer pitch.

Build a killer pitch based on Lil's formula. That's right—Lil has a brilliant formula you can follow. While not every pitch is going to be the same, you can set yourself up for success by following this format and knowing it inside and out.

PREPARE YOUR PITCH DECK

First, Lil likes to build the entire structure of the pitch around the pitch deck because it forces you to be more concise and to work within the constraints. Usually, you're going to have only about three minutes to communicate your message, so each word is extremely valuable. This comes out to about ten to fifteen slides in a slide deck, and you need to restrict yourself to *one thought* per slide, relying heavily on images to communicate. Each slide should have only five to seven words, which will require a lot of time for you to craft and hone in on the core of your message.

EVOKE EMOTION

Your front slide and introduction must evoke an emotion so that you can build rapport with the investor as soon as possible. As mentioned before, this helps you grab their attention early, sustain it throughout the pitch, and set you apart from others.

PROBLEM

Your second slide should define the problem, flowing out of the emotion.

SOLUTION

This is where you introduce your product or service, however you solve the problem. It's easy to get wordy at this point, so be cautious to keep it simple and to the point.

DEMO

Here you may devote a slide or two to your demo. A best practice is to not actually do a live demo but to have a recorded or animated demo running in the background on the slide for about ten seconds. What you *don't* want is try to do a live demo and have something go wrong—your prototype breaks or a shoddy internet connection causes the screen to freeze up. Nothing can kill a pitch faster.

It will also be tempting to go into all the features, especially if you have a software product, but doing so requires too many words and risks losing the attention of the investors. Or worse, you could end up confusing them.

Your next several slides should focus more on your business plan:

TOTAL ADDRESSABLE MARKET

This slide (or two) covers your ideal customer: Who can benefit? Where are you headed? Don't be vague here. You can even talk about your Stage Gates: "By next year, we want to have locations in these ten cities," or "In two quarters, we're looking to increase distribution to reach this group of customers." Specificity here is your friend.

COMPETITION/CHALLENGES

Simply put, who—or even what—are you up against? Who else is doing what you do? This is an opportunity to discuss your X factor or your Nearly Unbearable Brand Promise. And if you have no competitor in the marketplace, then what other obstacle is in the way of your growth? Tech limitations? Small staff size? Distribution?

BUSINESS MODEL

This is where you cover your financial business model—how you're making money. Are you customer-funded? If so, how? Product purchases? Subscriptions? While you may be tempted to also talk about future plans for making money, it's more important to stick with the proof of how you're *already* generating revenue. Investors are not interested in hypotheticals.

TEAM

Spend a moment talking about your people. Who do you have propelling the mission forward? Show that you've got the right team with the know-how and drive to carry out the business model and hit your Stage Gates. After all, the investors are not really investing in your product—they're investing in your team.

TRACTION

Again, this is where your proof comes in handy, because you can show investors who you're already serving, what kind of revenue you're already generating, and how additional funding will allow you to build on that. Provide specific examples of how you are solving problems to connect the pitch back to the emotion you started with.

YOUR ASK

What do you want from the investor? Once again, be succinct yet specific. What will it cost for you to scale in zeros, and how are they going to help you get there? Too many pitches fall apart at this crucial moment because the entrepreneur doesn't know *what* to ask for.

While a killer pitch deck by itself won't make you successful, following this formula will help you know exactly which details to discuss in a logical and concise order.

Prepare the deck and practice your pitch.

The first step in preparing for your pitch is to know who your audience is, as we discussed before. There may be tweaks you need to make based on the intended audience, and you might need a couple of versions in rotation for different situations.

Lil simplifies this by starting with Post-it notes. She writes down individual thoughts on Post-its based on the preceding formula and then rearranges them into the best, clearest order. As you do so, you'll revise your thoughts, cutting the fat along the way.

Once you've got the right order for your thoughts, it's time to translate those Post-its into the pitch deck and to find a designer who can assist you in creating powerful images that align with the emotional side of your message.

Next, you should type out *exactly* what you want to say and then print it out. This allows you to identify problem areas, like where you might be spending too much time—or not enough time. Once you can see it on paper, start cutting unnecessary and extra words for clarity and conciseness.

Finally, it's time to practice. Don't worry about the time at first. Focus on getting comfortable with the words, building your confidence, and making additional revisions. Once you've crafted a short but specific delivery that feels natural to you, it's time to practice with an actual clock. Lil suggests keeping the pitch to two minutes and forty-five seconds to give yourself a bit of leeway for when things don't go as planned—where a slide might freeze up or a microphone glitch requires you to repeat a thought.

As you practice, look for more ways that you can trim the pitch and enhance the emotion. Refine the deck more, getting your thoughts as clear as you can and becoming comfortable with the flow.

Once you have the words down, you have to also think about your physicality. Your stance needs to communicate confidence just as much as your tone should. Record yourself and study your feet, whether you pace in a way that looks uncomfortable or natural. If you tend to talk with your hands, be mindful of when gestures might be too big, and avoid pointing at people—a pitching sin I have committed. Pay attention to whether you're standing upright and the cadence of your breathing, and Lil even recommends ordering a clicker so that you can practice holding it at your side and using it discreetly rather than fiddling around with it.

Get feedback from people you trust.

You're likely too close to the material to be objective about where the holes might be, so you need to have people you trust who you can present to. Get their feedback and then incorporate that feedback. Or as Lil puts it, "Ask people to continuously rip you apart so you can refine your pitch."

This could be done through an incubator program that sets up practice pitch sessions, or you can approach a circle of advisors. As Lil says, "Nobody likes to hear their baby is ugly," but it's better that you hear it from people you trust when it's low risk instead of hearing it from an investor when there's more on the line for you.

One of the worst things you can do is ignore feedback. Take it to heart without taking it personally, make tweaks to your pitch based on what you've heard, practice your revised pitch, then go back to those same people for more feedback until they say, "You've got a winner!"

Focus on achieving the Three Cs.

Coming full circle to where we started, you have to be calm, confident, and credible. I know, I know—that's easier said than done. But it *is* achievable when you start prepping your pitch early and spend enough time with it until it's second nature. Although we're talking about this in Scale, it's entirely appropriate to begin this process in Start. The sooner, the better.

CALM

There's nothing wrong with being nervous about a pitch. Accepting this fact can immediately help you feel calmer. There are a variety of exercises you can practice to help channel any natural nervous energy into a state of calm, from breathing techniques to listening to a favorite song. Sometimes it's as simple as taking a moment to smile and breathe and remind yourself that you believe in your business.

I like to take a very deep breath before I speak, because I find that it slows me down. The number one mistake I see with inexperienced speakers is that they talk too fast because they're nervous. Anyone who has spoken in front of a crowd has done this. With experience and coaching, you can slow down your cadence, which demonstrates confidence.

CONFIDENCE

Do as much homework as possible ahead of time, especially where it concerns your audience. While you may not know who the exact people are in a crowded room, you can research why they are there or what problems they're facing. If it's a one-on-one pitch, there's a good chance you're going to get grilled on the spot, so you need to be ready to think on your feet.

Preparing ahead of time for these scenarios builds your confidence. Again, this is all the more reason for you to practice and receive feedback. If you might feel shaky, hearing from trusted advisors that your pitch is ready is a huge confidence boost. And if they say that it's not ready, then that also helps build confidence as you address those issues and strengthen the pitch. Practicing your stance and observing your body language is key in projecting confidence in addition to your tone. Lil is a fan of employing the power pose made famous by Amy Cuddy to help her feel and project confidence when headed into a pitch.

But a note on this—confidence is not the same as arrogance. In a 2021 study, it was found that entrepreneurs who showed humility in their pitches ended up almost twice as likely to get funded. As it turns out, the stereotypical picture of a boastful entrepreneur who presents as if they have all the answers ends up being more of a turnoff to investors than the entrepreneur who is willing to admit that they don't have everything figured out yet. Researchers interviewed fifty-seven venture capitalist investors who said that ambitious entrepreneurs who fail to display humility in their pitch come across as arrogant and therefore resistant to coaching.[12]

On the other hand, those who are willing to admit that they don't have all the answers ties in with our next C—credibility.

CREDIBILITY

Being calm and confident go a long way in helping you build rapport *and* credibility with your audience. Knowing your material inside and out, especially your numbers, is foundational for giving a credible pitch, but so is a sense of integrity. When you practice your pitch for others, encourage them to ask tough questions like a real investor would so that you can also practice your responses. A practice Q&A session may even help you discover some holes in your pitch or think of new proof points to add in.

In the end, the best way you can develop credibility is to find that human connection that links back to your purpose. "Don't do anything for money, because if you do it for money, you're not going to be successful," Lil says. "That's not your big why. You'll give up when it gets hard." If the investor can resonate with your why, then they'll know you're in it for the long haul and committed to scaling—with or without their help.

You won't get an investor every time you pitch, but following these tips will increase the likelihood of scoring an investor and, more importantly, will help you connect with the right investors who will really believe in what you're doing. Having an investor who truly wants to partner with you can be more valuable than the capital they provide.

> **" Having an investor who truly wants to partner with you can be more valuable than the capital they provide. "**

---

12   Carmine Gallo, "The Surprising Personality Trait That Investors Admire In Entrepreneurs," Inc.com, November 12, 2021, https://www.inc.com/carmine-gallo/the-surprising-personality-trait-that-investors-admire-in-entrepreneurs.html.

Also, keep in mind that the investor who tells you no today might say yes when you have more proof next time around, or they might tell you yes on your next venture. Leave people with a positive impression, whether they jump on board this time or not. You never know when they might turn up again.

Now that you know how to pitch, the question is, Who do you pitch to? Who are the investors you should be looking for? One mistake a lot of entrepreneurs make is pitching to the wrong investors. You might have the best pitch, but now you need to make certain you're delivering it to the right people.

CHAPTER 28

The Right Funding for the Right Situation at the Right Time

I THINK I CAN PREDICT your next question: "So where do I find these investors to pitch to? What's the best funding option out there?"

The good news is that there are lots of funding options available for scaling. The bad news is that because there are a lot of options, you'll really have to do your homework to figure out which one is the best fit for the specific season your company finds itself in.

When Hostopia was growing in the US, we reached a point where we needed to scale *fast* to stay ahead of our competition. Since we already had our platform running well, we didn't need money for R&D, but we needed funds to acquire new companies to add to the platform. We had a 75 percent margin, so it made sense for us to acquire companies and accelerate our growth that way.

Ultimately, we decided to go the IPO route to raise the $30 million we needed to scale. Our primary reasoning was to avoid the liquidation preference built into venture capital (VC) funding. We used VC funding when scaling the company in Canada, but in the US, it was a different story. I tend to be pretty paranoid of liquidation preference as the company builds up substantial value, so I avoid it like the plague, since I don't want to get pushed out of my own company.

When we finalized the details of the IPO, we issued common shares, which meant that shareholders had the same type of shares we held within the company—which meant they were taking the same risks as us. Long story short, it worked, and we were able to use the money to scale the company. I never sold any shares on the public market, but when it came time to exit, I cashed out during the sale of the company, which was a huge benefit we'll discuss more in Exit.

Most of this chapter is going to focus on giving you a list of funding options rather than a deep discussion of each one, because those discussions need to be held on an individual basis with an attorney who understands securities and investment law. There's no one-size-fits-all answer here. Each discussion will yield different pros and cons depending on who you are. I want to give you just enough so that you can do some deeper digging on your own, build your own pros and cons list, and have a discussion with your key people.

In other words, this is an overview, not specific legal or financial advice. Anything you research further, you need to discuss with an attorney to make sure you're doing everything the right way and in accordance with the law.

Jenny Kassan, a business attorney and author of the book *Raise Capital on Your Own Terms*, joined our podcast *Serial Entrepreneur: Secrets Revealed!* to discuss finding the right funding fit for your business. She expressed this by saying, "There's a tension between keeping things simple but also designing for your specific situation … the way you bring on investors is going to have a huge effect on your company … so it's worthwhile to take some time to think through what you want to do and not use an off-the-shelf document."

She explained that there are two main legal perspectives an entrepreneur has to keep in mind when seeking the right funding. First, what is it *exactly* that you're offering to the investor? This must be specific. And depending on the type of funding, you will encounter investors who have the condition of laying out their own terms. This is especially true with angel investors and VC funding, where Jenny says, "It's the investor who hands you the term sheet … they're going to tell *you* how they're going to invest."

Second, what security law-compliant strategy will you choose? In other words, you need to get legal advice to make sure you're doing things the *right* way. On this point, Jenny shared with us, "You have to be really careful what you do when you're looking for investors … people go to Clubhouse every day and break the law" without realizing it. You can't just go asking anyone and everyone for money willy-nilly!

Furthermore, you're nearly always going to be giving up some form of control when you invite investors into the company, whether they have a seat at the table in the decision-making or whether they own a piece of the company and have the freedom to trade it on the market. Thankfully, Jenny let us know that "there's so much flexibility in corporate law," in terms of the type of filing you go with and what terms you're allowed to set with investors, from how you price out the shares, to limiting how many shares an investor can own, to the liquidation preference. That's why, as we'll talk about in a moment, it's important to weigh *all* your funding options so that you can find the right fit for your situation.

It's also important to connect with the right investors. My colleague Jeff Sass once shared with our Clubhouse members, "It's important to not just take money from anyone but to seek out strategic partners who will have a vested interest in the company itself." In other words, your definition of your People has to grow to include *who* you want investing in the company, which will also factor into what kind of filing you choose.

You also need to ask, "Who is going to help us set the terms and stay within legal bounds?" It's at this stage when it's key to have someone who can guide this process. It's not enough to use just your CFO or accountant here. Yes, they need a seat at the table, but you really need an attorney who understands the legal ramifications and who can help you set up the best investor terms to protect your control.

Check the timing.

While writing this book, we saw what I sometimes describe as the tech wreck of 2022, where the value of many tech companies fell by over 60 to 70 percent, which reminded me a bit of the dot-com crash. This led to the IPO calendar for the year being rather dormant and the window closing for any major tech IPOs like what we've become accustomed to in the past decade. Although it took a few months to settle in, we began to see significantly lower valuations for private companies as VCs began to do rounds.

This serves as a good reminder that timing can be everything. When you're a small business wanting to raise money, it's easier to do so when things are frothy. We saw the signs in early 2022 with the NFT craze and GameStop buying. When things are entering an insanity stage, these generally are good times to raise money.

Sometimes you may not even need the money quite yet, but if things are going well, then it might just be the time to capitalize on the momentum. Raise money for scaling while the window is open, because once it closes, not only will it be more difficult but also the window might never reopen in time for you to remain solvent. When times are hard, money becomes much, much more expensive.

So while you don't want to rush into funding before you have a plan, you also don't want to wait too long and find that you've run out of oxygen. Regardless of your situation, the principle behind the best timing is that the funding is devoted to *growth*, not survival.

In another Startup Club session, Sheel Mohnot, cofounder of Better Tomorrow Ventures, shared his wisdom on this as he focuses on preseed and seed rounds for fintech companies. While the generic philosophy is to raise money when you need to scale, he gets more specific by suggesting, "Historically, it's been something like every eighteen months—or twelve to eighteen months—that you go out for a new round of funding."

Knowing this, the scaling business should build this into its business plan, which then allows you to better set goals related to the proof you need for each round. You can then proactively set your Stage Gates so that you're not waiting too long to evaluate your state of business, nor are you rushing into it. During that time, then, you need to be laying out the options of funding available to you and building those options into your game plan.

One big note on this: *Delaying is never a strategy.* Don't wait until you're thirty days away from running out of cash to start raising money. Because the longer you wait, the worse it gets and then you become desperate. If you're hemorrhaging money while seeking investors, it means you're not really raising funds—you're begging. I can guarantee that investors you pitch to will detect the desperation, which will hurt your fundraising efforts. Instead, you want

> " You want to be looking for investors to scale when you're still in a good place, not out of desperation. "

to be looking for investors to scale when you're still in a good place, not out of desperation.

On that note, some companies may opt to utilize factoring receivables or even taking out a high-interest loan, but I would say that both of these cash-creating methods should be considered last-case scenarios due to the extreme interest rates you end up dealing with.

I'm speaking from experience here from a company I helped acquire once. Before we acquired them, the company was in dire need of cash, so they got a high-interest loan, which took something to the effect of 20 percent interest, except it was based on percentage of revenue. When they hit a heavy sales period like Black Friday, the effective rate was closer to 50 percent. That company was in desperate straits, but these kind of situations often end up digging a bigger hole because the interest keeps you from generating the funding to move forward.

When the oxygen is running low, you'll have to make tough decisions—and you'll have to deal with the ramifications of the choices you make, whether that's entering one of these desperation deals or taking a second mortgage. Either way, both things can put your future—and your family's future—at risk.

Consider all your options.

None of the funding options listed next are necessarily better than any other. We've used many of these ourselves in scaling different businesses at different times. The funding you use to scale your current startup this round may not be the one you use next round. Different stages of scaling in the life of your company call for different forms of funding, so once you pick one, you're not married to it every time you scale.

Many entrepreneurs I've spoken with don't realize how many options there really are. As Jenny put it, "Most people think it's either VC, bootstrap (lifestyle business), or maybe get a bank loan." But the reality is there are many options that can—and should—be considered. That said, keep an open mind to all these choices and learn all their pros and cons.

REGULATION D, PRIVATE PLACEMENT MEMORANDUM

I'm going to inject my bias a little since this is my favorite funding option. Why? Because it can be relatively inexpensive and brings in top-notch, sophisticated investors. In short, these are private placements where only a small group of investors are given the opportunity to invest rather than opening it up to the general public.

The investors *must* to be accredited—that's key. It can't just be good old Uncle Bob, who has $100,000 he wants to give you. Within Reg D, there is something called the 506(c) Rule, which stipulates that you can advertise the opportunity publicly but only accept accredited investors.

To get .CLUB going, we needed to raise $7 million in thirty days, and we went with the 506(c) under Reg D. How did we execute it? I went to my LinkedIn account and used my contacts to inform them that we were launching a raise and asked if they were accredited and whether they would like to receive the offering memorandum. I created an official document that looked a lot like an S-1 (IPO document) to invoke trust with my prospects. It helped the raise, because it took an intangible concept and made it tangible to gain their interest. They could see that I knew what I was doing.

With this particular filing for .CLUB, we were able to clearly articulate the business plan, the risks, and the path to profitability. We even put in projections, which were probably a bit more optimistic than they should have been. The disease of optimism is rampant among us entrepreneurs. But I still think it's good to include projections because it's important to show prospects what you can achieve if everything goes well—and then build in some caveats. A lawyer will probably tell you that you can reduce your chances of being sued in the future by laying out all the risk factors. I'm not even certain all the investors read everything we put together, but the fact is, it looked professional and communicated the message, "Hey, we've done our homework and the train's leaving the station—are you getting on board?"

To do all this—create the documents, hire the law firm—cost $17,500. And it was only that low because we did a lot of advance work to keep the legal costs down. We looked at other similar companies and identified the risk factors, but, simply put, we knew the industry better than the lawyers did. We copied risk factors from similar companies, which is actually something that the SEC appreciates. So don't worry—you're not going to be accused of plagiarism like in college. Instead, it will save you time from trying to write it up yourself by taking what's already out there—even look at the risk factors your competitor has mentioned—and use those in your own private placement memorandum.

In fact, there are a number of platforms an entrepreneur can use to help raise money—like StartEngine and OurCrowd—which make it easier for startups to connect with investors. I'm a big fan of these options because it not only makes the connection easier but also you're more likely to attract investors who really connect with your Story and vision.

REGULATION A

While this specific method has been around for a while, changes in the law in 2012 mean that a company can raise up to $60 million through Reg A under certain conditions. Here the company can offer and sell securities without having to register them with the SEC. But to be clear, as Jenny explained to us, you still have to file the details of your offering with the SEC along with any state-mandated filings.

There are two tiers within Reg A: Tier 1 allows a company to raise $20 million within a twelve-month period, which has to be qualified by a state regulator. In Tier 2, a company can raise up to $50 million within a twelve-month period but does *not* have to be qualified by a state regulator.

The investors in a Reg A company either have to be accredited, or, if they're not, there are limits to how much they can invest. Nonaccredited investors can't invest more than 10 percent of their annual income or net worth, whichever is greater, with their net worth excluding the value of any properties they own.

REGULATION A+

Unlike Reg D, Regulation A+ means you can solicit funding from anyone in the public—nonaccredited investors—but there are limits and higher standards set by the SEC similar to what's described in Reg A. A key difference from either Reg D or Reg A is that a company can raise up to $75 million. Otherwise, it's similar to Reg D in terms of communicating your business plan and risks to your prospects.

In my experience, I see Reg A+ rarely used, but it could work well if you have a larger subscriber base. I look at it like doing a mini IPO without actually listing your stock.

One of the ways I've seen it used recently is through tokenizing real estate. I once got the chance to interview Daniel Fiske, an expert in the emerging field of real estate tokenization. He discussed with me how he works for a $2 billion construction firm and is tokenizing a ten-story building in Miami. To do this, he had to file a Reg A+, and now public investors can buy a token to invest in the building.

Daniel describes it like "converting an asset with a digital wrapper," where digitizing the asset makes real estate investing more accessible. In some ways, it's similar to what we see with NFTs, except there is a real physical asset behind the token. "You can specifically choose 'I want this asset in this market,' and you have more control and you're benefiting from cash flow," he explained. "Let's say you own one percent of that tokenized asset, [then] you receive one percent of the disbursements on a monthly basis."

This type of investing definitely represents a new wave and paradigm shift from traditional real estate investing. For those entrepreneurs who already have some of these physical assets available through other ventures, it may provide a new way to generate funding for the startup you're working to scale.

REGULATION CF (CROWDFUNDING)

I've already mentioned StartEngine and OurCrowd, but it's worth discussing this topic a bit more, especially as crowdfunding has become a staple for startups to either get off the ground or to scale. Crowdfunding through these platforms can overlap with Reg D or Reg A+, depending on what you're pursuing, but then there's also the donor-based Kickstarter and other platforms devoted to specific industries.

Reg CF was created in 2012 as part of the JOBS Act in the US, and it's essentially a more dressed-up version of Kickstarter. It can be used to raise funds online from supporters, but unlike Kickstarter, where you give the supporters some kind of perk, a Reg CF means that investors can get securities and equity in exchange for backing the campaign. Jenny clarified for us that because Kickstarter is donor-based, not investor-based, it's not regulated by securities law.

A key thing to note here is that under Reg CF, a private company can raise up to $5 million, so you do have to be aware of these limits. However, it does allow you to advertise your investment opportunity publicly and from anywhere in the country. Jenny also let us know that you'll need to go through some required financial reviews (usually two years' worth) and a possible audit depending on the specific amount raised, which in her words can be "onerous," but once it's done, there's a lot of flexibility on the other side.

We're considering this route currently with scaling one of our businesses because we have over one million existing customers, and it could be worth inviting them into the story of how we scale. Whereas traditional donor-based crowdfunding like Kickstarter is perfectly acceptable for raising *startup* money to get you going, Reg CF is designed more for scaling *after* you have generated proof.

ANGEL INVESTORS

Funding from angel investors is generally thought of as a startup funding source, but I believe it should be looked at for scaling too. There is usually a local angel investors group in your community that you can find through an incubator program, accelerator program, or innovation center near you, like what we discussed in Start.

I also recommend participating in pitch competitions in your community, as this both helps you sharpen your pitching skills and exposes you to angel investors attending the competition as they hunt for new opportunities. After all, the money isn't going to just come to you—you've got to go where the money is, which includes these competitions and incubator programs.

Once you've connected with angel investors, you can begin pitching to them, whether that's in a more formal setting to pitch multiple investors at a time or whether it's setting up one-on-one meetings. There's a nice personal touch with these groups that you can't get with the big VC types, as they love to see a local business thrive. Jenny pointed out to us that there is a strong overlap between angel investors and VC, though, she shared that "most angel investors are part of the VC ecosystem—it's the same model." Like with VC, many angel investors are going to want to have a say in *how* their money is being used and will have their own terms with which they expect you to comply before they buy in.

When people watch *Shark Tank*, they tend to think only about the money the entrepreneur is getting from the investors. What they don't think about is that the entrepreneur is giving up 33 percent of their future profits. Yes, they get other benefits—probably a bump in sales from the appearance on the show and some PR, media exposure, and so on—but those are short-term positives. Long term, it's like adding a new tax onto your company for the entire life of the business. And in some cases, investors want guaranteed ROI, so they offer the worst preferred shares with preferential rights over common shares. In some ways, to me, it's almost criminal.

Certainly you could count friends and family in this group too, but with a major caveat. In my opinion, you have to be really careful about bringing your friends and family in to invest too early in the scaling process because of the risk. My mom is always asking to invest in my various ventures, so I created something I call the mom test, which simply means that I won't let my mom invest in one of my companies until the concept has been proven.

Usually this isn't until the second or third round of investing, when the risk of investment is low, revenue is flowing, and I know there's a lower chance of our investors losing their investment. So while I think it's fine to bring in friends and family to invest for scaling, I also think you should use the mom test to reduce the risk for them. Regular savvy investors will come and go and know the risks they're taking, but you have to be more cautious with those closest to you. Trust me, you will keep more friends who would rather make less money than lose it all on a risky startup.

Instead, you can bring in angel investors early on in the scaling process to support the growth of the company without experiencing the onerous terms you'd normally have with VC funding. The most popular structure for this today is making a SAFE agreement—simple agreement for future equity—which documents the agreement between the investor and the company. Within SAFE, the investor gets the right to buy stock in a future equity round, usually at a discount.

Most SAFE investments have a cap so that if the valuation of the next round exceeds the cap, they can still convert at the cap rate, even if it is beyond the stated discount. Sometimes entrepreneurs set the cap too high on these agreements, so it's important to set a reasonable valuation on your company to help create a fair deal for both them and you to attract the investors. Either way, this signals to the investor that you're willing to share the upside and that if things go well, they're going to make good money with you, not just small returns.

As of the writing of this book I haven't used a SAFE agreement for any of my companies, but I have invested in companies with SAFE agreements, and I can say that in those investments, I was pushing for a lower cap to convert on future rounds. Jenny shared with us that a lot of people go with SAFE because it can seem like the simplest option, but she cautions that it still isn't the best fit for everyone's situation, so you need to make sure you do your homework before jumping into it. Again, given the nature of the investment, your investors will get paid out first on exit.

One of the reasons this section discussed proving your business right off the bat is that early-stage companies have challenges raising funds if they haven't proved their model yet. So no matter what filing you choose, you're still going to need to offer something to potential investors to show the proof of what you're presenting. Again, this is why you'll want to be certain you have someone to ensure that you're following the law.

GOVERNMENT OPTIONS

I won't rehash all this from Start, but the same options available to get your seed money can also be used to help you scale. Don't forget to look at what government options might be available, whether through local or state grants designed to boost the economy through small businesses or even SBA loans. People tend to think of these options for only the initial startup cash, but they can be used to scale too. Interest rates do apply—and they have risen sharply over the last couple of years. And of course you'll also need to pay it back, but if you've established a proven concept and have revenue coming in, then you can build repayment of the loan into your plan and use the money to scale faster than if you were to carry on without it.

Here's something to be aware of with the SBA loan. Since it's a guaranteed loan, you're putting your house or other personal assets up as collateral when you sign. But if you're comfortable with doing that because you have a proven model, then it's pretty much the cheapest money you can get in terms of repayment and not diluting ownership of the company.

In the midst of the COVID-19 pandemic, our team at Paw.com applied for the MSLP (Main Street Lending Program) loan, which was part of the CARES Act in 2020. The pandemic hit during our VC roadshow, forcing us to pull back and find an alternative. This funding allowed us to continue to grow during that tough season.

All this is to say that you can look into federal, state, and local government options. Some options don't require repayment, especially if you're able to become a government contractor through a grant and your services satisfy a need in the government.

INITIAL PUBLIC OFFERING

We'll discuss this more in Exit, but IPOs can also be an option for scaling. Certainly, in recent times, this has become a more difficult option until you're raking in billions in revenue, but it's still worth mentioning, as I've done it myself. Part of the strategy for both scaling and exiting Hostopia was our IPO. By taking the company public, we could raise the additional funding needed to accelerate our growth further.

The IPO process can be very, very intense, and if you're going to pursue one, you need to be prepared to go out on the road and set up dozens of meetings with institutions in a short period of time to create a sense of urgency and buzz in the marketplace. You want to generate the appearance that the train is leaving the station and that it's time to get on board.

NYSE and NASDAQ are not your only options either. If you have a smaller business that doesn't meet the parameters of an IPO through those name brand avenues, you can look at foreign options like the Toronto Stock Exchange or the London Stock Exchange. If you don't live in the country hosting the exchange, you'll have to deal with learning the international laws around this and the foreign jurisdictions and rules, but it could very well be worth the time, especially when you're not based in the US or you have a customer base in those countries.

While it's still gaining traction, SPACs have become more commonplace as an alternative way to go public. These special purpose acquisition companies, sometimes also referred to as blank check companies, serve as shell corporations that smaller businesses can combine together and enable them to go public. It's a bit of the best of both worlds in terms of private and public, and they're sometimes seen as having less risk than a traditional IPO, not to mention they offer better terms to the entrepreneur and shorten the process of going public. That being said, money was too easy, and too many SPACs from 2021 imploded in 2022, tainting this particular method of going public. I do hope over time that the reputation can recover, as it improves liquidity for entrepreneurs and provides alternatives to traditional VC or private equity.

A lot of entrepreneurs tend to romanticize the idea of an IPO, with its images of ringing the bell at the NYSE as a marker that they've arrived and everything will be smooth sailing from here on out. But the real marker of health no matter what is *liquidity*. If you've gone public but you don't have liquidity, then what have you really achieved? If you can keep liquidity in the forefront of your mind rather than the public appearance of success, then you can make a wiser decision about whether an IPO or a SPAC is right for you.

CRYPTOCURRENCY

A quick note here on using cryptocurrency. In our session with her, Jenny strongly cautioned against trying to circumvent security laws by using cryptocurrency in lieu of traditional securities. At the end of the day, she explained that even when you offer a cryptocurrency to investors, there is still an expectation by those investors of obtaining some kind of return in the end, therefore the practice still falls under securities law.

She stated that some entrepreneurs and investors have tried to get away with this in recent years, but "the arm of the law will eventually catch up" to you. I would add that recent events have shown the volatility and risk involved in cryptocurrency, which suggests it's not as stable as these other methods with more proven track records.

I know this is a ton of information to digest but that's a good thing. The more options you have on the table, the more freedom you have to pursue a plan that aligns with your values, your vision, and your team's talents. Narrowing down these options will automatically help you hone in on which investors to pursue so that you're not wasting time and resources pitching to the wrong people at the wrong time.

> **❝ The more options you have on the table, the more freedom you have to pursue a plan that aligns with your values, your vision, and your team's talents. ❞**

CHAPTER 29

The Problem with Venture (Vulture) Capital

I'VE KNOWN A COMPANY FOUNDER who's spent over a decade working to grow his company and has raised over $50 million in VC funding, which sounds like he should have it made, right? Yet the company is worth only a fraction of this amount, making it nearly impossible for him to ever see a cent.

It's a confusing world out there, especially when it comes to raising capital to scale. The fact is that less than 1 percent of startups actually get VC funding, yet this method receives a tremendous amount of publicity.[13] So many entrepreneurs I interact with have accepted the myth that venture capital is the only way they can scale their company, but most people don't realize some of the damage that VCs can cause. I've seen too much Silicon Valley carnage to stay silent on it.

> 66 **I've seen too many entrepreneurs get pushed toward venture capital and get eaten by it instead of looking into other options.** 77

While it *is* an option, I often refer to VC as vulture capital, because I've seen too many entrepreneurs get pushed toward venture capital and get eaten by it instead of looking into other options. To be clear, I'm not saying to never consider VC funding but instead that you should consider all of your options first.

In our session with Jenny, she shared some additional insights with us about VC, its history, and its purpose. Essentially, it came about in the 1950s and 1960s when the technology and computer industries were first taking off, which is why to this day we see it play such a role in the world of tech startups. This is also why it tends to make a lot more headlines than the methods we reviewed in the previous chapter. "The purpose of [VC] is to fund very high-growth companies that have the intention of dominating the market," she explained. "It's not a fit for 99.5 percent of companies."

As such, "When you're getting a VC, you're getting a boss," Jenny cautions. "They're going to dictate what you're doing in the company, and they don't always make the best decisions." I agree with her insights on this 100 percent, which is why before you go hunting for VC, you need to know *exactly* what you're getting into.

---

13   Laura Entis, "Where Startup Funding Really Comes From," Entrepreneur.com, November 20, 2013, https://www.entrepreneur.com/money-finance/where-startup-funding-really-comes-from-infographic/230011#.

You must understand your investors' risk versus reward equation.

My number one concern about VC is the way liquidation preference is standard in almost every VC agreement, which is something Jenny also pointed out to our members. Investopedia defines this as "a clause in a contract that dictates the payout order in case of a corporate liquidation."[14] Typically, the company's investors or preferred stockholders get their money back first, ahead of other kinds of stockholders or debtholders, in the event that the company must be liquidated.

Furthermore, "Liquidation preferences are frequently used in venture capital contracts, *hybrid debt instruments, promissory notes and other structured private capital transactions, to clarify what investors get paid and in which order during a liquidation event, such as the sale of the company.*"[15] Understand that liquidation preference isn't just for VCs—many crowdfunding platforms require it for their investors as well.

The good news is that the legal costs have come down a lot when raising money due to the fact that most of these agreements are pretty standard. But this also means they're going to follow the same playbook. Knowing this, I'm going to ask you to stop being an entrepreneur for the next minute. I want you to imagine that you are now proudly sporting an investment banker's hat when looking at your business.

There are three alternatives you have to consider:

---

14   Alexandra Twin, "Liquidation Preference: Definition, How It Works, Examples," Investopedia.com (Investopedia, November 29, 2020), https://www.investopedia.com/terms/l/liquidation-preference.asp#:~:text=A%20 liquidation%20preference%20is%20a,the%20company%20must%20be%20liquidated.

15   Alexandra Twin, "Liquidation Preference," Investopedia.com, November 29, 2020, https://www.investopedia. com/terms/l/liquidation-preference.asp.

➤ If the company fails, the VC gets paid out all the money first under liquidation. If there's nothing left over, oh well.

➤ If the company is a moderate success, the VC walks away with whatever they invested, and they might get some additional percentage, but they haven't lost anything. And there may or may not be some crumbs left for the founder.

➤ If the company is a huge success, the VC gets their percentage all the way up, and the founder walks away the hero, making a ton of money as well.

I will also add that too many entrepreneurs look at the big shiny number on the page the VC is offering. They might even think their company is worth that amount—heck, it's reported that way, right? Instead, start by looking at the liquidation preference terms. How is it going to impact you if the company fails? How will it impact you if the company is a moderate success? Don't get so distracted by the offer that you miss these red flags. Some VCs even add a guaranteed return on their investment, which I think for the most part is going too far. This was not popular in recent years, but with the market drop in 2022, we might see this come back in a bad way. Remember, money gets *way* more expensive in the tough times.

It's a huge trade-off you have to consider. Yes, you're getting funding, but you're also giving up a big chunk of money and control over the long term. It may be worth it to you, but at least know what you're giving up before it becomes a rude awakening.

VC can tempt you to forget the bottom line.

One of the dangers of VCs or large investments (outside of afore-mentioned concerns) is that some entrepreneurs seem to just throw the bottom line out the window when they get a VC deal. Suddenly, because they have other people's money to spend, they lose discipline when it comes to their finances. They look only at the top line, and a lot of waste occurs along the way. The mantra that it's all about growth sounds great—and then 2022 hit and the equation changed to it being all about growth *and* a clear path to profitability. VCs are notorious for pushing for growth at all costs. Of course they want the upside, as their downside is already protected, so why not push and gamble for a bigger outcome?

This is one of the issues addressed in the series *WeCrashed* that dramatizes the story of the startup WeWork. Here we see caution thrown to the wind with the influx of VC funding, and spending skyrockets to an unnatural level. Don't get me wrong—this is 100 percent the fault of the entrepreneur, not the venture capitalist.

It's like sending a teenager to the store with a hundred bucks when you just want them to buy a carton of ice cream for dessert. There's a good chance they'll walk out of there with ten types of ice cream, some sprinkles, chocolate syrup, and root beer to make floats—and then half of the ice cream melts on the way home because they also stop to pick up a friend along the way.

Instead, make sure you have a plan for *exactly* how that money is going to be used strictly to *scale* while keeping your daily expenses covered through your sales revenue. You can fight the temptation to overspend if you design some guardrails for yourself and if you always make sure to build in margins for the unexpected. At Hostopia one of our core values was "We spend it like our own." Even though we were public, we wanted everyone to think about ways to save money and run the company efficiently.

There is a time and a place for VC, but it must be strategic.

I'm not completely against venture capital. For me, the right time and place is when you have a situation where you need to grow *very* fast or else your competition is going to wipe you out. This is exactly the situation Clubhouse experienced, because if they didn't raise money quickly, they were going to get left behind, overtaken by competitors.

Now let's flip sides and look at it from the VC perspective. Hostopia would've never successfully scaled in Canada without our partnership with VC firm Telus Ventures, which is operated by the second largest telecom in Canada. Beyond the $2 million they invested, we were also getting high-quality expertise from some of their top people whom we added to our board.

As part of our growth strategy with them, we housed our servers in their data centers and then they outsourced their email and web hosting to us, which all added up to generating millions of dollars worth of transactions. It also brought us a ton of credibility, allowing us to win deals with nine of the top ten telecoms in Canada. Conquering the market there allowed us to then scale to the US.

To help gain some understanding on the venture capital side of the equation, we sat down to talk with Mathew George, who was our primary point person at Telus Ventures, to get a sense of their perspective. Mathew helped found Telus Ventures in 2001 because he saw few corporations in Canada involved in VC and believed it could be an arm to benefit the larger company's bottom line while also helping smaller companies gain traction.

Hostopia wasn't the only one they looked at, so what was it that set us apart?

"The biggest worry big companies have of using startups," he explained, "is whether they are still going to be around in five years or ten years." As part of their due diligence to ensure that a company was well run before providing funding, they would ask themselves these three questions:

1. Is this company run by experienced entrepreneurs who have had both successes and failures? Are they resilient?

2. Are they solving a real problem customers have?

3. Is there enough market share available? Is there still room for them to scale?

For Mathew, a key element of their decision to partner with us was looking at the core people in the company. "They had boot-strapped the company from scratch and had a clear understanding of what they needed to do," he shared. He appreciated that we knew in which direction we were headed and that we had a plan to get there, whether we received venture funding or not.

In our proof, we showed an understanding that VC would be an accelerant to our plans, not the thing that would make or break us. For him, this is first and foremost in his criteria: "Will this investment stand on its own feet? Will it provide a return?"

Second for him is this: "Does it fill a gap in the organization, something we can offer to our end customers?" If you can put these two things together, it can be a fantastic outcome.

But there is also a third criterion he considers, which sets Telus Ventures apart from some other VCs. "I saw it as an opportunity for up-and-coming employees to observe how an entrepreneurial unit could work," he said. He wanted the Telus team to learn from the entrepreneurial mindset because, while big companies have a different set of problems, he knew they could learn how to be more agile like a startup for continuous improvement.

Authenticity is key too. He said it's easy for entrepreneurs to say yes to everything a VC asks them for because they just want the deal, but he sees more value in an entrepreneur who is willing to speak up and say what they're *really* about—which goes back to the power of your Story.

Other common pitfalls he sees in entrepreneurs is when they display a lot of swagger but not a lot of proof of solving a real problem. "You have to do your homework ... you have to develop real proof points and show you can solve the problem," he advised. "If you could just show you can solve a problem, you could raise money quickly,"

On that note, he pointed out how they tend to focus on opportunities that have already been vetted through their colleagues or by industry veterans who have used the startup's offerings. So his next bit of advice for entrepreneurs was truly golden: "Take the time to not just go to the money ... go to the other places in the space who can validate what you're doing. Only approach VC after you have proof." In other words, prove yourself to those who have already built up trust within your industry.

These insights serve a twofold purpose: they de-risk the opportunity for Telus Ventures, but they also prove whether the company's success is repeatable. Sound familiar?

All this is to say that Telus Ventures viewed Hostopia as a true partnership that would benefit the economic ecosystem for both sides. The problem is that many VC agreements are centered only on the initial transaction instead of on setting a scaling strategy designed to create more profitable transactions over the long run.

So if you're going to enter into a VC agreement, make sure that you not only read the fine print about what you're giving up but also that there is a real strategy and partnership that will help lead to growth outside of the funding itself. And I do give credit to VCs who have expertise in a particular area, which can help a startup scale and, in some cases, even exit.

There are certainly other benefits to VCs, such as gaining some exposure and notoriety as well as bringing in some new expertise, new connections, and new customers. Some even consider VC a rite of passage in scaling a business, but I would still argue that all these perceived benefits hold lasting value only if they are connected to a clear scaling strategy.

In my opinion, one of the worst symptoms of Silicon Valley Disease is an addiction to VC funding. It's incredibly contagious because entrepreneurs look at the unicorns making headlines

> **If you're going to enter into a VC agreement, make sure that you not only read the fine print about what you're giving up but also that there is a real strategy and partnership that will help lead to growth outside of the funding itself.**

and think they need to make the same moves to mimic their success—and without knowing the details of what they're giving up.

You have to remember that your Story is different from those companies, and your People are different, so it stands to reason that your Money will be different too. And so-called unicorns like WeWork should serve as a stark reminder that VC funding in and of itself is no guarantee of success.

CHAPTER 30:

Raise Money by Saving Money

REMEMBER CUSTOMER-FUNDED STARTUP techniques from Start? All that applies here and more.

Most entrepreneurs focus on getting more sales and more revenue, which isn't necessarily wrong, as scaling requires you to become a sales-driven organization, as we'll discuss later. But few focus on the cost side when you really need to be managing both sides of the equation.

The idea of reducing costs is probably the least sexy within the topic of funding, but it's one of the most powerful, as it can help you accelerate your growth by redirecting your funding to growth drivers. I would argue that it's one the easiest ways to "raise" money for scaling, yet it's the most overlooked.

The addiction to VC funding that we see in Silicon Valley has crossed over into the wider entrepreneurship community. More often than not, entrepreneurs make the same mistake as others who have suddenly found themselves flush with cash—they create a Flamingo Hotel not unlike Bugsy Siegel and end up with almost no ownership in the end. The result is that entrepreneurs think the answer to growth is found only in getting outside money instead of having the ownership mindset to look *inside* the company to what they can control.

> **❝ There's nothing like being self-sufficient when you scale, and one of the most overlooked ways to free up money for scaling is to make cost reductions. ❞**

As I stated before, there's nothing like being self-sufficient when you scale, and one of the most overlooked ways to free up money for scaling is to make cost reductions. I've previously referred to how Hostopia was losing nearly $500,000 per month in the early days. Most of that loss was coming out of the pockets of my two business partners and myself. That's a lot of money to be burning each month.

Then we got hit with 9/11. Although we had survived the dot-com crash, we never anticipated an external event of that scale. Everything in the B2B market froze, and our losses at the company continued to pile up. Unfortunately, we had to make the tough choice of letting go of thirty people within a week of 9/11. It was emotionally devastating and definitely not a good time for the employees. Yet with hard work and more focus, something unexpected began to happen—we became more productive.

The remaining staff not only accepted the outcome but also felt relieved that the company was going to survive. And although we lost a third of our staff, we had retained the top performers in the remaining two-thirds and saw them generate an overall increase in productivity. Let me be clear here: We produced at a higher level of productivity with fewer people. And although it was still stressful and we were still in a money-losing position, we began to see the numbers change quarter by quarter until that magical day when we finally hit the breakeven point.

Ensure that your cost cuts feed actual growth.

When you make cost reductions—whether that's finding new suppliers, negotiating better deals with distributors, automating processes, or other ways to reduce your overhead—you'll only accelerate your growth if you make sure to redirect those funds to growth drivers. This might be ad spending or hiring new sales staff, but the point isn't just to reduce spending for the sake of reduction; it's to free up the funds to spur on growth.

Also, you can—and should—do this at any time. People usually consider cost reductions only when they've had a bad quarter or when the economy takes a downturn. But if you have a growth mindset to scale in zeros, you should be looking at making cost reductions all the time, especially during the good times, to capitalize on the growth and accelerate it further.

Make sure to always include your team in this process before you go hacking away at the budget with a cleaver. There may be expenses you want to cut that turn out to be vital for growth. I always enjoy adding a brainstorming session to our quarterly strategic planning meeting focused on cost reductions. If you're growing rapidly, they may think you're crazy, but let me tell you: when all the staff, or at least the executives get behind it, you will come up with some really cool ideas.

During your next strategy session, I challenge you to fill up a whiteboard with one hundred ideas.

One small cut won't make a difference, but a hundred small cuts will move the dial.

Every business loses money from time to time, some for longer than others. I have worked with dozens of small businesses where there is no magic bullet. But there are a hundred different moves or cost reductions you can make to break even or increase your margins.

It's the equivalent of someone revisiting their budget and thinking they can reduce their debt just by canceling their magazine subscription. No—it's going to take a lot more than that. It's going to take a hundred of these small ideas to help us get to break even. It means looking at your biggest expenses with the least impact and rebalancing to increase the spending in the areas with the biggest impact.

When you can make those cuts, as painful and uncomfortable as they may be, you can move the dial toward profitability and then accelerate both growth and profitability through another round of raising funds. This is something we practiced at .CLUB—I challenged our team to come up with cost-cutting ideas, including how we booked flights, ways to hack trade show expenses, moving into a shared office facility, and more. The key win for our team was renegotiating some big advertising contracts. Although our revenue grew year after year, our costs also went down year after year, increasing our overall profit margins.

Never sacrifice service or growth.

If there's one way to help you make the tough decisions between what to cut and what not to cut, it's to ask this question: "Is this cost related to service or growth?"

If it's yes, then don't cut it. If you can reduce the cost without sacrificing your service or growth, then by all means, do it. We've been frank with distributors before, telling them that our company was trying to break even and needed their help to do so but that their great service was something we weren't willing to sacrifice in order to maintain our reputation with customers. When you build strong relationships like these, you might be surprised by the deals people are willing to make to keep you on as a customer.

In 2003, Hostopia was experiencing hypergrowth, and we needed to hire more programmers and systems administrators. My brother, Bill, and Igor Nikolaichuk went to Ukraine to see if they could hire out a dozen programmers. They came back and said they hired fifty. Over the years, Hostopia would outsource hundreds of engineers and call center staff overseas—engineers primarily out of Ukraine and call center staff out of the Philippines.

This move gave the company a competitive edge and helped us eventually find our X factor. The lower costs allowed us to develop an incredible platform that none of our American competitors could come close to. Contrary to the popular belief that outsourcing means replacing your home staff, *none* of our employees were replaced. In fact, we expanded our core team in both Canada and the US. What we did was scale through outsourcing, allowing the company to grow efficiently.

Develop a business process outsourcing mindset.

At Paw.com, we do a daily report to closely track our return on ad spend ROAS. After receiving the same report every day from our accountant on staff, I made a recommendation to hire an accountant out of India to take over this task. Our bookkeeper's salary was about $75 per hour, and we could hire someone to fulfill this report-writing role for $7.50 per hour. I particularly want you to look at everything you do, and if you find repeatable aspects in the business, it's time to outsource those.

Another example I like to talk about was a situation that occurred at Meowingtons, a company in our incubator program. They have a very popular daily comic run by a quite talented artist based out of Austin. Eventually, though, she left the company, as Meowingtons couldn't afford to pay her rate anymore. Michele, my cohost on the podcast and the owner of Meowingtons, took the initiative to hire an agency in the Philippines to help find a replacement.

Yes, the concepts for the comic still have to be designed by the Florida team, which really isn't that time consuming, but each cartoon is now being drawn by the artist in the Philippines at a tenth of the cost it would be in the US, yet the quality is still amazing. Check it out at MiltontheCat.club—they're hilarious. She is so good, we even asked her to draw the illustrations for this book.

At Hostopia, our call center was blowing up, and while a place like the Philippines could also be used for a call center, at the time we wanted to keep it domestic for our business clients. We cut a deal with the New Brunswick government, who gave us over a million dollars in subsidies, and we hired hundreds of employees in Miramichi, New Brunswick.

Eastern Canada can be a great place to outsource onshore. In our experience, the people have wonderful, positive attitudes. And if I could add one more thing—they really like to party! Every year, the executives, including me, would fly up for the holiday party. One year, our plane was delayed, and we arrived at the event about two hours late only to find our staff quite happy, and my annual speech ended up becoming more like a comedy routine thanks to a vivacious audience. And given the pullback in the Canadian dollar in 2022, it makes for an even more desirable option for outsourcing.

Developing a business process outsourcing mindset can be one of the best ways that you can scale at a fraction of the cost of having all your employees local. What's ironic is that when we outsourced at Hostopia, we hired a lot more staff in Canada and the US. The more contracts we won, the more we hired.

> **" You might need the investor's money to scale in zeros, but that shouldn't stop you from finding dozens of ways to cut costs. "**

In short, don't wait for funding from outside sources to grow. While you're figuring out how to get the money to scale and who to pitch to, you can fund growth by reducing costs and reallocating funds to high-impact areas. You might need the investor's money to scale in zeros, but that shouldn't stop you from finding dozens of ways to cut costs. The lessons you learn in the process will help you be a better, wiser steward of the funding you eventually get from outside sources.

SYSTEMS

CHAPTER 31:

The Value of Coaching

ENTREPRENEURS CAN BE really good at creating excitement around an idea or a vision—and then getting others to follow. But entrepreneurs can be really bad at one important thing: following systems. This is especially true when they have succeeded by breaking conventions.

I often say that entrepreneurs are more like artists than operators. Although that's not true in all cases, it is for most. When you think of an artist, you think of an eccentric personality, one who can create an incredible vision yet who can't seem to monetize it. Entrepreneurs are better at the monetization piece but can be similar to artists in their eccentricities and adherence to a vision.

Remember the stat about half of all US businesses closing shop within five years? That's because the vast majority fail to scale. They simply don't have the right systems in place. They may have the vision and early successes, and they may even make a living, but they simply do not have the right systems to scale in zeros. And why would they? There isn't a college class I know of that teaches entrepreneurs what to do to scale companies. Instinct can get you only so far, but it isn't going to take you *all* the way.

In 2005, we were about to take Hostopia public when we ran into some major problems—in fact, the truth is that the wheels were beginning to come off the bus. Growth had stalled out at about $18 million in sales, and there was fighting among the executive team, including between my brother and I. We were missing numbers at the end of every quarter. We were simply running the company by fighting one fire at a time. The stress was killing me.

One day, a board member approached me to share his concerns about the company and suggested that I was in way over my head. Unfortunately, my original business partner had to part ways with the company, and my brother and I no longer controlled the board. We needed to find a way to avoid getting fired and to bring in new board members so that we could regain control over the company.

I was truly desperate when I first met my CEO coach, Patrick Thean, in Las Vegas and shared with him the challenges we were facing. "Patrick, I just need you to get the board off my back," I told him. "I can hire you for a couple sessions, assure the board we're making some changes, and that should be enough."

Patrick refused. "Colin, I can't do that," he said. "Maybe you're smarter than some of my other clients, but I don't know that we can succeed with what you're suggesting. But I *know* we can succeed if we do it my way."

This made me nervous because, deep down, I knew he was right. There was no going halfway on things if they were going to get fixed. But it meant convincing every executive to get on board with going through a full coaching program, making changes, and implementing new systems we'd never tried. It wasn't going to be easy. Especially given my track record with trying to implement other systems previously.

Too many times I'd go to a conference or event, come back to the office, and try to implement a number of concepts that would fall flat. The staff would literally cringe when they heard I was going to *another* conference, fearing what new things I would make them do, only to drop it a few months later. It wasn't until I met Patrick that he opened up a whole new world for me. Not only was I able to bring back these ideas but also I was able to institutionalize his systems to ensure that they would stick.

We kicked it off with a two-day strategic planning session off-site. Patrick flew to Fort Lauderdale where the team had gathered. I thought the first session was a disaster. Fights, politics, defensive postures, denial—it was so bad that on the ride back to the airport, I apologized to Patrick on behalf of the team. But something wonderful happened that day. We began to really address the brutal facts, the elephant—or in our case, *elephants*—in the room.

Everyone began to understand their place and what their expectations were. We started to figure out where we wanted to go *together*. For years, we had based all "strategy" on our instincts, and now our eyes were opened for the very first time that we needed some external systems to support us in scaling the company.

That's why coaching is a part of Systems and not People—because having a coach is really about putting systems into place. Think about

Olympic and professional-level athletes. They already have the raw talent and know-how for their sport. But they need a coach who can create a training program customized to their needs to help them push past the performance plateaus they face. And besides, if it wasn't for Patrick, I would still be wandering the desert looking for answers—or maybe I would've even died of thirst, metaphorically speaking.

Coaching creates accountability, planning, and alignment.

If you took a look at me, you wouldn't consider me a prime candidate for CrossFit. As of the writing of this book, I'm in my early fifties, and I've had to live with an autoimmune disease that fused my neck and spine over the last thirty years, reducing my mobility. Yeah, not fun.

A couple of years ago, I recognized that I needed help losing weight, building muscle mass, and improving my quality of life. But I simply didn't have the skills or systems to do it on my own.

I could've done a couple of things. I could've bought a home workout system—a video workout to follow along with or something like Peloton. Or I could've joined a class at a local gym. But in these, the instructor is speaking to an entire group. While this could have helped me some, I realized that having a personal trainer to focus on my *specific* goals and needs would be way more effective. So for the first time in my life, I decided to hire a personal trainer—Santiago.

I can't tell you how difficult that first workout was. It was *tough*, and in hindsight, he was not pushing me all that hard—as I've come to discover in the past couple of years! At the time, though, I thought I was going to injure myself and put myself out for months. But something magical happened: I did *not* injure myself, and to this day, even doing CrossFit three times a week, I have still not had a serious injury. I credit that to working directly with an expert to help me practice every move to ensure that I'm improving my form.

> **Having a CEO coach invites an outside perspective, one that is tailored to your situation.**

It's the same in business. Going to a conference or training course is like attending a group exercise class. It's definitely beneficial, but it's not tailored to you. Having a CEO coach invites an outside perspective, one that is tailored to your situation. I've learned several things from Santiago that I believe translate well to the need for CEO coaching:

→ *Accountability*: Santiago holds me accountable to a plan and to see him at a specific place and time to work on specific goals. Even when he's not training me on a particular skill, he's assigning my exact workout for that day.

→ *Commitment*: Having a coach usually drives a higher level of commitment. As Santiago once pointed out, "A lot of times we do things better for others than we do for ourselves."

→ *Results*: I'm not a fitness expert. Santiago is. I'm more likely to ensure results for myself by trusting in his expertise than trying to do it on my own because he has both the knowledge and the systems that I'm lacking.

→ *Transcendence*: With Santiago, there's an additional element of psychological and emotional support that can't be replicated by a group instructor or an at-home program. As he puts it, "Pushing ourselves outside of our comfort zones is where growth happens." But that means you have to be willing to face a level of discomfort where additional support is needed to get you to the other side. I felt this discomfort after that first workout and began to learn that it was okay to be sore afterward. In fact, sometimes if I'm not sore after a workout, I have to wonder if I exercised hard enough.

It's no different in my relationship with Patrick as my CEO coach. He also provides the level of accountability, commitment, results, and transcendence needed to grow. If I have bad form in a workout, Santiago points it out and helps me correct it to prevent an injury. If I have a blind spot holding me back, Patrick is able to point it out and help me correct it to prevent failure.

For Patrick, it all boils down to preventing failure, often by providing an external perspective. "In a crisis, we'll miss the simple and clear," he says. "Someone needs to help us see the obvious."

Greatness clusters.

Great athletes go after great coaches who they know won't let them settle for good enough. And you won't see someone trying to go to the Olympics competing against middle schoolers so that they can have an easy win. No. They want to both train under a coach who pushes them to greatness and compete against rivals who push them to greatness.

Having a coach is not cheap, but in my experience, if you're aiming for a high-performing environment with high performers, you can dramatically increase their performance by having one. Ultimately, this one investment can have the biggest ROI in your business.

Companies often make the mistake of focusing on weaknesses, falsely believing they can elevate people through learning and more training. But the big money is in taking great performers and making them perform even better.

Should you address weaknesses? Of course. But in terms of scaling, your greatest investment is in strengthening what's strong—and eliminating the weak.

Patrick shared on Startup Club that there are two competing ideas you have to hold in your head in order to succeed:

First, you have to believe you're going to change the world.

Second, you have to believe you could fail—so you need to have a plan B ready.

These sound contradictory, but the way these two thoughts work together is like the up and down of a piston on an engine. Great athletes are driven by the idea that they can be the best in the world. But they're equally driven by wanting to *avoid* failure and having a plan for how to handle it.

I've said it before, but I'll say it again—sometimes we entrepreneurs can be our own worst enemies. Sometimes we're too close to the problem to see the problem—especially when *we* are the problem! Our startups are like our babies. We are protective of them and can feel slighted when someone tells us what's wrong with our baby. But just like how you would take your child to the doctor if they're sick, or your car to the mechanic if it's stalling out, it's the same with business coaching.

> **❝ We have to know when to check our ego at the door and open our minds to a fresh perspective. ❞**

Patrick says that one of the greatest lessons he's learned from a mentor is this: "First, you have to survive before you can thrive." You can't scale if your company crashes. A good coach will provide the insights, systems, and tools designed to ensure survival while also developing the rhythms necessary to thrive.

For me, coaching was absolutely life-changing. It was like taking the red pill in *The Matrix*—it opened my eyes and experience to everything I hadn't seen before. Did we have some success beforehand? Of course we did. But coaching has made a huge difference by allowing us to scale things in a way we could never have done if we had kept flying solo. The impact doesn't end on a personal level either because one of the great values of coaching is that it allows you to amplify your impact across the company's culture too.

❝ A good coach will provide the insights, systems, and tools designed to ensure survival while also developing the rhythms necessary to thrive. ❞

CHAPTER 32:

Scale Your Culture

I MEET SO MANY entrepreneurs who have great ideas, great vision, great passion—but they lack the systems to be able to scale the company to the next level. While we've already discussed how to scale your team as well as some best practices in hiring, which absolutely will impact the culture of your company, here I want to go deeper into the systems you can use to scale your culture. Unfortunately, culture is an afterthought for entrepreneurs when it should be in the foreground.

Too often an assumption is made that company culture is something HR can worry about. While there's some truth to this, and you *should* have human resources involved in developing ideas on how to create a strong culture where people love to work, scaling that culture has to begin with the leadership team, or any system HR tries to put in place will fail. At the end of the day, your culture is a reflection of your company. I'll take it one step further—it's ultimately a reflection of yourself.

The culture of an early startup can be really fun. It's late nights, pizza, free-flowing creativity, and lots of energy. Everyone knows everyone, and everyone knows exactly how to behave in the environment. As your team grows larger and wider, you won't be able to have direct connections with everyone like in the early startup days. Therefore, the culture you establish among your direct reports has to be one that can scale throughout the organization as you grow.

You know you're hitting the point in your company as it scales when someone starts to say, "Remember the good old days? The company is just not the same anymore." Well, they're right. The company is not the same, and the culture that you were able to effort-lessly create in an office of ten people becomes increasingly difficult to maintain over time, especially in today's world when so many are working remotely.

> ❝ Scaling your culture can be one of the easiest, lowest-cost ways to increase your chances of success. ❞

Even so, scaling your culture can be one of the easiest, lowest-cost ways to increase your chances of success. While the culture of every workplace will be different by nature, there are some consistent principles I've observed that can help you scale it for success.

Core values are a reflection of you and your business.

Not many startups think about core values before they launch. For the most part, entrepreneurs begin to look at core values only when something goes off the rails during the scale phase. When you first start out and your team is small, everyone implicitly knows what will tick off the owner—or make them happy. But as you grow and scale, it becomes essential to define what those values are and to create clarity around them for everyone.

So while it overlaps and is related to scaling your Story, integrat-ing core values into your company is a system. In the same way that your why can drive motivation in Start, core values are the guardrails guiding the decision-making process throughout the life of the business. Startups that fail to follow their stated values may succeed in the short run by making a quick buck, but in my experience, they ultimately fail to scale because they've compromised on those values.

> **"Core values are the guardrails guiding the decision-making process throughout the life of the business."**

I once had the opportunity to visit the office for Zappos and saw a book sitting on the CFO's desk called *Mastering the Rockefeller Habits*, by Verne Harnish, in which he builds off some concepts from Jim Collins and others. In my opinion, Zappos has one of the best-defined culture stories of any startup in the last decade. They not only codified and promoted their core values through ten culture statements but also everyone lives out the values, as follows:

1. Deliver WOW through service.

2. Embrace and drive change.

3. Create fun and a little weirdness.

4. Be adventurous, creative, and open-minded.

5. Pursue growth and learning.

6. Build open and honest relationships with communication.

7. Build a positive team and family spirit.

8. Do more with less.

9. Be passionate and determined.

10. Be humble.[16]

---

16 Zappos.com, "What We Live By," accessed October 12, 2022, https://www.zappos.com/about/what-we-live-by.

During my struggles at Hostopia, I had the opportunity to read *Mastering the Rockefeller Habits* (which came out before Verne published *Scaling Up*), and I discovered how effective value statements can be in defining your culture. I learned how core values should be something people actually *use* day-to-day and become the language of the company. I also learned how they should form the basis for hiring, firing, driving growth, customer service, rules of engagement, and all other areas of major decision-making.

When you're trying to scale, you really need to bring your team together to define your values, or what I like to call your pillars. At Hostopia we developed them six to seven years after launch, but at .CLUB we established them over the first eighteen months, honing them rather than rushing into them. We knew these would be the values we would live and die by—the rules that could never be broken—and would serve as a reflection of the company itself.

When we had Verne Harnish on Startup Club via Clubhouse, he compared the creation of core values to parenting. "You as a parent hope [your children] take on certain attributes that you think are important, but sometimes you get a kid where you're not sure where they came from." Likewise, core values aren't there to squash an individual's personality or to turn them into a clone but to help you channel someone's individuality in the right direction to protect the integrity of the company.

The easier it is to remember your core values, the easier it is to follow them. Single words and long sentences can be ignored or forgotten, whereas short, punchy phrases can become part of the company's DNA and language. For example, at Hostopia, we came up with the following as our pillars:

➜ First and foremost is respect.

➜ Recognize greatness.

- We spend it like our own.

- When our customers succeed, we succeed.

At .CLUB we took it a little further:

- Only the obsessed change the world.

- Usage is everything.

- Integrity over money.

- Recognize greatness.

- Do crazy things, not stupid things.

Notice the rhythm of these statements. Verne and Patrick showed me how you can take a concept and make it memorable. It doesn't take a ton of brain power to memorize them, and yet they are flexible enough to be applied across many areas of the operation. It's fascinating to see how these common phrases can have such an impact on the team, and there wasn't a day that went by when someone didn't repeat one of them in a conversation. Unlike mindless mission statements hanging on a wall, these have become part of our lexicon, ingrained in our thinking, and therefore are guideposts for our decision-making.

Have you ever gone to a bowling alley and used the bumper guards for your kid? Or yourself? That's what core values are—if you get too close to the edge—*bump*—they send you back to where you need to be.

Sometimes this will bump you into some uncomfortable but necessary situations. If you hire someone who isn't meeting the core values, then they need to be fired. Sometimes that means you might make less money in the short term but you keep true to your values, which is far more important—and it's something your staff will remember. I've had to fire people before when it turned out they weren't following our core value of integrity over money.

On that note, knowing your personal values is a great place to start. Who wants to dedicate their life to a project incompatible with their own values? A few years back, I decided to take the work that Verne, Jim Collins, and others have done in this area and apply it personally. In asking myself, "What are my personal values?" I came up with six that are key for me:

➜ First and foremost is my health.

➜ Do it really well or don't do it at all.

➜ Live in the future.

➜ Integrity over money.

➜ Carpe diem/seize the day.

➜ Make a difference.

You can see how some of these personal values have transferred into our company values. Although stated differently, "Do crazy things, not stupid things" has the same message as "Carpe diem/ Seize the day."

While you don't simply copy and paste these onto the company, your personal values do have a strong influence on your ability to follow through on the company's pillars. Your values are a reflection of who you are as well as the team around you.

To get started, set up an exercise with your team at your next planning session. Spend a few hours trying to figure out what values are common among different people on the team. Discuss why certain people just did not fit within your organization. Why were they fired, or why did they leave?

Come up with four to six core values—no fewer, no more. Although Zappos has ten, the fewer there are, the more memorable they become. The company that sets up core values establishes a stronger relationship between the team members and the purpose. I'm convinced that everyone can thrive within that kind of culture, knowing you've got these guardrails in place.

Recognize greatness.

Call centers are a tough place to work. At Hostopia's call center, we had a Five Diamond Award system where we would give employees a diamond pendant for specific accomplishments. Then whenever they got five diamonds, they would receive an extra week of paid vacation and an entire day at the company named after them—including a celebration during which we would buy lunch for *everyone* in the company.

That's what I mean when I say to recognize greatness!

I know that what I'm about to say might offend a few people, but one of the things that irritates me is when companies recognize employees for three things: birthdays, tenure, and when they leave. Given the growth of Hostopia, there was a birthday almost every day. How many times can you sing "Happy Birthday" and eat cake? Call me the birthday Grinch, but someone had to put an end to it. We ultimately canceled the daily parties, moving them to once a month, and I think over time, even that faded away. But when an employee got that fifth star? That was a party to remember!

I'm not saying that these traditional ceremonies can't be good things to do, but when that's *all* that a company recognizes, what does it communicate about the culture? Instead, one of the greatest ways to scale a culture is to recognize greatness *as it happens*—and maybe just pull back a little on the traditional ones.

Recognizing greatness can't be haphazard or half-hearted—everyone needs to know what the expectations are and then those expectations must be met. Otherwise, it's just nice words and broken promises. But when it truly becomes a part of the company culture, then it also nurtures a high-performance culture. This should come as no surprise—everyone likes to be recognized when something great happens.

When Sara Blakely, the entrepreneur behind the clothing brand Spanx, announced the successful sale of the company to Blackstone, she paired it with recognizing the greatness of the team that had led to that moment. Beyond a simple "thanks for all the hard work" that too many leaders think suffices for proper recognition, she announced publicly on social media that every team member was going to get a $10,000 bonus and a paid, first-class vacation.

Without her having to say another word, team members flocked to social media to announce their plans for how to use the money and the trip and how her actions were going to personally impact them. Obviously, this was great PR for the company, but it was further proof of the value you create when you put your money where your mouth is and make recognition of greatness a defining attribute of the business.

CHAPTER 33:

Strategic Planning and Execution

WHEN FIRST STARTING a business, everything is ad hoc. We entrepreneurs can be found sitting in a coffee shop brainstorming the company name, figuring out how we'll make that first sale, and running around like a chicken with its head cut off to get that first dollar in the door.

However, this kind of adrenaline-fueled chaos can work against us as we begin to grow. As we discussed earlier, it happened to me when the wheels eventually came off the bus at Hostopia.

In your Start stage, you might write down ideas and tasks and then follow up on them. Your staff might meet on an ad hoc basis, and ideas just sort of come together from pure drive and rapport. But true strategic planning and execution has to go further than this if you intend to scale the company—it has to be tied to the goals and outcomes you're looking to achieve, backed by a regular rhythm of meetings. And the SMART-er, the better.

Develop a rhythm of executing your strategy.

Verne Harnish has said that a common pitfall for entrepreneurs is thinking that their company is too young for creating processes around strategy and structure. They assume wrongly that processes are only

> ** A common pitfall for entrepreneurs is thinking that their company is too young for creating processes around strategy and structure. **

for the big guys. But Verne's advice is that "if you get started in these processes and in this thinking early on in your business, it has extreme benefits going forward."

What does this mean? It means having a proper annual strategy meeting to document where you want the company to be in several years, defining your next 10X Stage Gate, and then looking at what needs to happen in the next three years, the next year, and the next three months at the company. Once the next quarter has been defined, you break it down into quarterly goals, then translate those into the individual projects and tasks that will accomplish those goals.

Before I started doing this, my team would end up in a cycle of having a lot of ad hoc discussions about doing this or that, but often it was just time wasted because we weren't truly focused on how those ideas fit into the long-term vision for the company or how it connected with our goals. Now I like to do my annual strategic meeting off-site, usually at one of my vacation rentals or even at my personal home, for a couple of days. I think it's helpful to get my core team out of the regular environment so that we're not distracted by the day-to-day. I have found that it also really helps team members bond and ideate better. We work hard, but we have some fun as well.

The pattern we follow for strategic planning typically looks like this:

PLANNING PHASE	PLANNING DURATION	EXECUTION TIMEFRAME
Annual Planning (Includes Q1)	2 days of offsite planning	Followed by 88 days of execution
Q2 Planning	1-2 days of offsite planning	Followed by 88 days of execution
Q3 Planning	1-2 days of offsite planning	Followed by 88 days of execution
Q4 Planning	1-2 days of offsite planning	Followed by 88 days of execution

This cycle ensures that every quarter we're checking in to make certain we're on track but focused on execution the majority of the time. As the company grows larger, it becomes essential to do at least two days of strategic planning per quarter. What's interesting about this cycle is that it *reduces* the amount of conversations you need to get everyone on the same page.

What you want to avoid in these sessions, though, are presentations from everyone where one person from each department stands up and gives a status report. If you need to do that, do it in a separate premeeting. Also, it can be easy to spend strategy sessions talking only about fixing problems, but what I find valuable is to focus on what's working well and trying to identify new opportunities.

When you do that, you'll inevitably fix a good chunk of the problems, but you'll also keep things in a positive space rather than drowning in complaints, which only makes the culture toxic over time.

> **" Spend at least 70 percent of your time in some form of ideation. "**

I would encourage you and your team to spend at least 70 percent of your time in some form of ideation. This is where the breakthroughs come in by harnessing the intelligence of the entire team.

In Start, your strategy is focused on Stage Gates, breaking even, and keeping oxygen in the tank. But here in Scale, it's focused more on making three to five very specific winning moves over the next five to ten years so that you can scale 10X, which is a bit different from the idea of setting goals. Eventually the strategy will translate into quarterly goals, individual goals, and KPIs, which we'll discuss in just a bit.

For example, with Hostopia, we strategized about how we were going to win major contracts like Verizon, setting dates to do so, determining the people who would be involved in winning it, and looking for the sales opportunities, where we needed to open conversations, and the tools and systems we needed in place to make it happen.

We also like to kick off our strategy sessions by having everyone prepare in advance their start-and-stop list. We like to use an app called Mural that allows executive team members to fill in their ideas on the app beforehand and then bring those into the strategy sessions.

Within the Mural app, each person lists their thoughts on what items they think we should *start* doing and those things we need to *stop*. There may also be some conversation on newer initiatives we need to *continue* doing, but that's usually obvious once you've determined the things that need to stop.

It's great to find the overlaps in everyone's lists to prioritize things, and it's fun to see when that one person finds the really big idea that no one else has thought of. Using the Mural app in this way prevents people from being influenced by others *during* the meeting and protects us from groupthink in the strategy sessions. If you don't use Mural, consider having your team members write out their start-and-stop list in advance.

Patrick taught me how it's important that you as the entrepreneur check your dominance at the door and wait to speak last. Hold yourself back and let others talk first to see what they come up with so that they aren't just agreeing with whatever you say. This fosters innovative and creative independent thought, which is perfect for producing those aha moments—the ideas that will be game changers for the company.

Here's a simple brainstorming tool Patrick taught us: *I encourage everyone on the team to just throw ideas out there. No idea is stupid—just throw it out there and put it on the board. After we've done that, we'll rank the top ten based on the ease of implementation and the overall impact of the idea by having each person on the team approach the board and vote on what they think the top ideas are.*

It's kind of like when the audience in *Who Wants to be a Millionaire?* votes on the answer—which, by the way, they end up being correct 91 percent of the time compared to 66 percent for the alternative of calling a friend.[17] The audience—your staff—can help make a difference here. Then we compile that list as the cream of the crop and assign someone who will be accountable for execution of the idea.

After we started implementing some of these things at Hostopia, I can't tell you how much of a difference it made. When we did all of these—and others that we'll discuss over the next few chapters—we saw Hostopia grow in revenue to 4X its size over three to four years. And we were well rewarded, selling the company for *seventeen times* EBITDA to a Fortune 500 company. But more on that story when we get to Exit.

Decide what you're *not* going to focus on.

This is all about focus. As Patrick astutely noted in the same session, "Most entrepreneurs have more opportunity than they can handle." He'll ask a CEO what their one big priority is for the year, and instead of giving him one thing, they almost always rattle off ten things in one continuous train of thought.

For Patrick, the key to focus is prioritization, or rather, *de-prioritization*. Entrepreneurs can have a hard time figuring out what their top priority needs to be, so sometimes it's easier to eliminate the items that are low impact and difficult to do.

Remember the start-and-stop list I mentioned? Patrick uses a two-by-two matrix technique with his clients to help them take the raw data of that list and transform it into strategic priorities. On one axis, he has clients rank items on their priority list based on how high of an impact they are—if it's high impact, it's a ten; if it's low impact, it's a one. On the other axis, he has them rank how easy it is

---

17   Freestak, "Who Wants to Ask the Audience: The Benefits and Pitfalls of Social Media," August 13, 2014, http://www.freestak.com/blogposts/who-wants-to-ask-the-audience-the-benefits-and-pitfalls-of-social-media/.

to do something. Those items that rank as high impact and easy to do became the focal points for the company.

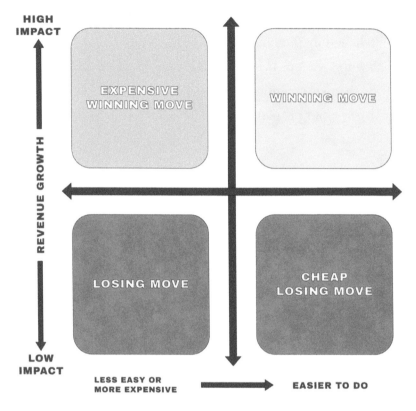

Thean, Patrick (2014). Rhythm: How to Achieve Breakthrough Execution and Accelerate Growth.

Certainly there can be exceptions. There may be items that are high impact and difficult, but they're necessary because they create a moat around the business or are more directly connected with the long-term strategy. You need to take those things into account, but according to Patrick, this exercise is really handy to help his clients de-prioritize all the ideas bouncing around their brains and to identify the top three. This often naturally leads them to realize what activities they need to stop if they're going to reallocate their focus to the goals that truly matter.

In the end, all three of these are interconnected—clarity, alignment, and focus. Without clarity, you'll struggle to create alignment, and you might end up focusing on the wrong things.

Having a system in place and employing a coach are keys to ensuring that you're aiming at the right target (your goals), with the right arrows (your people), and the right bow (your systems).

CHAPTER 34

Goal Setting

REMEMBER EARLIER WHEN I talked about going to conferences and returning with ideas to implement, only to have the team cringe at the practice? Over and over, the ideas just petered out. Well, that changed when I met Patrick, my CEO coach, and the implementation of strategic goal setting. By institutionalizing the changes we brought into the organization, all of sudden we had a system to provide accountability, transparency, and a sense of urgency.

Patrick once pointed out that only 2 percent of all companies get north of $2 million in revenue, and it's usually not because of a lack of strategy—but execution. Goals are at the heart of execution; they represent your target—what you're aiming for. As Patrick wisely puts it, "Breakthroughs come only when your dreams get executed."

During a session of *Serial Entrepreneur: Secrets Revealed!*, he shared a powerful story about one of his clients. This was a CEO for a company that does laundry in the healthcare industry, and during a review meeting, he said, "Patrick, every year I come to you with too many goals on my list, and I've finally learned to narrow it down. I'm just focusing on one thing this year—I want to increase our revenue per pound by one penny."

Patrick pushed back at this and said, "Only one penny? Is that all you can do?"

"You don't understand my financials," the CEO replied. "One penny per pound of laundry represents a million dollars for us."

Again, Patrick pushed on. "Why not shoot for two pennies per pound instead?"

"Fine," the CEO said. "You've taught me to have stretch goals, so we'll make it two pennies per pound, which would be an extra two million in revenue."

Patrick continued to work with them through the year, focusing on this simple goal, and in the end, the company increased their revenue by four pennies per pound. That's right, they had $4 million more in the bank than what the CEO was originally shooting for.

In that same session, Patrick shared with us some of the key principles for how companies effectively set and then achieve goals, no matter who they are.

You'll never achieve a goal you cannot see.

I've talked previously about the power of visualization, and it's fundamental with goal setting. A good goal is one you can see—otherwise, you have no idea what you're aiming for. As Patrick puts it, "You've got to have clarity."

> **The more vague a goal is, the harder it is to take action on it. The more specific and clear it is, the easier it is to take action.**

In the last chapter, we discussed the importance of creating a long-term strategy based on winning moves. When you combine that with transforming into a sales-driven culture, it will naturally push you to set goals aligned with your long-term scaling strategy. The more vague a goal is, the harder it is to take action on it. The more specific and clear it is, the easier it is to take action.

When we discussed strategy, I shared how I follow a 2/88 pattern—two days of strategic planning and eighty-eight days of execution. This allows us to take our big strategy and break it down into quarterly goals that are *action-based*. For quarterly goals, each person takes on four to six top priorities with a specific deadline and specific KPIs. Each goal comes from the employee themselves, increasing their sense of ownership in the goal.

For our weekly meetings, we track everyone's SMART goals with a Red, Yellow, Green system. If things are Green—great, keep at it! Yellow—we'll talk about how we can get things back on track and what additional support might be needed from other members of the team. And if Red—let's look at taking more drastic actions, maybe reprioritizing or tweaking the plan to make sure we can fix the problems quickly before they fester into bigger problems that spill over into other teams.

Smaller companies can do this with a simple spreadsheet, but if you're really beginning to scale, consider a cloud-based solution like Rhythm Systems, developed by Patrick's company. We used it religiously at both Hostopia and .CLUB to make sure we stayed on track with our expansion. In other words, you've got to look at what kind of system you're using to make your goals visual. Only with this kind of clarity can you define what you need to achieve and what you need to do to get there.

Create alignment around the goals.

Once you have clarity and visualization of your goals, it becomes much easier to create alignment in your team. As Patrick observes, "If you're only setting a goal for yourself, that's fine; you don't need alignment. But if it's a goal for a team? That's a completely different story."

Another reason it's important to have a system in place like Rhythms is that it forces greater transparency and accountability. If someone is headed in the opposite direction from the rest of the team, it's harder for that to go unnoticed when you're tracking activity and results. When you've got KPIs in place that you can connect back to specific actions, you allow the entire team to benefit by seeing what works best, creating further alignment.

In other words, setting a goal isn't enough in itself. You have to get buy-in from the team. According to one study, around 90 percent of businesses fail to reach all their strategic goals.[18] Why? Because they lack alignment. This is often because the C-suite fails to communicate the goals effectively or clearly, they focus on goals that don't matter to the team, they don't get feedback from the team, or they fail to utilize the strengths of the team.

I can't tell you how many times we'd be on track to hit the quarterly numbers and then, in the last week of the quarter, something goes wrong. With Rhythms' goal-setting tools, we were able to catch things going off the track much sooner so that we could make the necessary adjustments.

---

18   Jordan Erskine, "Why Goal-Setting Fails (and Four Ways to Fix It)," Forbes, April 6, 2021, https://www.forbes.com/sites/forbesbusinesscouncil/2021/04/06/why-goal-setting-fails-and-four-ways-to-fix-it/?sh=663f8e28283e.

CHAPTER 35:

Transforming into a Sales Organization

IN 2003/2004, HOSTOPIA was arriving at a crossroads. We had invested four years in developing what we believed to be the best platform in the world for selling hosting and email services for SMBs to telecoms. Then there came a day when we began to say, "Okay, now let's bring this ship to shore and focus on monetizing the platform." Likely this was due to years of financial loss taking their toll. We began to transform from primarily a tech company into a sales *and* tech company.

Our approach to growth dramatically changed. We began to hire the absolute best people in the industry who had a robust rolodex. We redirected IT resources to focus on customizations for new clients. We launched an eight-minute daily sales huddle at 8:50 a.m., which all the execs attended. We also put the CTO, COO, and myself on the road one to two weeks per month *with* the sales team to support their efforts. The results were huge!

To successfully scale, part of that strategic plan has to include transforming into a sales organization. Some startups do this really successfully in Start, as we've already discussed, and it's important to lay a sales foundation as early as you can. But one thing is for certain: no matter where you are in your business, you'll struggle to scale until you can transform into a sales-driven organization.

I'm not talking about an oily used car salesman type strategy. As I mentioned before, my own personal value of integrity over money has become a core value for companies I've started. During an episode of our podcast *Serial Entrepreneur: Secrets Revealed!*, a very successful entrepreneur and friend of mine Jim Bennett shared that to become super successful, you have to "step back, take a look at the business, stop always working *in* the business and work *on* the business … creating a sales culture is what I consider the most important thing I've ever done."

> **Even if you're really gifted in sales yourself, you can't be the only one responsible for landing deals if you're going to scale.**

In other words, even if you're really gifted in sales yourself, you can't be the only one responsible for landing deals if you're going to scale. And you're going to have to look to others on your team and the skills they have to set the sales team up for success.

Develop a sales playbook.

Jim was a collegiate athlete, so when he was building a sales team, he decided to create a playbook to operate by—a plan that would spell out the type of people he wanted on his team, the scripts they would use, the daily schedule, and the commission structure. In other words, it's about giving your sales strategy a clear structure so that it can thrive.

Jim shared that he "was trying to create a system around which people like me could become successful," so he targeted others who had played college sports, people who would be enthusiastic and competitive but who would also know what it meant to be a good teammate.

To spur on a positive competitiveness, he ran daily, monthly, and quarterly contests among the team, connecting them through a culture of friendly competition. To develop his team, he even held internal conferences when they were as small as ten people so that they could learn and grow. In short, he likes to find people with potential and train them to become rock stars.

His playbook included scripts of what was most successful for winning customers. Scripts often get a bad rap for making salespeople sound robotic, but here his scripts were designed to be alive and to help everyone improve. Their team would do role-playing exercises, where each salesperson would run through their script and get critiqued by their peers so that there could be mutual learning. "It wasn't just about the words," Jim explained, "but even the nuances of the words … you practice, practice, practice to become successful."

Eventually, the playbook you create can have a larger impact beyond the sales team. It was so effective in transforming the company culture, he said, that "I've got to do this for every position in the company ... the receptionist even had a playbook!"

Notice that this is a playbook, not a *rule* book. The difference is that a playbook must be focused on building a culture of who you want to be as a company and how you want to represent yourself to customers. A playbook will be improved and tweaked over time to make it better, which relies on feedback and input from the team. This is a common pitfall where entrepreneurs think they're creating a playbook and instead end up writing a list of iron-fisted rules.

As we previously discussed with hiring leaders, it's important here to spell out the expectations for the sales team, especially their commission structure, as this will be a huge part of their motivation to succeed. Even here, these shouldn't be set blindly but should be a discussion. What kind of commission truly motivates success? What kind of rewards system can be put in place outside of commission? And what kind of schedule increases the chances of success?

One other piece I'll add is to keep your commission plan *simple*.

Too many companies complicate it to the point where the salesperson doesn't understand it, which reduces the impact the commissions have on their motivation.

To make sure he covers all his bases in the playbook, Jim has a simple acronym for his formula: BANK.

If a playbook does all four of these things, then it sets you up for success. If it's missing one, then you need to go back to the drawing board. Jim has repeated this formula over and over at multiple companies with great success—and now his kids are doing it at their companies! Coupling a solid playbook with a daily sales huddle will be key to noticing the gaps—and filling them in—to transform into a sales-driven culture.

Find ways to make more money with less work.

One of my sales role models over the years has been Jack Daly, who also joined us on our weekly live show and podcast. When Hostopia was struggling to transition from being a tech-driven company to a sales-driven one, we deployed a number of his methods to design systems that would generate more leads and improve our craft. He once shared that one of the keys to his success has been to always ask himself, "How can I make more money with less work? How can I generate more business with less work?" In fact, our successful friend Jim worked with Jack to set up his sales playbook and methods.

A common misunderstanding in transforming into a sales-driven organization is that the more work you put in directly correlates to how much money you make. This is where the old sales analogy about catching more fish by casting out your fishing line more times falls apart. No matter how many times you cast your line out, you're going to catch only one fish at a time. Instead, you should look at trading in the rod for a net.

There are a couple of ways that Jack does this that should be incorporated into a playbook. The first one is to focus on high-payoff activities. The top salespeople in any organization do this. "More than fifty percent of a salesperson's time is spent on things that don't generate new sales or grow the [accounts] you have. They're doing things that someone else should be doing."

So instead of having a salesperson wasting time digging up new leads or doing data entry, you can delegate these activities to other people or even outsource them to another company or to automation. When scaling, look at how your salespeople are spending their time and enable them to focus on high-payoff activities like closing deals. Let others take care of the rest. In many ways this is good advice for any position, not just sales. As Jack puts it, "If you don't have an assistant, you are one."

Second, Jack says he likes to model the masters and copy what other top salespeople are doing rather than reinventing the wheel or sticking with a process that has stagnated. "I keep my antennae open," he says. "Where are the people that are knocking the ball out of the park? How do I do what they do?"

There are a few ways you can do this. One is to always be learning from your team what's working and what's not working and to tweak things based on this input.

There's also no shortage of online sales gurus to follow. Not all of them know what they're talking about, but try out some of their strategies to see what sticks. Another way is to poach high-performing salespeople from other companies and pay them top dollar, like we did at Hostopia when we were transforming to a sales-driven culture.

Jack's third best practice for increasing money with less work is all about his interaction with the prospects themselves. "My style is to be very up front with [them]. I view them as partners." In other words, one of the best ways to shorten the sales cycle and do less work to make more money has nothing to do with process; it's how your salesperson communicates to prospects. Are they selling a product? Or solving a problem? Making a transaction? Or building a partnership?

Instead of assuming that you know what the customer needs, this means listening to them first and figuring out what wins they're looking for. If you know what will make them win, then you will win too. If you're a tech or product company, build features for clients, not for you. Invest in new features that you know will get you an ROI. Do what you need to do to get the deal—so long as you're not violating your core values.

There are three truly golden ideas that need to be a part of your playbook because if you follow them, you'll be constantly tweaking and improving the playbook over time to make more money with less work. These ideas are: you need the best tech, the best scripts, and the best salespeople in the world. If you don't have them you will hit a wall in your growth.

Jim was smart to get help from Jack to create a sales program that works, including a great sales playbook. Unless you're a master at sales management, this is an area where getting extra support can have a phenomenal ROI.

Hold a daily sales huddle.

One of the best habits I learned from Verne Harnish was to institute a daily sales huddle. First, I should define what a daily sales huddle is *not*. It's *not* an opportunity for the manager to read off quotas and hound salespeople about their numbers. If you have an established playbook, your team

should already know this, and individual goals should be addressed individually.

During our IPO at Hostopia, I watched how the RBC investment bankers met twice per day, once at the beginning and then at the end. I don't think there is a more intensive sales group than investment bankers, given the high level at which they're expected to perform.

When we were at Hostopia, we held our daily sales huddle at 8:50 a.m. We would go around to each salesperson and ask, "What's your top priority today? What was your victory yesterday? Where are you stuck?"

Can you guess which of the three questions was the most powerful?

It was the second one: "What was your victory yesterday?"

I know this because I also had to show up with a victory the next morning, so it motivated me to find one. Everyone wants to tout a victory, so they feel left out if the rest of the team has one and they don't.

Meanwhile, as they answered these questions, all the executives—the CTO, the COO, all the key players—were listening in, but they were not allowed to talk while each salesperson presented. Generally, a sales huddle should take only about ten minutes because it's not about the details, just three quick items. Often, this last question of "Where are you stuck?" is the most helpful for the executives to hear, and usually the executive had the issue resolved within a day.

Because if there was an area where a salesperson was stuck, such as a tech issue not working, the CTO listening in would take note, fix it, and make the salesperson's job easier. Likewise, if it was an operations issue, the COO could address it. The sales huddle isn't just about staying on top of salespeople to make sure they're hitting numbers, as it's often used at companies. Instead, it's about making their job easier and more productive, which makes the entire company more productive. It's extremely useful to learn from the sales team what actions will make them more effective, since these points will drive sales and scale the business.

Too many startups fail to scale because they think the key to improving sales is hiring more salespeople or changing the comp plan. I've seen these methods used and abused far too often. In my experience, changing your comp plan has little impact on actual results. Instead, I recommend keeping your plan very simple and understandable for everyone. The more complex, the more it demotivates the team.

Until you have your ducks in a row, hold off on hiring a bunch of salespeople. First, hire an expert to help you build a solid playbook, figure out what kind of people you want to hire, set up your daily huddle, and figure out *who* your customers are.

That's really what it looks like to transform into a sales-driven culture, where it's everyone's job to think about how to make sales more effective, from the receptionist taking a message to the software programmer in charge of the Content Management System. As companies grow, it's easy for them to become more siloed and disconnected from other departments, but a sales-driven culture reaffirms the principle that the company exists to solve a problem, to connect customers to the solution for their problem, and to close that deal.

> ** A sales-driven culture reaffirms the principle that the company exists to solve a problem, to connect customers to the solution for their problem, and to close that deal. **

CHAPTER 36:

Growth through Acquisition

IN SCALE, YOU WANT TO ensure that all of your resources are being used to focus on internal growth drivers, like increasing distribution, sales, and product launches. Whatever it is that can drive your growth, you need to focus on first and foremost. That's essential in becoming a sales-driven organization. Then and only then should you also consider acquisitions as a way to accelerate growth.

Buy at the right price; leverage well.

I've previously mentioned my company Escape Club, where we buy properties and convert them to vacation rentals. The key to succeeding in real estate is a very simple one-two punch: you score your win by buying a property at a great price—and then leverage at a great rate. For the most part, all acquisitions follow this creed: buy at the right price, leverage well.

I have had the opportunity to acquire about thirty companies during my career, mostly small tuck-in acquisitions that supported a company's current growth strategy. Acquisitions have a notoriously high failure rate, so we want to be really careful in managing the process of acquiring companies to reduce the level of risk. Success with an acquisition can dramatically increase your growth rate and get you to your 10X goal faster. So I do believe it can help you, but we really need to find the right candidates.

> ❝ **Success with an acquisition can dramatically increase your growth rate and get you to your 10X goal faster.** ❞

While I was working at Deluxe following the Hostopia sale, we had the opportunity to acquire another large hosting company. The cost was high, but given the economies of scale, our ability to do the migration, and the low funding costs, it made sense. I believed it worked because we had an integration plan and system to migrate those customers over to our platform.

Running multiple platforms for similar services may make a lot of sense in the short term because you avoid a potential drop in customers from a migration. In the long run, though, it can be a deadly strategy by spiking your own IT costs dramatically. This case can be made for multiple brands and cultures. The sooner you can put the companies together, the better.

Buy companies that are a natural extension of what you currently do.

In most of the acquisitions at which we succeeded, we were usually able to fold the acquired company into our company relatively fast.

The ones that failed were the ones where we were buying a new technology or system that ultimately failed to integrate into our company.

For instance, we loved to buy subscribers we could then add to our platform because the cost of maintaining the platform remained the same. The key was to avoid *overpaying* for those subscribers and ensuring that we had the systems in place for a smooth migration.

I can't understate how important due diligence is here. Don't assume that a seller is telling you the truth. Before you sign the dotted line, verify *everything*.

Part of your due diligence here is also making sure that you're not making assumptions about what your own customer base is looking for.

Let's say that Paw.com had the opportunity to acquire another company in a related space (and I do mean *closely* related), then we could sell our products to their existing customer base and in turn sell the acquired inventory of products to our one million customers as well.

Where companies go wrong here is that they assume that "because my customer owns a dog, I can sell any other dog products." The key is that the products need to *connect* where one is a natural upgrade or extension of your existing products. For instance, just because we have a million customers who love our designer dog products, doesn't mean we can sell them all pet insurance too. Instead, we want to find those products that connect to what we are already known for in the market and then test them in advance to see how well they do with existing customers.

Buy your competitors with their own cash flow.

I also like to acquire competitors using their own revenue stream to buy them out. Sounds too good to be true? This is rare, but from time to time, competitors fizzle out for whatever reason. A highly motivated seller will cut deals, and sometimes these can be a bit messy, but I have been able to offer them a payout based on the company's future performance, reducing my risk on the transaction.

They like this option because they monetize their investment by eliminating all their costs and simply receive a check from us every month for the services. We like it because the acquisition becomes accretive to *our* bottom line by bulking up our customer base.

Acquisitions that are tuck-ins *can* scale your company, but the two key questions you have to ask are these: "Can it be integrated easily?" and "Is it truly strategic to the core of our business?" It's all too easy for an acquisition to be more about building up your ego than actually making a long-term impact. However, if you can answer those questions and prove that the acquisition is truly strategic and can be done at a reasonable price, then it may make sense for you to acquire that company.

> **❝ Acquisitions should always remain secondary to your core scaling strategy— the extra icing on the cake, not the main ingredient. ❞**

Even so, acquisitions should never be your primary means of growth, but our conversation on Scale would be incomplete if we didn't at least touch on the idea. At the end of the day, acquisitions should always remain secondary to your core scaling strategy—the extra icing on the cake, not the main ingredient. Instead, what you truly need to rely on for success in scaling are your systems.

CHAPTER 37:

Rely on Systems to Scale

WHEN FIRST STARTING OUT, if something goes wrong, you typically figure out how to solve the problem quickly. You don't think about creating official documentation or handbooks to guide company behaviors. But as your team grows, everything becomes more and more complex.

I remember when we launched and grew Internet Direct to about three hundred employees. Every year in Canada, there is a government holiday the Monday after the first weekend in August called Civic Holiday. Year after year, employees would ask whether it was a company holiday, and we had to explain to them—year after year—that they could use either one of their vacation days or one of their personal days but that it wasn't an official holiday.

As you might imagine, this led to a lot of confusion and frustration among the team every year: Which were the paid company holidays? What was the difference between a vacation day and a personal day?

Solve problems once and for all through policies.

Finally, I had an epiphany: Why not write out a policy on what the actual paid company holidays are, the vacation policy, and the definition of vacation days versus personal days? Groundbreaking, I know. 😤 We did this, and the next year when someone asked if Civic Holiday was a company holiday, we mentioned that they could refer to the posted holiday policies on our company intranet.

This is a very basic example; however, it can be applied to so many different areas within a growing company. When you notice problems repeating themselves, you can write a policy or procedure to address those issues once and for all. This reduces the noise, creates transparency, and allows companies to scale more successfully—no more two steps forward, one step back.

Companies that scale quickly rely on systems, not on people.

Rely on systems, not people. I know how cold this sounds, so let me explain. Let's take Ford Motors and McDonald's as examples. Both scaled through developing a system and then following it. I'm not saying that people aren't important—they are very important, which is why we had an entire discussion about People first!

> **No matter the issue, we as a company need to set up systems to allow for changes in personnel.**

However, one day that top salesperson might leave. Your CFO will decide to call it quits, or your CTO will move to Dubai. No matter the issue, we as a company need to set up systems to allow for changes in personnel. Of course, one of the most important changes is focusing on keeping our top players at the company. Setting up strong values and recognizing greatness is part of this, but we also want to set up systems in case they do leave.

We'll want to ensure that there is a proper handshake (separation plan) when people leave and that as many documents as reasonable are stored and organized well—preferably on a virtual drive. Many employee procedures can be documented so that if one day they leave, a new employee can hit the ground running. Training a new employee is very expensive; documenting the ins and outs of the role can dramatically reduce the time and money for that training.

As I mentioned, I like to set up a virtual drive to manage all the documents. I can't tell you how many times I have run into an issue with an old real estate purchase and find myself searching boxes to locate the original HUD/purchase documents. Virtual drives are so cheap, and when it comes time to sell, having these documents stored safely can make a huge difference.

We also need systems that don't rely on specific people so that we aren't held hostage. As an example, I really like online accounting software. The worst thing you can do is have accounting software reside on your accountant's computer. If you have to fire them one day, you won't be able to. They can hold you hostage, figuratively speaking.

On the other hand, if you have accounting online, then you can simply change the user login and password—been there, done that! Same goes for your domain and hosting accounts, CRM, pipeline software, bank accounts, network passwords, and so on. Let's make certain that you or someone you trust completely has the control of these key systems.

It is particularly important to develop systems to manage highly repeatable positions where there is a large turnover. Without it, you're done. And I'm not talking just about how to get the job done—I'm also talking about systemizing excellence in everything.

We hired a gentleman named George Walther to teach communication to our call center staff, first at Internet Direct and then again at Hostopia. He had developed a system to dramatically improve customer service simply through the use of language. This program was called Power Talk, and in it he explained how training your staff to change a few words can make a huge difference. For example, replacing "but" with "and," or replacing "I have to" with "I would be glad to." We used his system to train our call center staff at both companies, ensuring that our team members had the skills to communicate the best they could. They were not merely doing their job but doing it with excellence.

We were fortunate to get him to come onto our weekly show and podcast where he shared dozens of these very simple tricks. There are few speakers in my life who I can point to who have had a significant impact on me. Seeing George speak over twenty years ago literally changed me. Such a simple concept costs virtually nothing, yet it is so impactful.

I even used it in October 2022 when my twin brother called to let me know that he and his girlfriend of ten years would be getting married in thirty days. My first thought was "That selfish prick. He tells me this only thirty days in advance." See, our company had sponsored a car at NASCAR for the same day, and I was thrilled about the idea of going to race.

Given that I am his twin brother and there was no way I was getting out of it, I remembered what George had taught me about communication. So instead I answered him, "I would be thrilled to come to your event." And the wedding was fabulous, with everyone having a great time. Let's just hope he doesn't read the book ... 😫

Lastly, empower your people through systems. This may not sound intuitive, but basically you need to let your staff break the rules to make customers happy. You'll want to set up guidelines and limits, yes—that's what the system is for. But staff need to be trained on how to handle different situations so that they have the confidence to problem solve for customers without having to fetch a manager every time.

> **" Lastly, empower your people through systems. "**

I meet so many entrepreneurs who have great ideas, great vision, great passion—but they lack the systems to be able to scale the company to the next level. They're still operating in the ad hoc, frenetic energy of Start instead of becoming more organized so that things can benefit from growth that comes from both hard work and the occasional stroke of good luck.

CHAPTER 38:

Catching the Break: Maximize Luck

WE BEGAN THIS entire discussion asking whether success is just a matter of luck or whether there is a formula to follow. There may be a bit of both, but I would say that relying on systems when scaling helps you take the most advantage of luck when it comes along.

During a Startup Club session, Reebok founder Joe Foster shared the insight that "you need luck if you're going to start your business … but you've got to be willing to take on the problems." He went on to describe this mindset further: "You learn to look at a problem and say, 'Now how can I make this into an advantage?'"

> **Relying on systems when scaling helps you take the most advantage of luck when it comes along.**

The story of Reebok started with his grandfather, J. W. Foster, who invented the first spiked track shoe in 1895 when he was only fifteen years old. Eventually his shoes would be worn by the highest-class athletes, used to break world records and win gold medals, including Harold Abrahams and Eric Liddell, the two Olympic athletes profiled in the famous movie *Chariots of Fire*.

Fifty years later, though, the company was failing due to conflict between Joe's father and uncle, who had inherited the company. So in 1958, Joe and his brother, Jeff, decided to start their own shoe company. One of the first problems they faced was that they were based in the UK, where the biggest sport was football and that already had established brands. So they decided to try athletics, carving out a modest market.

But when looking to scale, they turned their eyes to America. In the late 1960s, a new wave of running fanaticism was washing over America, and they knew they needed to catch that wave. Joe took advantage of a government program to look for export opportunities in America and attended the NSGA trade show in Chicago. A lot of people showed interest in their shoes, but when Joe explained that they had to be exported from London, interest evaporated.

Problem number two: To scale in America, they had to find an American distributor. Joe recalled how he even went door-to-door at retail stores, trying to get independent stores to distribute, and owners would ask, "Why do I need Reebok? I've got Adidas." He realized, "I need to make them need Reebok." But how?

Over the next eleven years, they experienced six failed attempts to find a distributor in America. Finally, in 1979, they submitted some of their shoes for consideration by the popular magazine *Runner's World* for the annual shoe recommendations edition—and three of their shoes earned the coveted five star rating, which finally allowed them to secure a distributor.

Still, they had more problems to face as now they were encountering an athletic market dominated by the likes of established brands such as Adidas and Nike. While the running market had allowed them to scale to America, things had stagnated, and they needed to pivot. "Being an entrepreneur means taking risks," he observed, and one of the big risks they decided to take was when a key player on their team, Arnold, came across another new exercise wave: aerobics. They decided to create a couple hundred pairs of sneakers for women's aerobics and see what would happen.

Then one magical day, the actress and fitness instructor Jane Fonda wore a pair of Reeboks in her popular series of aerobics videos—and sales went crazy! First in the women's market but then the men wanted in on the action too. In five years, they went from $9 million in sales to almost $900 million. It's funny how even in the days before social media, influencers could still make a difference for your business. What's old is new again.

To the casual observer who doesn't know the background, it looks like luck that an influencer like Jane Fonda wore Reebok shoes. But in Joe's words, it was really about "looking around and trying to find that little bit of difference from someone else" to "make sure [luck] doesn't pass you by."

Create your own luck through systems.

I've cut out some of the amazing details that Joe shared in that session, but even so, reread the story and count just how many systems Joe implemented for them to scale—from pivoting, to catching the wave of aerobics, to using an established magazine to get noticed and secure their distribution agreement, to finding their X factor. Over and over again, each time they were facing a new problem, Joe and his brother were asking themselves, "What do we do next?" For each problem, they found an opportunity.

In terms of luck, the Reebok story goes to show that you can create your own luck through hard work and solving problems.

As a case in point, we thought our big break for .CLUB was going to happen a few years ago when singer Demi Lovato launched Lovato. club. Unfortunately, that ended up fizzling out, and as of the writing of this book, the site doesn't exist anymore. Thankfully, we weren't relying on Demi Lovato—or any other one personality—to scale.

One day, after eight years since founding .CLUB, Jeff and I were taking a walk around the block as a mental release. It just felt like nothing was easy with .CLUB. We had received an offer to buy the company, and while it was pretty close to what we were asking for, we just felt like .CLUB had never experienced a big break. It had been nothing but a tough slog all the way.

Within an hour after this walk, our big break finally came. It was truly unbelievable! Back at the office, we got a call from a good friend: "Have you seen what's happening on Clubhouse? People are buying .CLUB domains for Clubhouse like crazy!"

It turned out that digital marketing expert John Lee had bought a .CLUB extension for his new site and was promoting it on the

Clubhouse app as *the* domain to use. Sales exploded as it began a trend and turned into what Jeff has called a "twerking" moment. This term refers to the moment that Miley Cyrus twerked at an MTV Music Awards Ceremony. Few had heard of "twerking" before this.

And all we had done was follow the systems to grow the company and position ourselves for that big break moment, which included spending seven years to build out a global distribution network. I believe that if you do the hard work and you wait long enough, your big break will come, and it will accelerate the flywheel with better and better things happening. You may want to be a famous singer, and if you train and practice and keep releasing the songs you know are good and you find the right promoter, then eventually your time will come.

> **If you do the hard work and you wait long enough, your big break will come.**

Everyone's looking for their big break, but you can't control when it comes along. However, it's way more likely to happen if you use systems to nurture the opportunity for it to occur. That way, when the big break comes, it serves to accelerate the momentum your systems have already generated. One thing I've seen consistently with my own scaling experiences is that the "overnight success" usually takes ten years of really hard work and discipline. Even this book was ten years in the making.

The truth is, we have no idea when our big break will come. However, maximizing your systems—distribution, PR, sales, a killer X factor, and positioning for Geoffrey Moore's tornado—will allow you to maximize the impact when that big break does eventually hit. Not to mention that you can further maximize your luck through knowing how to hack your growth.

CHAPTER 39:

Minor Majors (a.k.a. Growth Hacks)

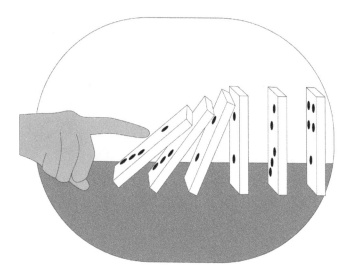

ONE OF MY FAVORITE concepts that I've picked up from my coach, Patrick, is called a "minor major," because it requires minimal effort and funding but can yield major impact for growth. Some call it growth hacks, but I think "minor major" is a better description of minor effort, major impact. Before we move on from Scale, I want to make sure you have some very practical ideas and systems on ways you can set yourself up for success.

All of these are actual growth strategies that either I have used or that other successful serial entrepreneurs I know have used. Better than that, all of them are action-based so that you can move beyond strategic ideas to actual execution without delay. I picked only a few of my favorites here or else we would have to double the size of the book. If you want to get more ideas, listen to our podcast *Serial Entrepreneur: Secrets Revealed!* on your favorite podcast app.

Surround yourself with great people.

While working on this book, my son was starting his third year in college as a junior, and yet he was stepping into a physical classroom for the first time ever. Because of the COVID-19 pandemic, colleges in Canada had been shut down to in-person meetings for two years, and his entire college career had been virtual up to this point.

I asked him about his experience after the first day of in-person learning and where he was sitting in the classroom. He answered, "Dad, not only am I sitting in the front row, but I'm sitting closest to the professor."

Years earlier, I had told him how doing this had impacted my own college career. I was so proud that he had listened to me, as this one small decision can have a major impact on his life. And it literally costs him nothing to choose to sit in the front row.

By choosing to do so, though, he has helped set himself up for success in life because it will force him to pay closer attention and engage more with the professor compared to hiding in a seat at the back. In addition, he surrounds himself with all the other keeners who eventually become his study partners and friends.

Likewise, who are you surrounding yourself with in the "classroom" of serial entrepreneurship? Are you in an incubator program? Are you connecting with other entrepreneurs who are at different stages of their journey than you? Have you joined the other million members on Startup Club? If you surround yourself with successful people, then success can become contagious.

> **❝ If you surround yourself with successful people, then success can become contagious. ❞**

Hack the trade show.

Like in the Reebok story, there's a good chance that attending a trade show is part of your scaling strategy. And it should be for most companies. There are several easy ways that you can hack the trade show to get the most out of your time there.

For starters, wear your swag as often as you can, whether it's a company T-shirt, hat, canvas bag, or whatever. This is so easy and is a great, inexpensive conversation starter. For years I have worn a .CLUB T-shirt at trade shows. In fact, I'm on a plane right now editing this section and just realized that I'm still wearing my .CLUB shirt even though we sold the company two years ago. I guess old habits are hard to break!

It's also a good idea to have not only your logo and web address on your swag but also a way for people to contact you. You might be surprised by how many people will take a photo of your swag and use it as a digital business card to reach out to you later on.

Whether I'm meeting people in the elevators or at the hotel bar, or if I'm being interviewed about something else, when I wear the T-shirt, people always ask, "What is .CLUB?" And frankly, it reduces my wardrobe costs and makes my decision of what to wear in the morning very easy.

And speaking of sitting in the front row, I can't say how many times we have attended shows and speeches and sat in the very front row and then the speaker referred to .CLUB in their speech. If two or three of us are sitting in the front row wearing our T-shirts, you can bet we're hard to miss!

On the flip side, I'm aghast at how many vain leaders don't wear their company shirts at conferences. A trade show is a show, and everyone, including the leader, needs to be dressed in their company wear. It's just common sense.

My colleague Jeff always carries around a pocketful of stickers because they're cheap and people like them. It's like carrying a billboard in your pocket because it can fit easily inside a wallet, you can leave extras in the glove compartment to have on hand, and you can conveniently leave some behind at the local cafe's billboard, tables at the trade show eating area, or wherever you are.

If you're at a session with a Q&A, come up with a question to ask. Then, when it's your turn to stand, always start off your question by first introducing yourself. "Hi, I'm Colin C. Campbell from Startup. club, and my question is …" I have been in sessions with a few dozen or even a few thousand and when given the opportunity to engage with the speaker by asking a question, you're bound to catch someone's attention who might be your next investor, distribution partner, or big customer.

Another easy way to save at a trade show is to join your supplier's or distributor's booth instead of having your own booth. We were spending on average about $20,000 per trade show at .CLUB. As part of our strategy to cut costs and focus on high-payoff activities, we pivoted to sponsoring SEDO, one of our distributors for .CLUB at over twenty trade shows globally. The sponsorship cost was about one-twentieth of what we would spend on getting the booth. In doing that, though, we had an agreement with them that we could attend the trade shows of our choosing with our company shirts, promoting .CLUB and getting access to thousands of prospects.

Finally, use the trade show as an opportunity to throw a party. Have some fun! People want to unwind, especially if they're a vendor who was required to attend every single day. This can often be cheaper than paying for an exhibit at the conference. We once hosted a VIP party on the last night of a conference for only $500, including using Uber Eats to order the wine and food.

Also, when people walk by a booth, it's a good icebreaker to invite them to your VIP party. Ask a few people to join you, and you'll be surprised how word of mouth will do the rest of the work for you. It's always a great opportunity to network and attract new customers or new partners. If you want more tips, check out "50 Ways to Shine at Trade Shows" on Startup.club.

Hack technology and social media.

Video has become the best way to get social media engagement on platforms like YouTube or TikTok, so why not create a viral video? I know this is easy to say, but you can't go viral if you don't make the videos to begin with! Film everything you do and start uploading. These don't need to be Oscar-worthy documentaries—just short clips that grab attention and can quickly get thousands of views.

I had the opportunity to interview enterprising nineteen-year-old Adam Khatib on *Serial Entrepreneur: Secrets Revealed!* Adam creates viral videos professionally and recently had a video with over 124 million views on TikTok for a client whose back cracker product is used to relieve back pain.

Since I would by no means consider myself a social media expert, here is Adam's "Wireframe for Social Media Success" that he shared with us:

- ➤ **Catch:** This is the hook or whatever draws viewers' attention—the first one-fourth to one-third of a second is the most important. "Catch has to be something that's a little bit out of place, sometimes that's intriguing," he said. "You can't *not* watch all the way through, because another thing about the algorithm is the most important thing is *watch time*." In the case of the back cracker viral video, he explained that the draw for viewers was simply placing the contraption on the ground. It looked so strange that it made viewers ask, "What is that?," which translated into them clicking to watch the entire video.

- ➤ **Keep:** Don't lose their attention! Give viewers a reason that they just *have* to watch to see what happens. Concerning the back cracker video, Adam said they placed the device on the ground and then had somebody lie on it. "We added a sound effect of … somebody's back cracking … and it was so satisfying and relieving from the stress that [the subject of the video] had to scream." In other words, viewers stuck around because they wanted to see how people would react to using the back cracker.

- ➤ **Wow factor:** This is all about converting viewers into customers. Adam explained that they showed off how people in the video really enjoyed the back cracker. If you've managed to hold a viewer's attention for this long, you want to make sure you leave them with a way to easily become a customer so that they can have the same experience as what they just witnessed.

Adam has applied this specific formula to all of his projects, and he has had remarkable success. If a video doesn't check all three boxes, then it's time to go back to the drawing board until it has all three elements—catch, keep, and wow factor—in place. Whether you use TikTok or some other means for advertising, I found this to be great general marketing advice no matter what.

I also like that videos give you the opportunity to explain concepts in your industry and to position you as an expert. Every video doesn't have to have a million followers like of Adam's. We just need it to get to *one* prospect or distributor to make a difference.

Did you know that you can hack images on Google? If you search for "new gTLDs" and click on "images" on Google, you're likely to see a picture we produced promoting .CLUB among a group of other domain extensions. More often than not, journalists or bloggers grab these types of images and place them in their articles, which gives us exposure to their audiences. At a minimum, this little trick has made .CLUB look bigger.

Another very simple thing you can do is review your SEO strategy. Because it sounds techy, many entrepreneurs leave this to the IT folks, which is really not a good idea. Instead, entrepreneurs should work *with* their tech folks to develop their SEO strategy. SEO is really more about knowing how your ideal customer thinks than it is about being tech-savvy.

Just like in Start, when we set up five or six key words that you want to own, we need to make certain that these words are in place on your website title tags and then review and update them from time to time. Again, this costs absolutely nothing and usually takes only a couple of minutes to do, but so few entrepreneurs do it correctly.

Think about what phrases your ideal customer is searching for and make that your tag for your site. For example, for the school we have in Fort Lauderdale, one of our title tags is "best Ft. Lauderdale Montessori school" because we know that's what people will search. Don't be afraid to put "best" in your tag to help Google find you. Just make sure you're able to back it up!

We have just scratched the surface of SEO here. It's a *huge* area, and most entrepreneurs don't spend enough time to really figure it out, yet it's one of the best ways to promote your business for almost no cost. We can't be experts in everything, but we can learn SEO enough to ask the right questions of the experts and ensure that we get the maximum benefit.

Hack the audience of other people.

On that note, you can promote your business through getting featured by others. Think about your favorite podcast, large or small, and how often they have a guest speaker. Did you know that you can position yourself as an expert in your industry and then connect with podcast hosts? We do this through a low-cost service called PodcastGuests.com founded by Andrew Alleman. This gets you exposure to potentially thousands of prospects, not just at the time of the show's release but for as long as that episode exists. We've done this dozens of times with .CLUB.

Really, you can get exposure through anyone with traffic—podcasts, bloggers, news sites—they're all candidates.

Some of these sites want to help sell your products and will put up an affiliate link. We're ramping up affiliate links for Paw.com and getting access to potentially thousands of users for zero upfront costs or commitments. If you work with creators and share a portion of the sale, you'll be surprised by the traction you can get from them.

You can even hack the news by issuing press releases on topics relevant to your industry, especially if it's about news in your industry. It could be as simple as making a statement about the most recent acquisition or regulatory change in your industry. Since journalists have to get work out as fast as possible, they tend to grab material for their article from the easiest sources. Not to mention this kind of content also boosts your SEO with Google.

Hack your customers.

We even like to find ways to have customers or potential customers "advertise" for us. This could be as simple as giving out free stickers like Jeff does. At Little Flower Montessori, we have given away car magnets for people to stick on their vehicles. If you have loyal customers, as is the case with the school, then people will be happy to display the magnet.

On that note, you can also go old school with traditional signs. These are inexpensive and incredibly undervalued, especially yard signs. We did this for our school as well, giving out signs to the parents because people like putting them up in their yards—and thousands of cars pass by these signs every day. We did this one time, and it helped us fill every available spot in the school.

Car wraps are another great form of signage. They're cheap and they maximize the benefit of the ad because you turn your car into a moving billboard without the monthly expense.

Want to make your company stand out? Then find ways to give them UMODs—unexpected moments of delight. I experienced this recently after my thirteen-and-a-half-year-old King Charles spaniel died. A few days later, I opened the door to a surprise—some flowers and a note on our doorstep. The note read, "Sorry for your loss." Who was it from? The pet care brand Chewy. And it didn't stop there—a few days later, they even sent us a drawn picture of him for us to remember him by, probably generated by an AI program, but still, it was the thought that counted.

I wondered to myself, "How did they know?" I asked my assistant how they would have known, and she mentioned that she had called to cancel his medications. During the call with their customer service rep, she told them of our dog's passing as the reason for the cancellation. Clearly, the rep had passed the word on. I was shocked by this—but in a good way. It was truly an unexpected moment of delight.

It doesn't have to be anything big, but look for how you can give customers something a little extra and a little bit different to make yourself memorable. For example, take Magic Castle Hotel, one of the top-rated hotels in Los Angeles. How have they achieved their ranking despite all the competition in LA? Through something called the Popsicle Hotline.

If guests of the hotel pick up the red phone on a poolside wall, they're greeted with, "Hello, Popsicle Hotline." They can then request their favorite flavored Popsicle, which will show up a few minutes later, delivered on a silver platter held by an employee in white gloves. It costs the guest nothing extra to do this—it's just a nice touch that has led to positive feelings and great word of mouth.

The guests there may not remember the brand or thread count of the sheets, but they'll always remember getting the Popsicle delivered to them. These UMODs are nice little touches that build good rapport between you and the customer so that they'll become your biggest fans and tell everyone how great you are. They're also one of the procedures you'll want to document for your staff so that they can be repeated. Although it may appear to be impromptu, it's far from it. It's all a part of the growth strategy.

One more thing about UMODs—the most important word is *unexpected*. And sometimes that can be a moving target. At one time, a chocolate on your pillow was a delightful surprise. Today, it doesn't cut it any more.

Focus on selling more to your existing customers.

As we've discussed previously, one of the best growth strategies is to get your current customers to buy something else from you. More often than not, we focus too much on customer acquisition and not enough on *selling more* to existing customers or working harder to retain existing customers. Why not figure out what other problems they have and develop more products, services, or features they want?

> **One of the best growth strategies is to get your current customers to buy something else from you.**

Even though we offered hosting and email services to telecoms at Hostopia, we eventually launched fax-to-email, a service our telecom customers desperately wanted to provide but had experienced difficulty in launching on their own given the complexity and patent issues involved. We launched it at Hostopia after licensing patents and developing the technology, then offered it to our existing clients and generated millions in profit for the company. Our cost of acquisition to sell to our existing customer base was almost nil, and we were able to make the sales of this new product at a much faster rate.

Become the expert in your industry.

One particular way to grow your business is to establish yourself as the expert in your industry so that industry journalists and bloggers will call you when they're running a story. Launching a study and then publishing it can get you *huge* media attention. Webinars are good as well but only if you can attract the audience.

One of the best ways to do this is to connect with trade shows months in advance. More often than not, they're looking for experts to speak at the show. Why not offer yourself up? To do this, don't pitch

yourself but instead pitch the topic and the insight you've gained from experience, customer data, or market research.

As we talked about earlier, consider going on podcasts as a guest or even coming onstage during shows on Clubhouse or Twitter Spaces.

Press releases are not that expensive to generate and can have an impact. One such example was when Jeff ran a press release for Paw.com's new products during the month of September, targeting "gift guides for your pet." Not only did our products get mentioned in a lot of different gift guides that holiday season but also we were contacted by *Good Morning America* to be part of their featured products prior to the holidays.

Hack anyone and everyone you can—including yourself.

I can be pretty shameless when it comes to self-promotion. I know that's not everyone's cup of tea, but if you don't promote yourself, who will? As long as you're providing real value and real solutions—and not breaking the law—then it's okay to think outside the box.

You've heard about my logoed polo shirts, but you probably don't know that I also wrapped my car with our company name. I can't tell you how many times someone asks about my business or one day says, "I see that car all over town." I know it can irritate my family a bit, but I think they've gotten used to it by now.

At .CLUB, we had the opportunity to meet the person who runs the South Florida Tech Corridor and publishes a poster featuring logos from tech companies in South Florida. These posters then end up on every wall in every school and throughout government buildings. We explained who we

were and simply asked them to put us on the poster. Although we were small compared to others featured on the poster (like Microsoft and Magic Leap), they agreed to add us. I knew this minor major worked one day when my son came home from high school saying he saw a poster with .CLUB on it. Again, this cost us nothing.

Look at your suppliers too. Is there a way they can help you? At Hostopia, not only did our VC Telus Ventures fund us and contract out our services but also they had a global tech division that helped us get leads on new customers. And they didn't charge us a penny for that.

Hack your systems.

There are many little systems you can implement that can help you scale profitability outside of your sales if you just take the time to examine them. For example, at Paw.com we experienced explosive growth hitting *Inc.* magazine's fastest-growing companies list three years in a row. Yeah, we had done a great job growing through sales, but that explosive growth resulted in a lot of inefficiencies. It wasn't until after the pandemic had cleared and our sales began to stall that we started thinking about ways to generate additional profits by optimizing our systems.

One example was taking some extra time deciding which credit card we would use for the company—one that paid a 2 percent cash dividend. By doing this, we selected a card that generates an *extra $240,000 of profit* for us totally unrelated to selling our products but just from the regular payments we need to make to run the business.

Where things tend to slow down is when you have to look for those systems or build them if they don't exist yet. Or in the case of the credit card example, you don't take the time to look at the hundred tiny actions you can take to scale profitability or cut costs. The earlier you establish those systems, the quicker you can scale.

Maybe the ultimate minor major is simply to always be learning. Learn from the mistakes of others and also from how others have succeeded. Startup Club on Clubhouse and *Serial Entrepreneur: Secrets Revealed!* are both free to join or listen to if you want to keep learning more hacks like these.

While some of these systems cost money, a lot of them don't. The point is that you don't have to do huge things to grow. You can use these minor majors to take small actions that can then convert into major opportunities. Like we said in the pitching chapter, you never know who's going to be in the room, walking down the street, or clicking on the website. A few small changes can make a massive difference. If you make enough of them, it can be transformative.

CHAPTER 40:

Why Startups Fail to Scale

NO BEATING AROUND THE BUSH HERE—the vast majority of companies fail to scale. Why is that?

The entrepreneur is in the way.

I believe the main reason that startups fail to scale is the entrepreneur. They become their own worst enemy and simply cannot get themselves out of the way. As we mentioned previously, when you're scaling, you're no longer delegating tasks but responsibilities. The personality traits that helped them launch and be successful in Start won't get them to Scale.

Why?

Because scaling is a different formula from starting. In Start, it required the talents, effort, personality, and leadership directly from the entrepreneur. In Scale, the entrepreneur needs to transform themselves, check their ego at the door, and learn to lead leaders, become a coach, focus on strategy, and allow others to execute and—dare I say—fail.

They fail to find the people to grow.

During a Startup Club session, Jeff Sass shared a situation in which he had difficulty with scaling. The company consisted of himself and his business partner with a proof of concept. Even so, they were able to raise $7 million and were already publicly traded. With that much money in the bank, they assumed that scaling would be a piece of cake.

Since they were a tech company, they decided that their first move would be to hire a CTO. Before putting out any job description, though, his business partner made an acquaintance at a shoe store, and long story short, they decided to hire the sales clerk's boyfriend for the role. Again, they thought, "This is so easy. We didn't even have to go through a time-consuming or expensive recruitment and hiring process."

But then, at ten o'clock the night before their new hire that was supposed to start, he called Jeff and said, "Sorry, but my current employer made me a better offer."

"We had no backup plan," Jeff admitted. "Not even a résumé on a desk."

How were they going to scale the company without a CTO?

Realizing that hiring was going to be much more difficult than they originally anticipated, they decided to hire an HR person instead. They found someone who had been with a successful recruiting agency and had the insight and experience to lead the hiring process. With her help, they were able to grow from two to nine and start making headway.

Too much funding.

If you were to ask entrepreneurs why they have failed to scale, the vast majority would say that they just couldn't raise the money. Certainly, money can be a reason a company fails to scale, but in my experience the lack of funding is not the primary cause. In Jeff's story, their scaling troubles had nothing to do with money at all but with finding the right people.

I believe that too much funding can also be dangerous. I know this sounds odd, but again, I've seen too much Silicon Valley carnage on the startup highway. Companies that raise money feel flush with cash and begin to make decisions that can lead to their peril. In 2021, the trend was growth at all costs, not too dissimilar to how things were in 1999 with the focus on eyeballs at any cost. In both 2000 and 2022, the paradigm changed, and the companies that focused on a clear path to profitability fared well while the rest got slaughtered.

This is not to say that there isn't a plan around growth. When I was an advisor to PasswordBox, which ultimately sold to Intel for a very successful exit, I was critical of their plan to simply grow through their user base. But I learned that if you can build a user base quickly and sell before the music stops, it can be an effective plan—just not something to bank on.

The smarter companies find ways to monetize sooner rather than later and are ready for winter when it inevitably comes. Having too much money will most certainly lead to bigger and bigger losses. Meanwhile, surviving on less and being a lean startup forces innovation and problem-solving compared to an environment where there is too much money.

Misalignment around the vision.

In the startup phase, it's easy to align people around a common vision. It's probably the vision for the company that attracted people to you in the first place. It's fairly safe to assume that everyone knows the vision already, but in the transition from Start to Scale, those assumptions can become problematic. As new challenges come along, each person might start forming their own vision until there are more visions of what the company should be than there are people in the company.

This can be especially problematic if you have multiple founders. Ultimately, the vision for the company needs to become *one*, with one leader at the top making the final decision. It wasn't easy for my brother and I to always work together when our competing visions came into play. But when the wheels began to fall off the bus, we brought in a coach, and it all came together, resulting in effectively scaling the company.

Failure to expand the story.

Remember, your Story in Scale may not be the same as in Start. You have to reassess how the story has changed and how the vision needs to change and truly find your X factor. Many times the vision of the company in Start is too narrow and too small for Scale.

> **Many times the vision of the company in Start is too narrow and too small for Scale.**

For example, Microsoft's vision statement used to be "A microcomputer on every desk and in every home." But as that vision became a reality, they had to expand the story. Now it's "To empower every person and every organization on the planet to achieve more." Amazon was simply a book reseller, and now they're an e-commerce behemoth because they continually tweak their Story to scale.

If you're doing things right, then your vision should be adjusted—but with that adjustment, you have to make sure that it's communicated well and that everyone understands it. If you're not on the same track, then how can you possibly arrive at the same destination?

This ties into the values you set, your pillars, the kind of culture you want to develop, and what is going to motivate people. Not everyone may be able to sync with the new vision. In the busyness and complexity that comes with scaling, it's easy to miss the Story expansion that needs to take place—which is why you must be hyper-vigilant to be on the lookout for it.

They hold on to their original staff too long.

Sometimes the people you had early on—maybe even the people who have been with you since the beginning—simply don't have the runway to help you scale in zeros. It's because they're not just employees at this point; these are your friends. You've been through the trenches together.

You have to be brutally honest with yourself and ask these two questions: "Is everyone up for the challenge to scale?" and "Are they capable of scaling in zeros?" If not, there has to be a willingness to make painful changes and say, "We have to bring someone else in." They may change their role in the company or exit early, so in these cases, I do my best to ensure that these employees continue to be advisors and maintain some stock ownership in the company.

When your company is scaling, you can count on growing pains; you might need to change the entire management structure. In fact, investors may mandate that you bring in new people. And a lot of companies fail to scale because they're not willing to face those growing pains and make the tough changes.

On the flipside, sometimes it's not about replacing people; it's a matter of bringing in the people who can add more strength to your team. As Jeff's story pointed out, hiring is tough and time consuming.

When you're strategically scaling, you're going to need extra help in finding the right people, so hire an HR person who can lead the process. Assuming that you can find the right people on your own could be disastrous, not to mention that your time is probably better spent on strategy and closing new deals.

They don't kill failures fast enough.

This is really the same concept that we discussed back in Start—companies spend too much time developing bad ideas and pouring resources into failed products instead of killing them quickly. In Scale, this is especially true when you're trying out a new idea for a product. If a new product isn't working, then cut and run. Kill failures quickly so that they won't slow you down from further scaling.

Sometimes at Paw.com, we get a product that's a dud despite our best efforts. We could use email marketing to get rid of these at a discounted rate, but often it makes more sense to liquidate the duds and focus our resources on more popular items that get a better return. Or better yet, we can make certain that we're testing out new products or ideas so that we don't sink a ton of money into them without knowing whether they'll sell or not. If Paw.com develops five new products and four fail while one takes off, we can still make a killing as long as we test well, kill failures fast, and focus on scaling the one that succeeds.

You'll have failure, but even in those moments, get as much value as you can from that failure. Especially when you consider that your reputation as a company is on the line and that throwing your weight behind a bad product could lead to turning away customers. As entrepreneurs, we don't like to give up, and sometimes we stick with things longer than we should. Add that to the list of problems associated with our egos. Instead, it's better to acknowledge the failed product or idea as quickly as possible and move on. Holding on for too long is a death trap.

They don't use systems to scale.

All of these reasons usually land back here—not having the right systems in place to keep things on track. At the beginning of this Scale section, I talked about how the wheels were coming off the bus in 2005 at Hostopia. Without Patrick, the strategy sessions, getting the right people into the right positions, goal setting, daily sales huddles, and all the other systems we implemented, I really believe the company would have either stalled or imploded. Instead, we adopted those systems, which led us to a public offering and eventually a successful sale to a Fortune 500 company.

> **The entrepreneurs who successfully scale are the ones who take ownership of the outcome, even as they simultaneously let go of individual responsibilities.**

There will always be things that happen outside your control, and time and time again, we see startups crash and entrepreneurs blame others—the markets, competitors, lack of funding. But pointing the finger falls apart when there are others who grow in spite of facing these same setbacks and challenges. Why? Because the entrepreneurs who successfully scale are the ones who take ownership of the outcome, even as they simultaneously let go of individual responsibilities. It's a delicate balance, yes. But the good news is that it *can* be achieved with the right Story, People, Money, and Systems in place.

START.
SCALE.
EXIT.
REPEAT.

In 1998, at twenty-eight years old, my partners and I found ourselves in our lawyer's office, signing the closing documents to sell Tucows Interactive for $30 million plus a 10 percent share of the company. It had been a phenomenal ride—from purchasing the site with literally no revenue a few years earlier to building it up to become a global brand for software downloads and one of *PC Magazine*'s Top 100 websites at the time.

After six hours of signing documents, we were driving home at one in the morning, laughing all the way to the bank. My brother then slammed on the brakes and nearly got us killed, and my other partner said, "Man, that would suck if we got killed now after finally getting our big break."

The night got even more surreal when I climbed the stairs of my tiny house to enter our bedroom where my wife was fast asleep. I brushed her on the shoulder and handed her a check for $22 million. Bleary-eyed, she couldn't comprehend what she was looking at—there were just too many zeroes on the check.

She looked at it, and over and over again, said, "I don't understand. I don't understand. I don't understand." There were so many zeros, she could not comprehend what was happening. I know she believed in me, yet she had no idea that I really was going to pull this off. That very moment was a defining one for me in my life. All my crazy ideas and hard work had finally paid off.

My wife knew that I was running internet companies and that I'd been trying to sell one, but she just didn't think it was that big of a deal. We had little to no wealth in our names prior to receiving that check. It was our first deal, and even though I received only a portion of it, this was the deal that moved us from entrepreneurial poverty to extreme wealth at the age of twenty-eight. I hope everyone reading this can experience the same surreal moment.

Just stop for a minute here and imagine the moment for yourself ...

You've worked hard to start and scale your company. But is it time to sell? Is it time to exit and find the next venture? Or find a way to sell off a portion of your company to secure your family and improve your lifestyle? Or maybe you're going to have to sell your company due to unforeseen circumstances?

In this third part, we're going to explore the answers to these questions and the actions you need to take for a successful Exit. It's possible to start well and scale well and then suddenly trip at the finish line. I know because it's happened to me. It doesn't have to happen to you.

Maybe you haven't even begun your first venture yet. This section is still important, as you want to have an Exit mindset from the day you start the company. It's a lot easier to think that way from day one.

STORY

CHAPTER 41:

The Case for Selling

BEFORE WE CAN ANSWER the question, "Is it time to sell?" it's worth first asking, "Why sell at all?" Why not just keep on growing and driving profits? There are different philosophies to how you answer those questions for yourself, and the decision to sell or not to sell is one you will have to come to terms with. I have made a career from following the pattern of Start, Scale, Exit, and Repeat over and over. This formula has worked for me, and I believe it is a much less risky approach than Start, Scale, Keep.

I want to tell you about a dinner I had in late 2022 with Joe Foster, the founder of Reebok, who we talked about in chapter 38. He was joined by his lovely wife, Julie, and together they had recently launched his book, *Shoemaker*, which chronicles his incredible story as to how he and his brother built Reebok. I told him about my book and had a fun discussion with him in regard to my philosophies.

He pushed back a bit and explained how he went from zero, spent almost twenty years building the company to get it up to $9 million, and then within five years of that mark, how they hit $900 million after they focused on aerobics and hit their big break when Jane Fonda wore a pair of Reeboks on national television. Talk about scaling in zeros!

Joe made the conscious choice to Start, Scale, Keep. Had he sold in 1979, he would have lost out on what would become a unicorn— although that term didn't exist at the time, of course. The point is this: There are always counterarguments, so I don't want you to think that my way is the only way. Start, Scale, Keep has worked for some, but I'm making the case that it's the exception. For most, it is a very risky way to build wealth, and a more certain path for economic freedom lies in Start, Scale, Exit, Repeat.

My philosophy has always been what I call "laddering up" wealth: once you get some entrepreneurial success, take some chips off the table, then rinse and repeat.

The world can change. Your life can change.

There are a couple of reasons why I find this method superior to keeping a company. Probably the most pronounced is that the world

changes. What is thriving today may not be applicable ten years from now. After all, there's a reason that most of us don't buy CDs anymore. Sometimes keeping a company can set you up to get stuck, like a wooly mammoth trapped in a tar pit. Instead of moving forward, you could go extinct.

There's not much you can do when the world moves on and decides it doesn't need you and your company anymore. Instead, it makes more sense to be aware that the world is always in a state of change and to be on the lookout for the next wave that you can catch. It's hard to be watching for those waves when you're on the beach trying to patch together the sand castle being washed away.

> **What is thriving today may not be applicable ten years from now.**

Then there are external events and changes that must be considered. For example, 2022 was a brutal year for startups and company owners. The war in Ukraine, high inflation, doubling in borrowing costs, tech wreck, crypto crash, stock market drop, and then, to top it off, Hurricane Ian in the US. And believe it or not, somehow my companies got hit hard by all these events.

Our IT services company is primarily located in Ukraine, Paw.com had to pay 5X in costs for containers from China, our loan costs doubled, my tech shares, along with my bitcoin and my stock portfolio, crashed and then my vacation rental business took a direct hit when Ian, an almost CAT-5 hurricane, made landfall on the islands where my properties were located. Yeah, not a fun year.

Lastly, life can throw us a few curve balls we don't expect. In 2022, my dear mother-in-law went instantly blind due to an eye stroke. Already somewhat immobile, she is facing a challenging life moving forward. Fortunately we have the resources to help her, but even so, the time commitment for us is significant, taking time from my wife to run the school and myself to run the businesses. Whether it's childcare, eldercare, or health issues, life has a way of hitting hard sometimes.

Despite the external hits and the life changes, we survived the tumultuous year, and I'm now looking for buying opportunities given the current market conditions. But had any of these events destroyed one of my companies, my life still would not have substantially changed. I call it laddering up wealth for a reason—Start. Scale. Exit. Take some money off the table. Repeat.

> ❝ **Start. Scale. Exit. Take some money off the table. Repeat.** ❞

Laddering up is not giving up. It's simply choosing to sell your business to provide security and wealth over a career. I believe your identity should never be based on one company. For many successful entrepreneurs, it's hard to imagine that they won't be the CEO of their company. I admit that there's something special about running a six-hundred-person company or being recognized as a leader in your industry. But selling is not the end. It's simply the beginning of your next venture and that venture might come more easily than you think. We'll talk more about that in Repeat, but you have to keep this one thing in focus:

❝ Your trade is entrepreneurship. ❞

This is the ultimate reason for exiting instead of keeping. We just need to make certain that when we sell, we do so at the right time and to the right buyers for the highest possible dollar.

The best business plan in the world can only do so much to protect you from such market change or external forces. In the next chapter, we'll discuss how you can at least mitigate these unexpected changes when they happen. Not *if* they happen but *when*.

Consider the financial benefits of exiting versus keeping. To get practical, there are tax benefits to earning income as capital gains rather than as income. In the US—and in most Western world countries— income is taxed at almost double the rate of capital gains. Why pay the government more than you have to? This alone can help you augment your wealth long term compared to keeping a business and shelling out the income taxes.

In some countries like Canada, you can get an exemption from tax on the first million in capital gains. In the US, there is a structure that allows you to pay zero tax for up to $10 million in capital gains for Section 1202 eligible stocks. But *please* check with your accountants and lawyers to dig deeper here. I am not recommending that you choose one structure over another. I am just letting you know that options exist. Work with your lawyer and accountants to figure this out. This is one of those Exit lessons you should be working on in Start, which is why it's important to have an Exit mentality from day one.

Finally, I would add that your company is likely worth a lot more to a strategic buyer than it is as a stand-alone. Strategic buyers will pay a higher price based on the net benefit that the acquisition brings to their organization. When we sold both .CLUB and Hostopia, it was at a substantial multiple of earnings because the buyers determined that it made sense for them to acquire these companies based on their capabilities and how they could leverage their company to produce much higher revenue and earnings after the acquisition.

CHAPTER 42:

When the Rules Change, Change with the Rules

AROUND 1993, I WAS running my first startup with my brother, Bill. Since we were running a software rental company, business was booming. But then Bill Gates convinced the US government to put in a provision to the pending NAFTA agreement that would make renting software illegal in Canada.

Obviously, this was a death knell for us. It was like we were a bar at the time of Prohibition. We could've just closed our doors and said, "Well, it was fun while it lasted," but instead we decided to embrace the change.

Since NAFTA was going into effect on January 1, 1994, we decided to do whatever we could to maximize our profits on exit. We ran full-page ads in local computer papers announcing the new legislation, telling everyone that our business was about to become illegal, and sure enough it created huge demand, and we had lines of people coming to our stores.

When January 1 hit, we ran other ads saying, "We're going bankrupt—our business has been outlawed." In other words, we shared the horrible story with our customers. The result? We saw lines out the door for days as people clamored to buy our software. Even after a month of this, we still had some items left, so we ran one last full-page ad saying that we were going to do a final auction of our remaining inventory. In the end, we had about a hundred people show up, and we sold off our entire inventory. All in all, it was a profitable exit for us, and we used those funds to support our next business.

Emotionally, when your business isn't working out, it may feel easier to shut the doors and walk away. I have seen this happen too many times with entrepreneurs. Instead, when you're getting to the point when you're saying, "I'm done," it's time to mitigate by taking actions to quickly monetize as much as possible.

Embrace change.

I don't always like to think of change as good or bad; it's just change.

> **Change is the enemy to big corporations, but it can be a friend to the entrepreneur if you know what to do with it, even if it's unexpected.**

It's going to happen, and at some point, a change is going to come for your business, so you'll need to know how to handle it. As we talked about before, change is the enemy to big corporations, but it can be a friend to the entrepreneur if you know what to do with it, even if it's unexpected.

Like we did with our software rental business, you can make change a part of your story too. A colleague once shared with me a story about a Chick-fil-A franchise located inside a mall and how they survived the early days of the COVID-19 pandemic.

They had always been dependent on foot traffic in the mall, but with all the other stores in the mall closed, they appeared to be in trouble. Unlike the other Chick-fil-A franchises across town, they didn't have a drive-through to still serve people. But instead of fearing this change, the franchisee embraced it.

He put up cones and a couple of tents at the nearest mall entrance and stationed a couple of team members at the closest intersections with signs reading, "We're Still Here!" He assigned a couple of team members at the tent with tablets to take orders and another team that would transport food from the kitchen, down the hallway, and out the mall doors to the tent.

The franchisee shared with my colleague, "This ended up being our most profitable year. People who hadn't been to the mall in years started coming by because they didn't want to drive across town to the other location. I actually had to hire more people to keep up with the demand."

Mitigate losses; maximize returns.

The death of our software rental company wasn't the only time we had to mitigate loss. At one time, I was part of a company that did taxi tops in Toronto and Montreal—you know, the ads on top of taxis. But we got hit hard by Uber and had to accept the fact that the company wasn't going to be able to move forward and was on its way out, along with the taxis in town.

We looked for a buyer but couldn't find anyone interested, so we decided to get to know one of our competitors. Instead of selling the company to them, we brokered a deal to hand the company over in exchange for 15 percent ownership in the combined entity and an earnout.

We'd spent around $1.5 million on the company and sold it for no cash, just a potential payout. In the first couple years of this arrangement, we did pretty well, generating about 30 percent of our initial investment back from the earnout.

Instead of just walking away when we knew it was not going to be a success and we couldn't make much from selling it, we monetized it by moving it to someone else's hands. If you get to the point where you're frustrated with the business because it isn't scaling, then it's better to spend a little bit of effort to mitigate your losses and maximize the exit.

You won't be able to control the next legal change or the next financial crisis, but when the rules change, you have the opportunity to either complain about them or make the first move. Doing so might just change your business and your life. If Bill Gates hadn't convinced the US government to make software rental illegal, who knows where I'd be now? But that change opened the door to all the opportunities I've had since then—both failures and successes.

> **You won't be able to control the next legal change or the next financial crisis, but when the rules change, you have the opportunity to either complain about them or make the first move.**

CHAPTER 43

Types of Buyers

A SUCCESSFUL EXIT has to answer the questions of who, why, when, and how.

I've been on both sides of the line here. I've had the opportunity to sell companies and the opportunity to buy companies. In my life, I've probably bought over thirty companies. I was on one side of the equation when selling Internet Direct to Look Communication in the 1990s and Hostopia to Deluxe in the 2000s, but as part of both deals, I continued to work for the companies after the sale with duties that included acquiring our competitors. From that experience, I really learned the thinking process that goes on behind the curtain for acquiring companies.

When selling, there are three types of buyers out there: cash flow buyers, competitors, and strategic buyers.

Cash flow buyers are your last resort.

These are usually private equity or family offices hunting for companies generating cash flow that they can use to bolster the firm's overall revenue and earnings. At several of the companies we owned, I would get a call at least twice a month from these types of private equity firms wanting to buy us. But these buyers are looking only at your cash flow against their financing costs and then offering a valuation at fair market value—maybe slightly above if you're lucky.

But the fact of the matter is that they often take the soul right out of the companies they acquire and turn them into what I characterize as zombie companies. It's tempting to take the offer and run, but my two cents is to think about the employees, the customers, and all those you will leave behind.

The new owners may look at the company only for cash flow and with the sole purpose of making interest payments so that one day the company can be repackaged and sold off to probably *another* private equity firm if it is successful. They likely don't really connect with the story or purpose you established, so it can quickly turn into a pretty demotivating environment for people.

From an employee perspective, it's not really a great option. And even from the entrepreneur's perspective, it's really not great for valuation because they're looking only at the company in terms of cash flow, which often leads you down the path of the lowest common denominator for a startup—an earnings multiple.

This isn't to say that all private equity firms operate this way. I've seen some where they do have expertise and embrace the owner. They may be consolidating an industry or have a strategic reason for the acquisition. But these tend to be the exception, which is why I'm generally leery of them. However, if your only option is a cash flow private equity buyer, it makes sense to consider the deal. That being said, let's try to look at two other better alternatives.

Selling to competitors is your second-best alternative.

More often than not, a competitor is going to be looking at your company in terms of how they can save money and gain market share. In that way, it can be a better option than private equity because they're willing to pay a premium for the long-term cost savings and not just the value based on current earnings. They'll often achieve those savings by eliminating staff or any duplication in expenses during the integration of your company into theirs. And although they won't give you the benefit for all the cost savings, they often will find a midpoint between your current value and the economic benefit to their company.

When GoDaddy Registry bought .CLUB, this was partially the case. They were already running their own top-level domains like .co, .biz, and .us, so they didn't need to bring over any new staff. Not only did the staff at .CLUB know that the acquisition was going to happen but also they were happy about it! They would all benefit, since we had given everyone options in the company when setting things up.

They had worked hard for this moment and were excited about the outcome, even though they were all going to lose their jobs. I will admit that it was a bit of an emotional end, as most of us had set out together on this journey and had grown close to one another. The show had come to an end. The curtain was being drawn and tears flowed.

This was also true when we sold the taxicab advertising company to our competitor, as I described in the last chapter. In fact, when you're done with your business, your competitor may be your best option. My business partner and I had been discussing just shutting it down, but we had gotten to know the other operator well, and in wanting to maximize our exit, we struck a deal with him to buy the company for one dollar with some ownership and earnout. At the end of the day, this was valuable to our buyer simply because he could acquire our business assets for only one dollar, allowing him to gain 85 percent of the revenue we had been getting as his competitor. And it was valuable for us in that we were able to exit a business we were tired of.

Strategic buyers are the holy grail of buyers.

The third type of buyer—and my favorite—will look at your earnings multiple (the EBITDA), but they'll also look at your Story and how they can leverage your products or services within their existing infrastructure, their distribution channels, and/or their customer base. They'll want to demonstrate to their upper management that buying your company will provide them with a substantial benefit because of the leverage they can create, even if they're paying a higher multiple and offering a higher valuation.

They're looking at how much they can boost their revenue and ultimately their earnings on the play, which is why they'll pay a premium. They'll look at your current market value and then the projected value of merging the entity and will likely pay somewhere in the midrange.

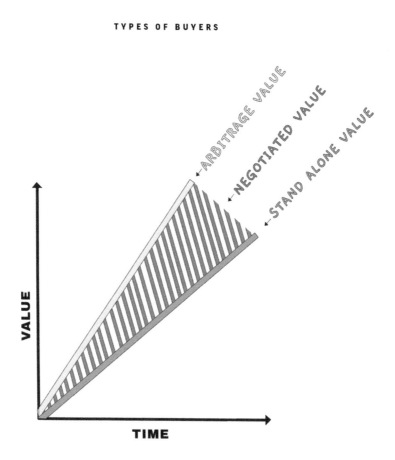

To me, this is the key and why I consider them the number one buyer to look for. Earlier I mentioned that selling .CLUB was partially a competitor buyout. GoDaddy Registry also has the ability to leverage a much broader distribution network by simply selling .CLUB through their network, increasing their ability to monetize the asset far greater than we could do on our own. This lent itself to a better valuation overall.

Sometimes strategic buyers can come from outside of your industry because they want to get *into* the industry. This is a cost savings for them as well because they can just carry on with what you've already built rather than having to build it themselves to enter your industry. In the case of Hostopia, Deluxe retained all the staff, and many of them have continued to work at the company over the last fifteen years, all improving their careers in the process. In fact, staff can be a critical asset to help gain additional value.

> **Staff can be a critical asset to help gain additional value.**

The sale of Tucows was a similar situation. Honestly, it wasn't even terribly strategic in the traditional sense. The buyer wanted to get into the industry because it was the late 1990s and everyone was going crazy for internet companies. Still, it ended up being worth it for them, as the company hit at a valuation of over $500 million several years later.

Make a list of your potential buyers.

As you're scaling and looking toward an exit, you'll want to make a list of who your potential buyers are. I recommend breaking them into the three categories of cash flow buyers, competitors, and strategic buyers.

From the list, let's look for the logical buyers. Who does it make sense to sell to? Who would most benefit and get value from what you're doing?

Find out what appeals to the buyer.

There are lots of reasons a buyer might pursue an acquisition, so gaining some insights into who they are and what their vision is around acquisitions can help you understand what they're wanting to accomplish. Understanding the buyers also helps you figure out how you need to adjust your story. The story of your company is what must sell here, so the story needs to be sexy yet still authentic. This is *not* a time to hold back.

That is, you have to know what story is going to appeal to the buyers. If the company has a sexy story, it will attract more buyers at a higher valuation. Sometimes this is as simple as figuring out the hot terms being used within your industry.

When Lil Roberts was doing one of her rounds of raising money, she came to me to talk over her pitch. I advised her to really hone in on terms like *AI* and *cloud*, since Xendoo really is an AI-powered, cloud-based platform. I said, "You should use those terms freely, since they're hot terms your ideal investor will be looking for."

Still, there is a balance. You have to be careful to not go too far and be overdependent on those terms. For example, I saw lots of people using the term *Web3* before the 2022 crypto crash and Meta meltdown, so now it has some bad connotations instead of being a selling point. If we really *aren't* something, we don't have to change things or pretend. Authenticity is better.

At Hostopia, we started out as a hosting company, which we later changed to an application service provider (or ASP), which we later changed to a software as a service company (or SaaS), which was later changed to a cloud-computing company. In each case, the industry had shifted, and we wanted to be perceived in the market as a leader in each new space by using the relevant language.

The key thing here is that no matter who the buyer is, you don't want them to see you simply as a cash flow company. When you're pitching the sale, it's not about how the sale benefits you or how great you are; it has to be about how great the benefit will be to *them*. That's how you get a higher valuation.

> " When you're pitching the sale, it's not about how the sale benefits you or how great you are; it has to be about how great the benefit will be to *them*. That's how you get a higher valuation. "

Know what scares the buyer.

Knowing what a potential buyer is afraid of can be just as valuable as knowing what will appeal to them. The biggest fear companies have in an acquisition is the merger itself. In technical acquisitions, their gravest concern can be the migration because so many things can go wrong. Sometimes the risks associated with these integrations are enough to deter a buyer from a deal. After all, they're asking themselves, "Why would I do a deal and if something goes wrong, I get fired?"

Knowing that reality, you can plan ahead with a migration or an integration strategy for the potential purchaser. The easier it is for your company to merge into another company, the higher the chance of a sale and the higher the valuation you'll get. This is a good reason to think about the exit from the start. Companies utilizing standard technology in the hosting industry had a better time being acquired versus companies that used their own platform because the acquirers knew what they were buying and how to do the migration.

Second, companies are afraid of the culture clash that can result from acquiring a company and the existing team. That's why sometimes they won't even take the team at all—they simply don't want to deal with what they see as an inevitable HR nightmare. Again, understand the individuals behind this decision first and foremost: If they mess up this acquisition, they'll look extremely bad within their organization. Acquisitions can be very risky. Remember, larger companies fear changes and risks, and those who rise often do so by avoiding risks—not by taking them.

The third thing buyers fear is that the entrepreneur is kooky. That's fair. When I was buying companies myself, every entrepreneur

I worked with seemed a little kooky. Every single one of them! And most of the time, the entrepreneur won't stick around, but if they do, it can be a problem of whether they can fit into the new culture or if they'll become a thorn in the company's side. And guess what? The savvy buyers already know this.

I experienced this personally when I worked for three years at Deluxe as part of the Hostopia acquisition. I really have to give their CEO Lee Schram a lot of credit because he allowed me to attend executive team meetings, and he wanted me to have a say, but I think a lot of the other executives in there wanted me out because I was just too direct for their liking—and maybe they found me a little kooky. Certainly, I was opinionated, a risk-taker, and a very direct communicator who held almost nothing back, which doesn't always gel within a Fortune 500 company.

It's easy for an Exit to fail when you can't see things from the buyer's perspective. But if you can get to know who your potential buyers are, what they value, and what they're afraid of, you can start molding your offering to increase your value in their eyes and to secure the deal you want. It's really not so different from understanding your ideal customer—what problem do they have, and how can you solve it?

CHAPTER 44:

Timing Is Half the Value

ONCE YOU KNOW the who and the why of your buyer, it's time to turn your attention to the when. Since Tucows was our first big sale, we didn't completely know what we were doing. We didn't have a broker involved, and yet we found ourselves in the middle of a bidding war between several potential buyers. Auctions—or even the fear of auctions—can help generate maximum value for a company. In fact, Deluxe paid a premium for Hostopia to avoid our shopping the deal on the market.

During the first sale of Tucows, the Asian flu crisis hit. The markets dropped rapidly, and even though we had agreed to a price with a potential buyer, they ended up dropping their offer by 75 percent to reflect the market. Long story short, the deal was canceled within minutes of this conversation, and somehow this became a good thing for us in the long run, as we sold for a significantly higher valuation within a couple of years.

Our eventual deal for Tucows was with a group controlled by billionaire Beny Steinmetz. He wasn't in our space at all, but given the times, he wanted to have a play in the burgeoning internet industry. He ended up flying in eight members of his team to meet with us over the course of twenty-one days.

> **" There are no free evenings and no weekends when a deal is in motion. "**

And when I say twenty-one days, I mean we were working literally around the clock and closed the deal in twenty-one days. Unprecedented, even in my career. There are no free evenings and no weekends when a deal is in motion. The negotiation took over our lives, but I'm glad it did. I learned a valuable lesson from Beny's urgency to close the deal: timing is half the value.

There's a need for speed.

As I saw with the potential buyer during the Asian flu crisis who had backed out, it's unwise to drag things out once you have an interested buyer. Change is inevitable, and it's only a matter of time before a major change can drop out of the sky and totally derail things.

I've thought about this in context with some of my other successful exits. The dot-com crash in 2000 would have wiped out our chances of a sale for Tucows. The Lehman crisis of 2008 would likely have prevented the sale of Hostopia if we had not closed the deal just weeks before. Likewise, the crypto crash, stock market drop, and Fed-induced slowdown of 2022 would have probably prevented the sale of .CLUB. In all these scenarios, we appear to have dodged a bullet.

> ** When it takes too long to close a transaction, you're in trouble. **

When it takes too long to close a transaction, you're in trouble. When you're in sell mode, it's go mode. It's not at the same pace as when you're running the company. You have to constantly move things forward, constantly push everyone in the organization to get the necessary documents being requested. And you have to get that football across the line—no matter what it takes—before the clock runs out.

There is a great danger in underestimating how much time this all takes. In one situation, I told my lawyer that the schedules to the contract were going to be the biggest issue he would face. Schedules cover details like the integration plan, lists of the organization's assets, liabilities, and so on. They take a lot of time to write, and they're not easy to put together—but they're essential to close a deal.

Apparently he didn't believe me, though. Just a couple of weeks from closing, I thought he had the schedules under control when one Saturday afternoon he informed me that he hadn't even started them yet. "We'll get them done quickly," he assured me.

"No, you won't," I replied, probably trying to hide my frustration. "They're not that easy."

He got so buried in putting the schedules together that I had to hire an additional lawyer who specialized in schedules to help him get everything ready in time for the close. Seriously—don't underestimate the work involved in the legal schedules in the contract to close.

To avoid failure from an extended sales process, it can be prudent to have people work on things simultaneously or to bring in extra resources to ensure that you can get things done quickly rather than drag out the process. This is not the time to be cheap.

If you've got the deal, then you need to close it before the world falls apart. I can't tell you how it seems like every time we're selling a company, the financial world seems to collapse. But more on that in Repeat.

When times are really good, exit quietly stage left.

The best time to sell is when the market is frothy, which means you need to measure the sentiment in the market. I usually say, "When the show is going well, exit quietly stage left."

In other words, look for the cues (or signs) in the market for when you should exit. To me, one sign in 2021 was the NFT craze, SPAC surge, and GameStop mania. We all saw what was happening, yet few acted on it. The insanity had hit, and yet the laws of economics seemed like they were no longer relevant.

In general, though, the easiest way to gauge the market is to look at how many IPOs are happening. Even if your company is not publicly traded, if there is a window open where IPOs are happening constantly, then that's a strong sign that it might be time to sell.

According to Ernst & Young, the volume of IPOs dropped by 44 percent in 2022, with the US market in particular set to record its lowest returns in nearly twenty years.[19] Selling a company in 2022 became increasingly difficult as the year progressed. When the market falls, IPOs freeze, prices for new acquisitions come down, and deals

> 66 The best time to sell is when the market is frothy, which means you need to measure the sentiment in the market. 99

dry up. Although some private equity deals were still being done, by the end of 2022, most private equity firms were concerned about supporting their own portfolio.

The difficulty here is that this can feel counterintuitive. You might think that it's not the time to sell because "things are going well," and you're enjoying seeing the numbers grow larger and larger. "Let's see where we are next year," you might say, but the fact is that your sales might not be as high next year. Something could go wrong, the economy could collapse, and the window could close on you.

It can be a real high to be the surfer riding the wave, but wait too long and the wave crashes down on you in a wipeout instead of carrying you to the shore. Bloodied and bruised, you might then think it's time to sell when, in fact, it likely isn't. Remember, "overnight" startup successes take many years. Let's not panic in tough times and instead do what we can to survive and eventually thrive when we come out the other end.

We made the mistake of waiting too long with Paw.com during the pandemic. Sales were going really well, and we had been featured in the *Inc.* 5000 list of fastest-growing companies for three years in a

---

19   Paul Go, "How Do You Prepare for When the Time Is Right?" EY.com, September 28, 2022. https://www. ey.com/en_gl/ipo/trends#:~:text=Year%2Dto%2Ddate%20(,year%20(YOY)%2C%20respectively.

row. As more people were spending time with their pets at home and the pandemic dragged on, we benefited greatly. Even though some opportunities to sell came along, we stalled, thinking, "Things are going well, the company is growing, and it's really too early for us to consider selling ..."

Another good friend of mine, Joseph Martin, ran the e-commerce company BoxyCharm and managed to pull off a deal to sell his company for a valuation of roughly $500 million in 2021. Today, that company would command a fraction of the value, with some of the publicly traded e-commerce companies declined 70 to 90 percent by late 2022. Talk about getting the timing right!

Meanwhile, for us, January 2022 came along and Paw.com got whacked by inflation like many other e-commerce businesses. Additionally, demand for our products experienced a drastic dropoff in the postpandemic world. Had I followed my own advice, we could have quietly exited stage left by selling the company at a higher valuation while the market was frothy. Nevertheless, as of the writing of this book, the company is bouncing back and, hopefully, like Tucows, this will turn out for the best.

Again, I'm not advocating that you take the first offer to come your way. You still need to do your due diligence to make sure you're getting the best deal that's right for you, for the buyer, and for the team. But once you're confident about those details, there's no sense in delaying. You're more likely to regret the delay than you are to be grateful for it. Some of us have learned this the hard way—so learn from our mistakes. And by the way, if others make a killing from buying your company and selling it again at a higher valuation, hats off to them. Just as long you did well on your exit and made some money, you never have to look back.

CHAPTER 45:

Maximize the Value of the Exit

AS WE STARTED to look ahead to our exit for .CLUB, there were a couple of things we did in the year before. One move we made was to reduce costs, including staff. We simply looked at ways that we could become more efficient with a smaller team. If someone left to pursue another opportunity, we took a hard look at their role and how we could still get the same output but with fewer people.

Besides, since we had a list of potential buyers—which included GoDaddy Registry—we knew the likelihood was that whoever acquired the company wouldn't be taking the staff along anyway. Please note that a number of our staff members have been hired in the industry by other companies as well. They were part of a great success that in turn benefited their reputations.

When we were in the process of selling Hostopia, my brother, Bill, was serving as CTO, and in the negotiations, I said, "Bill won't be coming with the company. He's decided to move on, so we can cut his $250,000 salary out of the sale." I know that sounds cruel, but we did this to increase our EBITDA. When the deal finally closed, we got seventeen times EBITDA, which means cutting Bill's salary made us an additional $4,250,000 in the sale. His share of that was worth way more than the salary he had "lost." Although I admit that his ego was a little bruised.

> **" The best thing you can do in preparation for the exit is to use the twelve to twenty-four months prior to the sale to become as efficient as possible. "**

Like we discussed in Scale, cost cutting is an incredible tool for increasing overall earnings. In the context of Exit, it can make a substantial impact on the offer you receive. Sometimes the market is looking at your growth of sales, but more often than not, it's looking at earnings multiples. Knowing that, the best thing you can do in preparation for the exit is to use the twelve to twenty-four months prior to the sale to become as efficient as possible. Feel free to reread the chapter on cost reductions again (chapter 30) but this time with the view of preparing your company for sale.

Continue to run the business as if you'll have it forever.

A word of warning, though—there is a delicate balance you have to find with becoming more efficient. You don't want to cut costs so much that you lose momentum and then your earnings drop. Don't become so obsessed with the idea of selling that you forget to keep running the business.

In some companies, you will want to position some of the staff as experts, which can help the combined entity thrive, and that same staff will help you increase the value of the company.

Every situation is different, but you want to run the business almost as though you'll never sell it. Because even if that was true, you would still want to look for ways to reduce costs and/or increase your revenues. When you're looking to exit, it's not the time to start slacking. Instead, you should be doubling down on activities and decisions that make the company more profitable and therefore more valuable.

If you're closing a deal where there is a multiyear earnout, this idea becomes even more important. You want to run the business so well that even as it changes hands, it not only remains profitable but also continues to grow, as this will increase the value of those earnings.

Align your strategy with the metrics of the industry.

Part of the balancing act with maximizing your company's value even comes down to what kind of initiatives you pursue. For example, if potential buyers in your industry are more concerned with overall growth versus earnings, then you may want to focus your sales strategy on greater initiatives, going after larger accounts, even if they take longer.

On the other hand, let's say that it takes you three years to acquire a large customer and your industry values EBITDA earnings over growth, then it's more prudent to pull back on some of the big initiatives and instead go after some smaller accounts that can close faster and can have an impact on earnings quickly. Doing so will accelerate your growth and therefore valuation more in preparation for the exit than trying to go after only the big dogs.

Or let's say you're a subscription-based business. It makes more sense to shift more of your budget toward acquisitions. This will allow you to accelerate your subscription numbers as much as possible to get the higher valuation. Also, never forget to focus on how you can make more money from your existing subscribers. Are there new services you can offer? Or can you build in price increases without spending more to maintain services to those subscribers?

This was something we brought up in our discussions for the sale of .CLUB—how part of our strategic plan was to increase the price of the domain by a dollar a year forever. This was particularly powerful because it cost us very little to keep those customers once we had them, and yet we could continue to earn more year over year just by maintaining the number of customers and increasing the price. Any increase in subscriptions would be the icing on the cake.

Fifty percent of the value of the business is building it; 50 percent is in exiting it.

As I have said, with so many companies, it takes ten years to make an "overnight" success happen. Entrepreneurs spend a lot of their energy, effort, and emotions on building the company, but they give far too little thought to the exit. Too often, they just hand it over to a broker and say, "Go sell it."

I have nothing against brokers; I've used them plenty of times. But it's best if you don't rely on them to handle *all* the details of the exit to the point where you're completely hands off.

Instead, there should be a clear action-based strategy around the exit before a broker ever enters the picture if you choose to use one. At a minimum, you should be putting this together a year or two before you exit. Even better, you should be thinking about it from the very beginning—what is your endgame with the business? Is it the company you're going to keep until your dying day? Or do you want to make it so valuable that others are fighting to take it off your hands for an eventual sale?

As we discussed already, timing is half the value. In the case of Joseph Martin with BoxyCharm, you could argue that it was much greater than half the value. Since you can't always predict when the market is going to be frothy for a high-valuation sale, you have to be thinking of this far ahead of time.

Therefore, here are a few things you can focus on long before a buyer comes knocking on your door. First, identify the important metrics in your industry. Is it overall growth, market earnings, or some other metric providing the highest valuations? Then make sure that these KPIs are in your strategy. Your budget should be diverted to action items directly connected to those KPIs. For example, if you're a subscription business like we were at .CLUB, you're focusing on things like number of subscribers, churn rate, scheduled price increases, and so on.

Next, as we discussed before, put together your list of strategic buyers, competitors, and (even grudgingly) private equity. Once you have that list, focus on finding ways to get their attention and attract them to you. Sometimes this can be done through PR efforts—making press releases, being featured in a study within your industry, attending trade shows, doing interviews or webinars to position yourself as an expert and thought leader in your industry.

Basically, you're going to do anything you can to make yourself attractive to those strategic buyers so that they come to *you*. Going to them and asking, "Hey, wanna buy us out?" could smack of desperation.

If they do take the bait, they'll be far more willing to close the deal and/or buy your company at a higher rate because it was *their* idea.

In addition, these strategies are not just good for the sale but good for business, whether you're in selling mode or not. Thinking as early as possible about why and how you want to exit someday will help you focus your energy in the right places, because you recognize a significant part of the value is in how you perform in the remaining months of the company, not just the years you invested building it.

> **" Thinking as early as possible about why and how you want to exit someday will help you focus your energy in the right places. "**

At the end of the day, what is the Story you want your business to tell? Did you half-ass things because you knew you would be getting rid of it? One where you have no idea what buyers are looking for, so you end up spending your time, energy, and resources heading in the wrong direction? Or one where the actions you take reflect long-term thinking that profits the company, the team, the buyer, and yourself?

PEOPLE

CHAPTER 46:

It's Not about You

A WHILE AGO, I was sitting down with a potential buyer for one of my companies. We discussed the obvious things: the company's story, the financials, and the future projections. But then the conversation turned to people. The potential buyer asked me about the CEO, and I happily discussed his role in scaling the company and hiring a great sales team.

"That's great," they replied. "What about you, Colin? What do you do?"

"Me?" I shrugged. "I don't really do anything."

They were a bit shocked by my answer. "What do you mean you don't really do anything?"

"I mean, I helped set up the company," I admitted, "and I helped a bit with some of the board structure and initial funding. Sometimes I come in for a meeting with potential investors to support, but really, in the day-to-day, I don't do anything. It's everyone else making things run."

You may recall back in Scale that we discussed the importance of checking your ego at the door. In Exit, it's time to multiply that concept by about a hundred. When you're at the negotiating table and the conversation turns to you, your job as the entrepreneur is to minimize your role and to emphasize your people. Minimizing the value of *you* maximizes the value of the *company*.

> 66 Minimizing the value of you maximizes the value of the company. 99

Check your ego in both word and deed.

Exit isn't the time to have a big ego, which sounds counterintuitive. After all, as an entrepreneur who has successfully scaled a company, it's natural to want some recognition for all the hard work and sacrifices you've made to get it to this point. Maybe you've even won deals in the past through the force of your personality, so it's natural to think the same strategy will work here.

But the negotiating table is a completely different ball game than pitching to investors. In fact, it's a different sport altogether. Here you'll want to do the opposite of what you're used to doing in pitching. Instead of being bold and promoting yourself and your vision, you're going to want to play down your role in things. Check your ego at the door and diminish your own importance.

In fact, when possible, you need to go a step beyond this and be able to back up your words with actual deeds. If you want to be able to say, "I really don't do anything," then don't lie about it—be authentic by taking the actions beforehand that will make this statement the truth.

As you prepare for the exit, start looking at how you can remove yourself from the equation of the company. If you're the CEO or president, replace yourself. If you're taking a salary, then stop. This increases the overall EBITDA, as we've already discussed, but it also serves as proof to say, "I'm not on the payroll because I don't do anything that deserves being on the payroll."

If that's not the case, though, and if you are still integral to the company's operation, then you need to be up front about it. But you also must be able to present a plan for how that can change. If you intend to stay on with the company after the sale, such as an earnout situation, be open about it and discuss the details.

And be honest with yourself. Can you be content in a role with a corporation where you aren't in charge anymore and where you'll have to go along with whatever decision gets made? If you're in an earnout scenario, it's better to have a seat at the table where decisions are made so that you can still contribute your voice. If that's what you want, you need to make it clear. Some buyers will be open to this while others are going to be very wary of having you around the other executives. And even if you do get a seat at the table, you still have to decide how comfortable you are with your advice being ignored or being outvoted on something.

There is an exception to this rule: If you don't have a new gig yet or you're not sure what your next startup will be, it might be worth sticking around with the buyer. Staying in the industry can allow you to explore new opportunities. It's far easier to start a new business in the industry you already know than it is to try to jump into a brand-new space. And besides, you can earn a salary and moonlight on the side to start that next company. But we'll chat more about that when we get to Repeat.

Demote yourself; promote your people.

The buyers are the ones who have to run the company after the entrepreneur is long gone, and the vast majority of entrepreneurs are completely out of the picture within three years of the sale. That means the buyers are thinking about all the other people in the company.

Rather than talk about your accomplishments, your focus should be on what the team has done—how amazing the leadership team is, how hardworking the salespeople are, how talented your IT people are, and so on. As you demote yourself, you promote your people.

You want to lift others up because this will increase the value of the acquisition in the buyer's eyes. If you turn their attention to the worth of the talent they'll be acquiring, then you raise the value of the company. Generally speaking, the less a company relies on the entrepreneur, the higher the valuation.

One time we bought a small security company simply so that we could acquire their talent for Hostopia. We didn't use any of their other assets whatsoever—we just wanted their people. That's how good of a job the owner did at elevating his people in our conversations.

And it paid off for us because those five people ended up becoming significant shareholders and key employees in the company, helping lead us to a successful exit.

Additionally, you want to make sure you don't overplay one individual but instead focus on the team as a whole. Even if you're not promoting yourself but singling out one person, you run the risk of making them think the company could implode if they lose that individual.

Always put the company first.

If all you do is talk about yourself, the more likely it is that the potential buyer will close their laptops, extend their hand, and say, "Thanks for your time" rather than continue the conversation. Putting yourself first is a good way to commit self-sabotage. Making decisions for personal gain often backfires, reducing both the morale *and* the valuation of the company.

That's why I've always lived by the credo, "If it's good for the company, it's good for me—even if it doesn't always appear so good for me."

Whether you're close to exiting or not, the company must come first in every decision. The company has all the value, not you.

> **Whether you're close to exiting or not, the company must come first in every decision. The company has all the value, not you.**

I sometimes refer to the company as the mothership, and we all have to support the mothership before ourselves. Be willing to sacrifice yourself for the good of the company, the employees, and the investors. For example, if the company runs into financial difficulty, be willing to cut your own salary. In the long run, doing so will reap benefits. It's for this reason that I've always preferred to take options in the company rather than a salary. For one thing, the taxes are lower, but it also means I'm not taking away any oxygen from the company—that is, cash. When nearing Exit, we want to think that way as well. But to be clear here, if you're integral in the company and not taking a salary, they'll add back a salary for that position in the valuation of the company. So you really need to find a way to remove yourself or at least find ways to minimize yourself within the organization.

You might say, "But, Colin, don't I deserve some credit for all my hard work?"

Sure you do. No one is saying that you don't deserve credit. But here's my question to you: "How do you want to receive that credit? In the form of ego or in the form of a twenty-two- million-dollar check?" A lot of times, you can't have both. One of those serves only yourself (ego), and the other one can serve not only yourself but also your entire team when they get to share in the success—not to mention your family.

MONEY

CHAPTER 47:

Liquidity or Control

LIQUIDITY   **CONTROL**

WE BEGAN THIS CONVERSATION on Exit with a really fun story of us getting a huge check in 1998 from our first successful sale. But now it's time for a not so fun story. As I've said before, we can always learn from our failures, and it's no different here. While I've alluded to this story previously, now it's time for all the gory details. People seem to think I'm some kind of genius because of how we sold Tucows, Hostopia, and .CLUB before the crashes that followed each. But it wasn't genius; it was simply paranoia. Paranoia born out of a real business tragedy.

As I talked about earlier, I study cycles and look for signs of froth in the market. Following the successful sale of Tucows, I let my guard down a bit. Too much, to be honest. My brother and I had also been running Internet Direct for eight years at that point, so in 1999, it was already a publicly traded company. We were approached by Look Communications, a privately run Canadian cable company that was interested in buying it. I was all fired up again.

The valuation of the company was approximately $80 million prior to the merger. After the announcement, the valuation doubled. Remember, it was 1999 and *internet* was the big buzzword. Internet Direct was the number one fastest-growing company in Canada after being the seventh-fastest the year before. As a result, I have to admit that I was living the good life with my newfound wealth—smoking the proverbial cigars, enjoying some attention from a cover story with *Profit* magazine along with my business partners after we were named the fastest-growing company in Canada.

As I've discussed before, we often give options to our team so that they have some ownership in the company too. This was exactly the case with Internet Direct, but in doing this transaction to sell to Look Communications, we agreed that we wouldn't sell any of the stock for eighteen months, which I now realize is a long hold to agree to. At twenty-nine years old, I thought I knew what I was doing and felt that I couldn't go wrong after selling Tucows. This internet thing was never going to stop! So we moved forward with the deal, forgoing both liquidity and control in the company for eighteen months.

Since I've always been very particular about employees getting the upside in profit sharing, I felt like this deal was in their best interests too. After all, we had just applied for a license for fixed internet in Canada at no cost to our newly combined entity. This may sound strange, but Canada was trying to promote competition and was willing to give away extremely valuable licenses to encourage competition. The side effect of this deal was that it made our stock jump to a valuation within months of the sale to well over a billion dollars.

What could go wrong?

Anything can happen at any time to derail your world. Well, this is the lesson that made me aware of it. And I hope that no one ever has to go through this but instead simply learns from this story.

In March 2000, a US court decided to break up Microsoft—and the Nasdaq responded by falling hard and fast from 5000 to 4000. Since we had given up control of the company, there was nothing I could do to help mitigate the impact of this as it hit our stock. As a result, Look decided to retract a secondary $50 million offering to wait for the market to bounce back. But if you remember that time, the Nasdaq continued to plummet and fall below 1200—and it took fifteen years for it to recuperate.

The music had stopped, and growth was now out. Only profitable companies would survive what became known as the dot-com crash. And remember, all our shareholders—including our employees—were locked in for eighteen months, and we were still twelve months out from being able to touch our stock at this point.

Long story short, around a year later, we knew that the company would have to head into receivership, and we filed for bankruptcy protection. But the market had predicted this even before the announcement. Our stock hit a low of six cents from what was once over nineteen dollars a share on an intraday high. And yet we were still locked up with no ability to sell our shares.

Everything we had built for ten years crumbled.

And who got hurt the worst by it? Sure, you could say that my partners and I took the brunt of it. But really our employees and our investors also lost pretty much everything as a result of the deal we had made. Everyone who had believed in us and in our company and who had worked hard to build it up for a decade—we'd let them all down, including my mom. It was a tough conversation to have with people, to say the least, and it's now considered one of the biggest internet company failures in Canada during the dot-com crash. From number one fastest growing … to last place finish.

One particular person impacted was Howard Bell, our chief of operations, who I'll talk about again later on. Because of his share in the company, it personally cost him $1 million. One day I was sharing this story onstage, and he came to hear me speak. When I saw him at the back of the room, the emotion overcame me, and I began to tear up as I remembered the human impact of our decision.

You need to keep liquidity or control.

There are a couple of big lessons I took away from this. First and foremost: Liquidity or control—don't ever give up both in a deal, no matter how good it sounds. You need to retain one of those in any deal you make.

> **Liquidity or control—don't ever give up both in a deal, no matter how good it sounds. You need to retain one of those in any deal you make.**

Don't get me wrong, there are examples of people who have done these kinds of consolidations and who have been successful and made a lot of money from it. But as a result of the Internet Direct nightmare, I won't do a deal unless I have either liquidity or control.

After making the deal, I quickly discovered the pain that came with giving up control. I was constantly fighting with the new CEO because

I felt like they were spending far too much money. For example, they didn't even own the building they were based in, yet they spent $7 million to renovate the space. When I tried to weigh in on why I felt this was unwise, what I would hear back is, "You're being cheap. You're still young and don't know the value of this." Yes, at that age I was accused of being young and naive a few too many times. Meanwhile, the CEO had come over from another large cable company and was simply repeating the same practices they had done at that multibillion-dollar company.

Since I had given up the rights to the major decisions, all I could do was watch and make recommendations—or, being less politically correct, fight with them. This wouldn't have been so bad if we'd gotten liquidity. If we had just cashed out, taken the money or tradeable stock and fully exited, then it would have been out of our hands. Then I wouldn't have cared how they were spending the money. Even if I still believed in the company, I would have had the choice of whether to hold or sell.

> **When giving up control of the company, you have to truly understand that you're in the back seat; you're *not* the decision maker anymore.**

When giving up control of the company, you have to truly understand that you're in the back seat; you're *not* the decision maker anymore. Even if the buyer puts you on the board and grants you a seat at the table, sometimes it's just for show. The best-case scenario is that you still get a vote, but it doesn't count as much as it used to. The reason a lot of acquisitions end up failing is that the buyer doesn't understand the culture of the business that's been built while it was under your control. If you're giving up control to get the liquidity, you have to be all right with the fact that they might run things into the ground.

Instead, at Internet Direct we had neither control nor cash. We were just clock watching, counting down the minutes until we could cash out, but as you already know, that moment never came. We crashed out instead of cashing out.

On that note, if you're going with liquidity rather than control, make sure it's *true* liquidity—not penny stocks or over-the-counter stocks—something that you can actually trade on the market for cash. When you have the ability to liquidate within a day or two, at least then you and your team can walk away with something for all your hard work, even if things start to crumble and you stop believing in the company.

As a side note, I should mention earnouts as well. In general, I advise caution with earnouts. This really depends on how strong your company is at the sale. As I said before, I did an earnout when we sold our taxicab ad company, but this was because it was either walk away with nothing or walk away with a little something. If you can get a 100 percent deal, then great.

If you feel extremely confident that the business will hit the necessary goals to satisfy the earnout criteria for extra compensation, then it can certainly be on the table. But you should know that earnouts can be *very* complicated, so before you pursue one, you need to make sure that the terms are very clearly defined and that they leave no room for ambiguity with what's expected. The ideal scenario for a healthy company is that 80 to 90 percent comes off the table first and then you can consider the earnout as icing on the cake. Don't confuse this with the holdback. Sometimes companies will hold back around 5 to 10 percent to ensure that everything you committed to in the contract is accurate.

How do you pick up the pieces after an epic failure like Internet Direct? Personally losing over $100 million at the age of twenty-nine, destroying the economic lives of your employees, and hurting investors who trusted you? There was only one thing left to do: follow what I loved about technology—its potential to change the world.

Watch out for the thieves.

Prior to this failed merger, we had another offer come along for Internet Direct in 1996. It was designed as a reverse takeover, sort of a SPAC deal of the time. However, when the interested party couldn't deliver in a year and a half, we canceled the contract.

Four years later, after we had signed the deal with Look Communications and sold Tucows, these thieves came out of the woodwork with a $750 million lawsuit claiming that we hadn't done things correctly when canceling our deal with them. We received the lawsuit Friday at 4:00 p.m., shortly after the stock market closed. Remember, we were a publicly traded company. We had a very good lawyer in Toronto who built a case for us within twenty-four hours. I don't think we (or he) slept at all. He pulled some strings to get a judge to hear the case *before* the market opened so that we could do a settlement with them and mitigate any impact to our stock.

Did we really want to settle? No. Not at all. In my opinion, it was clear that they were trying to blackmail us, and the judge could see that as plain as day. But if we didn't settle, it would be more damaging to our company's stock. The settlement was in the millions, which hit us particularly hard, as our stock had already been collapsing and our wealth was evaporating.

It cost us money, but it was still in the best interests of the company we loved. If we had carried on with the lawsuit, it would have become even more expensive. Our stock would have fallen in the midst of the offering to raise money at the time, and we could have received more lawsuits from investors. Even though, in my opinion, we were 100 percent in the right, settling was the safest option for us. Devotion to our staff, our investors, and our families helped us know which battle was truly worth fighting.

My friend was hit with another scam involving a penny stock public company offering to buy his company. Upon the announcement of the negotiation, the penny stock shot up, which brought a lot of attention to it. The negotiation started dragging and dragging, and after a number of months, the company broke off the negotiations only to see their stock collapse despite the many shares that had been traded in the meantime. Obviously, this is fraud, but it's hard to prove when your state of mind is focused on making the deal happen.

It boils down to this:

❝ Be paranoid of the scammers and thieves. ❞

There are a couple of solid side lessons that we can also take away from this. First, watch out for the thieves—they're everywhere—and sometimes they show up in nice suits and ties and big dollars signs on contracts. With Internet Direct, we saw two different versions of how these types can appear, and it's taught me to be on guard with future exits. And remember, we were prime targets, as I was only in my midtwenties and still wet behind the ears.

I'd be lying if I said that I don't regret how things went down with Internet Direct. It continues to be a sore spot for me, and I consider it my greatest failure because of the number of people I hurt. But it did teach me a valuable lesson. From the ashes of the situation, my brother and I refocused on our love for the tech industry, and that passion became the genesis for Hostopia. We were committed to the idea that the next time we were at a negotiating table, things would be different. From now on, we would accept only liquidity or control. And in the case of Hostopia, we sold it for all cash.

CHAPTER 48:

The Negotiation

A STICKY SITUATION arose during the sale of Tucows. That's bound to happen at the negotiating table when you're having to lay everything out, and the lawyers and business executives are reviewing every bit of documentation available.

In this case, a question came up regarding a discrepancy in the page views our website was receiving, which sounds innocuous at first glance. But on the first morning of negotiating with the eventual buyer, their team dropped some documents on the table in a grand gotcha! moment and proclaimed, "It appears your website traffic fell thirty percent from what you reported to us!"

My mind started racing, and I became extremely stressed out by the charts and graphs now staring up at me from the table. I'm sure it showed as my face went pale and I stammered whatever response came out first. I probably said something like "I'm so sorry. Let our team look into what happened here," but I honestly don't remember because I was thrown off so much. And that was probably the whole purpose—it was just a tactic to throw us off our game.

How do I know this? Because I took the graphs and charts to my team to get an explanation, and no one could understand where these numbers had come from or verify it in any way. When I brought this information back to the negotiating table the next morning, they said, "Oh, never mind. You're right. We made a mistake. The traffic you reported was correct."

Be highly aware of the information presented at the negotiation.

This was our first sale, so we hadn't learned this lesson yet. And their tactic had worked 100 percent because we immediately lost confidence in our own information. But their admission to their "mistake" didn't change the fact that we had already made some concessions the previous day that I normally wouldn't have agreed to.

Don't get me wrong—I still have a high respect for our buyer. It was their job to get the best deal they could, and this was part of their strategy. I didn't know then what I know now—that the brokers and lawyers employ these kind of methods to cajole you in the direction they want. It doesn't mean that the decision maker on the other end has directed them to do this—more on that in a minute. But you can bet that they'll adjust their tactics based on how you respond to certain information.

There are a couple of other lessons that we can learn here. First, you need to have a high level of confidence in the information *you're* bringing to the table. If they find errors in your data, even if it is not material, they may question *all* of your numbers. If you're confident that you're correct, then when it's questioned by the other side, you can stand your ground and say, "We've triple-checked this and can stand by it a thousand percent." Had I been more confident in our own information, my response would have been different. I would have politely said, "I'm sorry, but I don't think your information here is correct. Where did this come from? Can our team look at this more in depth with your team?" In other words, I could've called their bluff.

Second, it's all right to be skeptical of the information the other side brings. As you saw with Internet Direct, not every buyer with whom you meet will have good intentions. It's hard to know that in the very early stages. Every transaction is eventually executed on trust, but that trust has to be built on both sides. So it's okay for you to want to double-check the information they bring and to have your team look at things to make sure it holds up.

Chances are that this isn't the buyer's first rodeo, so you're not going to offend them or scare them away by asking for proof. However, if asking to verify their information does offend them or scare them away, then they probably weren't the buyer for you anyway and didn't have the best intentions. You may have just dodged a bullet.

On the other hand, a good buyer is more likely to be impressed by your skepticism and see it as a sign of how savvy you are. You may actually be laying the foundation for a solid, long-term partnership and a profitable business relationship. It may even help uncover new information to increase your valuation at the negotiating table. When used properly, stats can be our friend to prove value.

Don't let there be a wall between you and the key decision makers.

Let's talk a bit more about trust between you and the buyer. In any deal, you have to remember that no matter who shows up at the negotiating table, you're doing a deal with the key decision maker, not the brokers and lawyers.

That's not to say that brokers and lawyers aren't important—they are. Having been on both sides of the deal myself, you need them there. But brokers and lawyers like there to be a wall between the entrepreneurs and the decision maker they represent. They can get in the way of getting the terms you want and kill the deal if you're inexperienced.

Instead, if you have a relationship with the real buyer, the real decision maker, then at the eleventh hour, when the brokers and lawyers are making things sticky or are stonewalling, you can pick up the phone and talk directly to the buyer based on the trust you've built with them.

This came in particularly handy at Hostopia when we were preparing for our IPO. We were coming out at eight dollars a share, but we still lacked a lead institution for the underwriting. Despite the objections from our brokers at RBC, I called the decision maker at one particular institution who we'd gone back and forth with. No lawyers, no brokers. Just the two of us on the phone.

With the trust we'd built up, he got very frank and said, "Colin, I just think this deal is too expensive."

"Okay," I replied. "What if we cut down the IPO to six dollars per share? Would you do it then?"

"Absolutely," he answered. And just like that, we had a lead institution signed on, and the last roadblock to our IPO was out of the way.

Likewise, when we sold Hostopia to Deluxe, I had built enough trust with Lee Schram, their CEO, to go directly to him and work things out when it wasn't happening at the negotiating table. The same could be said for our experience selling .CLUB to GoDaddy Registry. You can't really put a price on having that kind of trust and openness between yourself and the buyer.

> **One of the best ways to build trust is to be willing to admit some of your mistakes and faults to the buyer.**

One of the best ways to build trust is to be willing to admit some of your mistakes and faults to the buyer. This is yet another opportunity to check your ego at the door instead of walking into every meeting claiming everything that is "Great, great, great!" When you can be frank about your missteps, missed opportunities, and failures, it adds value to the process in the form of trust.

Generate goodwill with the buyer whenever possible.

You're not going to get everything you want at the negotiating table, so you need to go in knowing which things to fight for and which things to concede on ahead of time. You don't have to announce those all up front, but you must have them clearly prioritized for yourself so that you don't fight over the wrong things and end up killing an otherwise good deal.

> **Don't fight over the wrong things and end up killing an otherwise good deal.**

There will come times when you will need to override your lawyer or broker too. During the .CLUB negotiations, I probably had to override our lawyer a dozen times because he was going too far on issues I wasn't willing to turn into an ultimatum. Sometimes what matters to the lawyers and brokers isn't what really matters to us, so I had to say, "Hey, I'm not willing to risk the deal over this point, so let's move past it." Sometimes I would do this during negotiations. This surprised the other side and made their chief negotiator look great. A seasoned lawyer won't take offense, especially if you warn them beforehand.

In getting the deal done, you still have to be extremely cautious in what you say and what you do so as to not overstep legal bounds and commit any kind of fraud. Obviously, this is where brokers and lawyers add true value because they can protect you from saying or doing something that would not only kill the deal but also land you with a lawsuit or in jail.

When you're in the negotiating stage, it takes over your life. You'll be going through contracts and clauses with the brokers and lawyers daily, with lots of back and forth on the phone over every tiny detail, honing in on what are the key points to fight for and the small points to concede. Fight for big things, not small things.

As for the small things? They can turn into leverage to generate goodwill with the buyer.

This in particular can be very powerful when done publicly in a large negotiation with their lead negotiator in attendance. There's nothing like saying directly to the buyer, "Look, I've given you this and this. Now I need you to come back and give me something here." The goodwill you generate with small concessions can really help you when you're arguing over the things you want the most.

Prepare for the exit as early as possible.

There are a number of strategies I've used to help me prepare for a strong exit.

- *Use one-liners.* I've practiced stating one-liners with my trusted advisors to get feedback on what I needed to say when pitching the company. One-liners must answer the question, "What message do I want to make sure is delivered back to the decision maker to increase the value of the deal?" As you do this, you'll want to ensure that you're not just selling adjectives and buzzwords but actual *facts*—proof detailed in statistics and analysis. These must be concrete statements—and you must repeat these same statements on more than one occasion so that they sink in.

- *Get an exit coach.* I used a business colleague and friend of mine, Gordon Stula, to help me with a previous sale. Even though I'd sold companies before, having an external set of eyes with a different perspective, a different negotiating style, and a different track record of success in closing deals helped me improve my skills at negotiating. Not only that, but a good coach can also help you spot the possible roadblocks before they can kill the deal. Gordon had a wealth of experience with exits, so he was also a great resource for practicing my one-liners.

- *Identify early on what you have that a potential buyer* doesn't *have.* What quality about you can they leverage for their own success? Make what's obvious to you obvious to the buyer. For example, with .CLUB, we had some particular international relationships that were of value to GoDaddy Registry. They didn't realize this about us when negotiations started, but as soon as it came out, it definitely upped the appeal of our offering. There could be aspects of distribution, technology assets, or your human resources that need to be made obvious to the buyer. Don't assume that they know everything about you. And don't assume that because you tell one person in the company, now everyone knows. Companies are large and diverse. More often than not, you might need to repeat these unseen benefits in several different meetings.

➔ *Create a virtual drive for every single major contract as soon as you start the business.* This one simple strategy makes it so much easier for you to sell the company when the time for information sharing arrives. You can simply say, "Here, you can have access to everything we've done." This kind of ongoing due diligence can be exhausting, but it will save you time during the negotiation, especially since you probably won't have as many people at your disposal as the potential buyer. When we were headed into negotiations to sell Hostopia to Deluxe, we had maybe three people devoted to the transaction—meanwhile, they had around a couple of dozen. The same happened at .CLUB. Having your documentation in order helps you and your team move much quicker through the process. It's absolutely *critical* to make the time from signing the letter of intent to the time to close as short as possible.

When timing is half the value, you want to have these items prepped in your tool belt to help keep things moving at a good pace so that they don't drag out and then die. You want to close as fast as you possibly can once you've got a good deal on the table because, as my own failures have shown, circumstances can change to derail the process. Remember the four key ingredients for the negotiation—build trust, gain goodwill, close fast, and don't allow the broker or lawyer to destroy the deal.

Always ask for more after the deal has been done.

I know that asking to increase the price *after* receiving a full-price offer might appear crazy. I was faced with this when my fellow board member, friend, and mentor Michael Cytrynbaum pushed for an extra fifty-five cents per share to close the Hostopia sale. Simply an extra $6.8 million when you do the math. I was so scared that this move would derail the deal.

But he made the case that we had a fiduciary requirement to maximize the value for shareholders. We were a publicly traded company, and we had to make certain that we maximized value on exit. It was actually a legal requirement!

So we reached out to RBC and asked them how much the buyer would have to increase the price upon sale that would get us out of the competitor bids. They came back at ten dollars and fifty-five cents per share. We went back to Deluxe and they agreed. So even when you agree to an offer, there might be an opportunity to go for a little bit more.

SYSTEMS

CHAPTER 49:

Sell Your Systems

WHILE PRESENTING TO A BOARDROOM of about fifteen people during the negotiations for Hostopia, I talked about all the systems we implemented. I discussed our core values, philosophy, strategic planning sessions, daily sales huddle, annual goals, and quarterly and weekly goals.

When I was finally done, the CEO of Deluxe at the time, Lee Schram, turned to his people, pointed his finger at the screen, and emphatically stated, "That's exactly the kind of culture we want to bring to this company!" There are not enough words to say how incredible I felt to hear that after all the work we'd put into our various systems. And remember, none of these had been implemented years earlier until I had brought in Patrick the coach.

If your company is running like a Swiss clock, that alone will increase its appeal and valuation to a buyer. No one wants to come in and have to do an immediate renovation. Your potential buyer is going to be imagining *their* ability to run the company postacquisition based not only on your product or even your people but also on the systems in place.

Systems don't change; people change.

In the previous story, Lee's comment wasn't about our quarterly reports or our revenue projections. These are important, obviously, but he was talking about the systems we had in place, which were generating both a healthy culture and a healthy bottom line. One of the greatest fears buyers have is that when something big changes with a company—like the ownership—then they won't be able to continue the growth rate.

Coupled with this fear is the concern that the success of the company is built around a specific person, which is why in Scale we discussed the importance of relying on *systems* to scale and building a strong leadership team. If we can put the right systems in place to help the company scale and also have the right checks and balances in place to *keep* the company scaling, it provides immense confidence for the buyer. Then they can approach you, ready to pay the premium you're asking for because you have those systems in place already, and they don't have to build a thing.

Lee understood this, and what he appreciated about Hostopia was that there were systems in place that would keep it a healthy company because the success wasn't dependent on one person or even a group of people. This both assuaged the common buying fears and increased the value of the company to them.

❝ The value is ultimately in how the company is run more than what you make or who your talent is. ❞

The book *The E-Myth Revisited*, by Michael E. Gerber espouses this same concept, emphasizing that a business runs on systems and people run those systems. "If your business depends on you, you don't own a business—you have a job," he writes. "And it's the worst job in the world because you're working for a lunatic."[20]

The value is ultimately in *how* the company is run more than *what* you make or *who* your talent is. Even if a deal falls through or you decide not to sell, this philosophy only serves to make the company better. ╱

Create confidence through proof.

Create confidence with your metrics. We touched on this one in the last chapter, but it's worth revisiting as a concept here. What systems do you have in place for tracking your KPIs? How are you documenting your return on ad spend? Customer churn rate? Lifetime value of a customer? In the process of exiting, these items can't be afterthoughts because the better the systems you have in place to track them, the higher the chance you have of selling the company for a greater value. When buyers are confident with the numbers, the deal is more likely to happen. The higher the confidence, the higher the value on exit.

When presenting pro forma projections to a potential buyer, you don't want to create false confidence by offering only aspirational targets. You build more confidence by showing budget-based targets *and* aspirational targets. This is what some people call goals and stretch goals. More critical than this is showing *how* you will get to those projections—what systems are in place that make hitting those numbers practical, not just hopeful.

In the process of selling .CLUB, one of my go-to proofs was to make the case that the company would continue to grow at a healthy pace based solely on distribution through registrars, even if

---

20   Michael Gerber, *The E-Myth Revisited: Why Most Small Businesses Don't Work and What to Do About It* (New York, NY: Harper Business, 2004).

we didn't increase any ad spending. On top of this, we used a real case study of how we raised prices twice in the past with no impact on churn rate.

In other words, we made a real business case with documentation of what was possible through our systems, not just pie-in-the-sky empty promises or adjectives: "Best this, best that, blah, blah, blah." Instead, we laid it out: "We had X customers, X churn, X lifetime value, X COA," simply sharing the facts and evidence. If you're not hitting your numbers because you went too aspirational with your estimations, it could destroy your credibility and derail the deal.

> **If a deal doesn't go through, either because you pull the plug or they do, you can still continue to hone your systems and scale as you await the next buyer.**

Remember, it can take a long time to close the transaction and make things official, so it's all right to be on the conservative side of your projections because you need to make certain that you hit your numbers during the first year of selling. If you go above those projections, it only makes it easier for you to get through to the end of the transaction. If you go below before the close, it can derail the deal.

Failing to Exit is a completely different story from failing to Start or failing to Scale. If a deal doesn't go through, either because you pull the plug or they do, you can still continue to hone your systems and scale as you await the next buyer. Remember, it can take a decade to build an "overnight" success, so when you reach this point, you don't want to rush it and make the same kind of mistakes we did with Internet Direct.

Instead, you want to pay attention to the details and make sure you don't do anything that will destroy all the hard work you've put into it. Sometimes that means walking away from a deal. And it absolutely requires putting the systems in place as early as possible to increase your success in both scaling and achieving the valuation you want when the right deal comes along.

Still, our conversation here isn't quite over yet. Now that you've made your first Exit … what's next?

START.
SCALE.
EXIT.
REPEAT.

Here is where we prove to the world—and, more importantly, to ourselves—that we have what it takes to be a serial entrepreneur.

We've all heard of the one-hit wonders, bands that release one great song and then, for whatever reason, can't seem to put two chords together to create another great song.

Think about the opposite. Those classic artists that have produced one great song after another: Louis Armstrong, the Beatles, U2, Adele, Bob Marley, Taylor Swift, Lady Gaga, Daddy Yankee, Coldplay, and my favorite, The Killers. They all have produced one hit after another, repeating their success time and again.

For entrepreneurs, a similar phenomenon exists. It's one thing to successfully Start, Scale, and then Exit. It's a whole other thing to Repeat it over again.

I have seen too many one-hit entrepreneurs in my time. Over the last twenty-five years, I have met and worked closely with dozens of entrepreneurs on their businesses and interviewed hundreds more. I have seen highly successful entrepreneurs sell their companies for millions and then spend years talking about different ideas but never actually pulling the trigger on one.

The specific reasons for this differ from one entrepreneur to the next, but there are a couple of common trends that I see.

First, I think that many have the lifestyle they've always wanted and decide that they just don't want to roll the dice one more time. Here the fear of going back to poverty or economic mediocrity outweighs their desire to make more money. The lightning struck once, so they just don't count on it striking again.

In other cases, it just may be too uncomfortable to reengage with a new venture that will inevitably lead to sleepless nights, relationship problems, loss of family time, health problems—do I need to go on?

It's that simple.

There is nothing wrong with either of these views. In fact, I have many friends who were multimillionaires who then lost it all. I am no exception, having once *almost* lost it all during the dot-com crash. So why in hell would you ever go through the same pain and potentially risk it all again?

I can't be certain what propels all serial entrepreneurs to keep rolling the dice one more time, but for me it's this: I truly believe that I have calculated all the odds and have the confidence of new success based on the systems and knowledge gained from prior successes. It's not naivete. It's the belief that if you can deliver on the four areas I've talked about throughout this book—Story, People, Money, Systems—then your chances of success are extremely high.

My prior experiences taught me that if I line up these four things—the right story, the right people, the right funding, and the right systems—and execute them correctly at each stage, from starting, to scaling, to exiting, it will dramatically increase my chances of success. When I do fail in one of my investments or ventures, I can usually see which of the four areas I missed out on—usually it's the people I put in charge who end up taking the startup down.

To go back to the very beginning of this book—it's not about luck, although we know luck plays a role like it did with Joe Foster and Jane Fonda. It's about following a formula. So once we have that formula and have successfully followed it, how can we then Repeat it? How can we use both the wins and the failures of our past adventures in entrepreneurship to begin the next one?

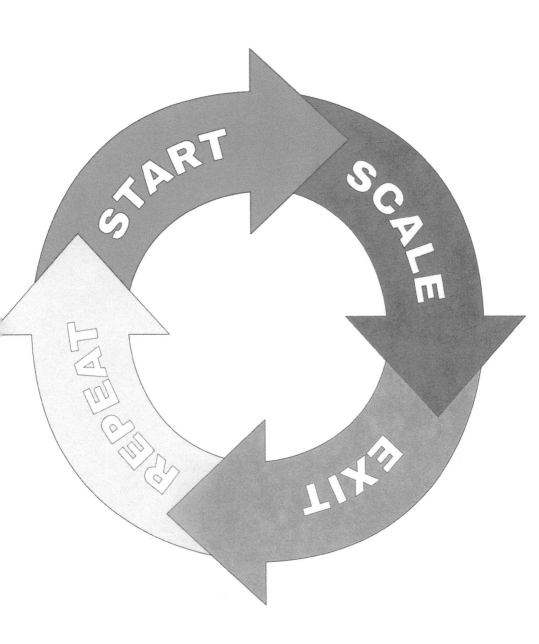

If you can deliver on the four areas I've talked about throughout this book—Story, People, Money, Systems—then your chances of success are extremely high.

STORY

CHAPTER 50

What Propels a Serial Entrepreneur

I ORIGINALLY WROTE this portion of the book in 2012 prior to the launch of .CLUB. Looking back at it now, it truly captures my thoughts and emotions prior to even knowing the outcome:

> I am fond of the great director Alfred Hitchcock who produced the movie *Psycho* … Alfred Hitchcock risked his wealth to the point of bankruptcy to fund his latest project. One scene captures him cleaning the pool because he had to lay off his domestic staff to fund the movie … not what you would suspect after a storied career. No studios wanted to support it, but he had a vision, and he put it all on the line one last time. History proved him right, and he walked away extremely wealthy from this venture.

> .CLUB is a highly scalable concept.

> I do like businesses with unlimited inventory. Which is probably why .CLUB is one of my favorite business ideas.

Our only limiting factor is the ability of the team and myself to execute. Success depends solely on our efforts. Will there be external forces? Yes, but we will guide the ship through the storms, including hundreds of new domain extensions launching, a regulator who has tied one hand behind our back, and an incumbent elephant bent on keeping us from succeeding (.com). Sound familiar?

Success depends solely on our efforts.

We have the confidence to step forward because we have all four of the pieces in place (Story, People, Money, Systems). I believe these efforts will result in success and help change the world in one small way by giving startups and clubs more options to brand their organizations.

And truthfully I find the whole experience absolutely exhilarating.

It's funny to look at the text written the day before .CLUB launched. After writing this, the company started, then scaled, and then ultimately exited almost ten years later. I believe it's additional proof that the theories we've been working on here are real and effective and stand the test of time.

CHAPTER 61

Ideas Are Everywhere Again

SO WHILE IT MAY be obvious that ideas are still everywhere, the question is more about how to get ideas for new companies. How do you know which ideas are the right ones to pursue versus a pipe dream?

It's a lot easier to see opportunity in your present company than to do it after you've sold your company.

First, you need to be thinking about your next company while at your *current* company that you intend to exit over the next few years. In Exit, I mentioned how sometimes it can be worth sticking around at a company as part of the acquisition deal, especially if you don't have a new idea yet. While it can be hard to give up control, it does at least provide you the chance to be on the lookout for new opportunities.

While running our software rental business Megachoice Software back in 1992, we launched ComputerLink, the free BBS service we had specifically made for our customers. ComputerLink outgrew Megachoice, which was good for us when software rental was outlawed through NAFTA, as I mentioned earlier in the book.

By the time we closed down Megachoice, we had a base of users for ComputerLink, leading us to become the largest social BBS in Canada. But it was through our experiences at ComputerLink that we found out about this thing called an internet browser, which led us to launch Internet Direct. As you might recall, we just didn't have the money to run both ComputerLink and Internet Direct—and we had a lot more demand and love for the latter.

Within Internet Direct, we launched Tucows and also the idea for Hostopia was hatched—incidentally, all three companies eventually went public.

At Hostopia, we launched the global IT company GeeksForLess, which today has over eight hundred people. Originally, their development center was set up to support our needs at Hostopia, but now they serve businesses across the globe. After selling Hostopia, I remained as CEO, and during that time, I was able to analyze and figure out which opportunities I wanted to pursue next. In particular, I studied new domain extension alternatives to .com, .net, and .org, and I had my eyes set on one called .club.

And lastly, before selling .CLUB to GoDaddy, we found an opportunity to promote .club domains in Clubhouse, which led us to acquire the domain Startup.club and running the largest club on Clubhouse with over one million members. Not to mention there were several other smaller companies started, spun off, and sold as a result of these companies.

Are you seeing the picture? One idea led to the next, which led to the next, which led to the next. By being *inside* these companies, it gave us knowledge and leverage to launch our next company, increasing our chances of success and *accelerating* our time frame from Start to Exit. The partnerships, distribution channels, and relationships built in each company could help accelerate the growth of the next. I was an *employee* when I conceived the idea of .CLUB, so you don't even have to own a company to see opportunities. You just need to be in the industry you love.

As I mentioned in Exit, the idea of selling yourself off in an acquisition can be a great entrepreneurial strategy if you don't have your next play lined up yet. It's better to stay engaged in the industry and to figure out either what other bottlenecks exist there and/or where the next wave is coming from. And the cool thing is that you can be collecting a salary while trying to determine the next big idea!

> If you fail to lay out plans for your new venture while at your prior company, you could be caught without a concept or an idea.

If you fail to lay out plans for your new venture while at your prior company, you could be caught without a concept or an idea. The longer it takes to come up with a new idea after selling your company, the harder it becomes—especially if you've been out of the loop for a couple of years.

Meanwhile, opportunities are everywhere when you're in the thick of it. So even if you plan on selling your business, you should work to identify some other opportunities that exist within your industry.

However, I will caution that selling yourself off can be a miserable experience. I have sold myself off twice in my life, and both experiences were a horrible exercise in perseverance for me. I've yet to meet an entrepreneur who works for a company they sold off who loves their job. I should also add that it can slow the process of launching new startups because of your time commitments to your employer. If you're stuck and miserable, it's time to launch that startup *outside* of your work hours—time for some entrepreneurial moonlighting.

Recently, I registered a number of .club, .shop, and .com domains with the thoughts of one day launching new companies around them. I find that this helps me visualize and solidify my business ideas, making them more real, like we discussed in taking action on your ideas (chapter 2). Most entrepreneurs I know have registered dozens, if not hundreds, of domain names.

The price of good domain names has increased dramatically over the past twenty-five years. Paw.com was registered for seventy dollars in the nineties, and we bought it for a heck of a lot more zeros. Over time the supply of great brand-able names will deplete, so grabbing names early on has proven to be well worth it for entrepreneurs. In fact, grabbing names has become part of the process for me, and I get a bit of a kick out of it. Yup, I am also a serial domain buyer. Probably another serial entrepreneur addiction.

Don't chase the latest trend or fad at the expense of your core business.

Still, acting on launching a new company while at an existing one has both major pros and cons that you must think through. Timing is critical to success, and you need to strictly follow one key philosophy that I see many serial entrepreneurs break: don't chase the latest trend or fad at the expense of your core business.

When launching new companies, always take care of your core company first.

What do I mean by taking care of your core business first? I have seen too many ADHD serial entrepreneurs launch way too many projects at once in what I refer to as the machine-gun approach. And you know what? It doesn't work.

I have seen serial entrepreneurs who have a great company then go and mess up their core company because they divert too much funding, talent, and time to new ventures.

However, when a company reaches a certain stage, there are signs that you may be ready to think about launching another venture. The first sign may be boredom, but be careful with this one. Sometimes boredom is just a signal that you're not challenging the status quo enough to achieve your next breakthrough within that company.

Then there's the kind of boredom resulting from successfully delegating roles and responsibilities to the point where you aren't as necessary to the company's success anymore. You've put the right leaders and systems in place that allow the company to scale without your full and undivided attention—that's not a bad place to be! But it does mean that your plate is emptier than you're used to, and you start to get fidgety.

Assuming that you have your core business performing well, now it is time to *act* on new ideas before that boredom becomes complacency. Since ideas are still everywhere, the point is to position yourself in a way that you can see those ideas and investigate the ones that have the greatest chance of success through scaling.

With your new ideas, think scalability, defensibility, and catching that next wave.

This goes back to the concepts we introduced way back in Start—you should choose ideas that can scale, that you can build a moat around, and, whenever possible, where you can ride the next wave.

For example, what made .CLUB so scalable was that it had unlimited inventory. You punch in a credit card on GoDaddy and buy a name. The company also had a ready-made moat in that not even Google or Amazon could directly compete with us. Google and Amazon had registered alternate names, but if you wanted a .club name, we were your only option.

Lastly, the business came about based on a regulatory change opening up new domain extensions. By paying attention to the industry, we were able to embrace the change and catch the wave at the right time. While it took us a little longer to ride the wave to shore than we initially thought, we still got there.

Whatever you do, do it really well—or don't do it at all.

Be honest with yourself here. Are you in a position to give this new idea *everything* you've got to make it successful? Are you ready to devote every waking hour to it? Are you ready for the stress of the startup roller coaster again? Are you willing and able to ask your family and friends to stand with you through it again?

I have a theory as to why we always hear about twentysomethings launching successful tech companies. First, they live closer to the trends and new technology waves or paradigm shifts than my generation. I was watching a movie with my son and saw that he was making faces every couple of minutes and sending them to his girlfriend via Snapchat. To me it seemed so vain, but for his generation, this relationship with technology is completely normal. Today, well over half of kids are using Roblox—and it's going to be one of those kids who really launches the metaverse.

Second, younger entrepreneurs have unlimited time with few distractions: no spouses or kids to take away their attention from their idea. The opportunity for this kind of intense focus can really pay off.

Every new company (especially tech) requires extreme intensity and focus during the launch and early scaling. Even if you are not a twentysomething, this intensity can be replicated for short periods of time. But let's face it, for those out there with family, it's going to require sacrificing time with them—and asking *them* to make sacrifices too. Are you prepared to ask this of them?

If you're not willing or able to do so, there is nothing wrong with that. Only you can decide this for yourself. Whatever decision you make, you'll be the one who has to live with it.

On that note, having support really makes all the difference in whether you can successfully Repeat. Which is why beyond the support of friends and family, you will still need to have the right People working alongside you or even to partner with.

PEOPLE

CHAPTER 52

Track Your A Players

I HAVE STARTED COMPANIES with myself at the helm and *without* myself at the helm. Despite what you might think about startups, starting and launching them can be such a slow process. The truth is, I generally find the first year of a new business very slow and boring, so I usually like to get others to do the heavy lifting in the early stages. Spinning Jim Collins's flywheel is just so tough at the beginning and so slow. Scaling companies with a defined formula is where I get the most enjoyment.

In the same way that we had to check our ego at the door in Scale and remember that it's not all about us in Exit, the same is true in Repeat. Regardless of how involved you are at the start of your new venture, you're going to need People.

Back in Start, we talked about the importance of finding those DIY individuals, but by the time you reach Repeat, this should be simpler because now you should have a roster of all-stars to draw from. It's not your first rodeo, so why not make those people your A players?

Track your A players from company to company.

Remember Howard Bell? I mentioned him when discussing the disaster story of Internet Direct and how he personally lost the equivalent of $1 million when everything crumbled. This particularly hurt me because he is definitely one of my all-stars.

Howard is extremely loyal, humble, hardworking, and knowledgeable in many different areas—a real Renaissance man, if you will. We first hired him in 1993 to work for our software rental business for a year or two. Then when Megachoice was shut down, he worked for us at ComputerLink. After we closed ComputerLink, we brought him along for Internet Direct, running the call center until 1999 when we sold the company.

Then he left us for a couple of years, but when Hostopia was ramping up, we had a huge need for someone to run the call center. Who did I call? Howard!

After selling Hostopia, he pursued other ventures for a few years. But when .CLUB was getting up and going, and I needed someone who could help me run operations—you can probably guess where this is going—I called Howard! And as much as this is starting to sound like a broken record, when I needed someone for the Paw.com call center, I called him up yet again.

And don't just think about your employees. We hired a consultant named Jamie Grant in 1996 to help us with our graphics. He ran his own graphics firm, and although he is pretty much a one-man show, he was not exclusive to any of the companies. He continues to work for us today at Escape Club and has worked on pretty much every company in which I have been a major shareholder for over the last twenty-five years. When we find good talent, suppliers, or consultants, we can be a little bit more liberal in our pursuit of them venture after venture, as they are not as tethered to the prior companies like an employee typically is.

I'm not saying that there's not a time to bring in fresh blood to your new ventures, especially if you need someone with a specific skill or complementary profile. But I'm not going to lose track of my A players who I know will bring their A game to the new company. I'm going to keep track of them via LinkedIn and social events, get together for catch-up lunches every so often, and make sure I maintain a real relationship with them.

People are so key to your company's success that it's just common sense that you increase your chances of repeating when you can reengage the strengths of the people who helped you succeed in the

> **People are so key to your company's success that it's just common sense that you increase your chances of repeating when you can reengage the strengths of the people who helped you succeed in the past.**

past. This is also why it's so important to treat people well, recognize greatness, share the wealth, and delegate well—you want to always give people a reason to say yes when you have a new opportunity for them that can benefit you both.

Instead of delegating responsibilities, consider delegating companies.

We entrepreneurs like to be hands-on, but sometimes the best way you can Repeat success with your new venture is to identify the people who can run something *for* you. The great thing about finding those DIY-ers back in Start is that they're generally people with an entrepreneurial spirit. If they have never been entrepreneurs before, now may be the time you help them become one.

Let's say that you have another company you're still running but that you want to embark on a new venture. There's a time and a place for that, but as I said in the last chapter, you need to make sure your core company is taken care of first.

You have some options for doing this well. Either you find an entrepreneur who can help you run that core company so that you're freed up to focus on the new venture, or, vice versa, you remain with the core company and identify another entrepreneur you can partner with to take the lead on the new venture.

With .CLUB, I decided to run it myself until a couple of years before the exit. But with most of the companies I have partnered with—including Sharkfin, GeeksForLess, Startup Club, Escape Club, Hip Optical, US SDS, Paw.com, and Tucows—I either partnered with a leader or hired an A player with an entrepreneurial mindset and let them run with it. Partnering with entrepreneurs can accelerate your Repeat strategy.

Consider partnering with other entrepreneurs.

I was at dinner a few years back with several successful serial entrepreneurs, including one of my mentors, Lance Tracey. I asked the group a question: "What is the hardest part of launching a new company— putting up the money, getting the person to run it, setting up the systems, or coming up with the story?"

The answer almost unanimously was getting the right person to run it. Believe it or not, the rarest commodity of the four is getting the right person, which bodes well for young entrepreneurs who don't have the money to launch a venture. If they have the desire, they can partner with successful serial entrepreneurs or investors from the get-go.

How have I succeeded at partnering? First, I have identified employees who have entrepreneurial mindsets, and after successfully launching my prior company, I work with these individuals to spawn new ventures. I no longer consider them employees at this point. In fact, today many of them are my dear friends and business partners who have created substantial wealth for themselves and for my family.

You can find entrepreneurs to partner with you if you are on the lookout for them throughout all stages of your company. If you have a great idea, the right leverage, the right money, and the right systems, you can *hire out* the entrepreneur. Previously I said that you can't replace the entrepreneur, but keep in mind that we're at a different stage in Repeat. This isn't your first venture, and if you find a way to hire out the entrepreneur, this allows you to work on the next company.

This also points back to the importance of profiling your people: Who has the specific set of skills to take over the core company or to lead the new venture? Constantly profiling to find the gems within a company has been my key to success with the next company. I look for those employees who have dominant instincts. Find the right leaders, and eventually they could become your future partners for new ventures.

Find the right leaders, and eventually they could become your future partners for new ventures.

I want to state a caveat here about the ethics of rehiring or partnering with your A players. I do not hire or partner with employees from the companies I have sold unless they have already left that company on their own. For example, Howard had left every one of the companies that I sold off before I rehired him. Most entrepreneurial-minded individuals will move on from the sold company anyway, but it still needs to be mentioned as a part of good entrepreneurial ethics.

Not to mention that poaching like this would impact my reputation. No matter how desirable it might be to bring the old team back together again, there have to be limits. Integrity over money.

This goes back to why I track them on LinkedIn, though. As soon as they switch to another company, LinkedIn informs me. Now they're fair game for me to hunt and track down if I want to. The success rate of starting a new corporate job can be pretty low, so when they're offered the chance to do something that includes more freedom and ownership with a lot of upside, they are often enticed to come over to our team. Not to speak for him, but I'm confident that's why Howard has continued to come back to work for me at six different companies over the past twenty-five years.

MONEY

CHAPTER 53

Dress for Success

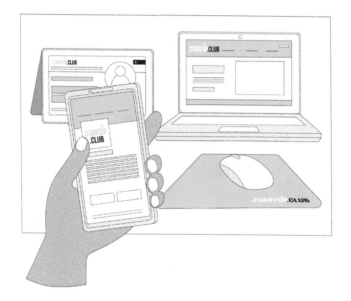

WE HAVE ALL HEARD the phrase dress for success. Well, it could not apply better than when you need to raise money for your next venture. For those who don't know me, I don't mean a literal dress code for success. I can usually be found sporting a logoed black polo and jeans as my wardrobe mainstays, whether I'm taking my dogs for a walk or presenting to a board.

> **Dressing for success isn't about outward appearances—it's all about reputation.**

Dressing for success isn't about outward appearances—it's all about reputation. As a serial entrepreneur, my reputation is my greatest asset, especially when it comes to funding my next venture. And frankly, I think it's the same for everyone else.

Reputation is your greatest asset.

Nothing is more important for raising money than your reputation. Your ability to point to prior successes is crucial. Even one misstep can almost spell the end for your new venture. I don't know too many investors who have invested in an entrepreneur, lost money, and then wanted to go for another round. Would you invest in another company from the FTX founder Sam Bankman-Fried?

The key here is to not misfire. And the best way to ensure that you don't is to have Story, People, Money, and Systems all in place.

Remember when I raised $7 million within thirty days from less than fifty contacts on LinkedIn with no broker involved? This had less to do with my presentation skills and more to do with my reputation. Of course, I lined up everything correctly in terms of a business plan and memorandum for them to review (more on that in a minute), but none of these people would have invested without believing in me as the result of my reputation.

If you're not 'dressed' with a good reputation, you could end up a one-hit wonder.

You can have the most expensive outfit and the snazziest hairdo out there. You can use all the buzzwords and fancy presentations. But if you're not "dressed" with a good reputation, you could end up a one-hit wonder.

Dress yourself for success online.

I'd be foolish to suggest that all of my success in fundraising has been based on my reputation from the past. There are external components as well, which is exactly why you have to be thinking about your online presence too.

On the internet today, everyone is on show all the time. Everything you tweet or post, your LinkedIn bio, every recorded speech you make on Clubhouse, or even a dedicated website about you all represent who you are on the internet. So leverage it!

There are several things you should consider. My personal favorite is LinkedIn. Don't be afraid to ask your contacts for a reference when building out your profile. When I left Hostopia, I sent a request to my contacts to get references from employees, suppliers, customers, and even friends and family. As a result, I received over fifty positive reviews, and I also reciprocated with a positive review for each of these individuals.

I told you before that I'm not afraid of self-promotion, so here's a shameless plug to make the point: If you've really liked what you've read in this book and have adopted at least one idea, I'd be forever in your debt if you submitted an Amazon review for the book. Or if you are so inclined, check out our podcast *Serial Entrepreneur: Secrets Revealed!* and leave us a review there.

Second, set up a Twitter account and become a leading voice in your industry. I was slow to get on the Twitter bandwagon, but as .CLUB approached launch, I began to realize the value in it. I had fewer than fifty Twitter followers, but they were mostly industry media, so when I tweeted something, it was then retweeted to thousands of other people. Today I have thousands of followers, as I'm constantly sharing more entrepreneurial ideas through the profiles @colindotclub or @startupclub_hq.

Next, consider a listing on Wikipedia. Granted, this can be challenging given the high notability requirements for the site, but it's not impossible, especially if you've done the work to have prior press releases that can be used as supporting references to back up your legitimacy. With that kind of credibility, it becomes much easier to raise money.

Fifty percent of business is show business.

Oscar DiVeroli, a fellow serial entrepreneur and friend, taught me the benefit of the mantra that 50 percent of business is show business. When I had to raise $7 million in thirty days via LinkedIn, this show business piece is exactly what I had to do. Why?

The startup had absolutely no revenue, virtually no employees, and was simply an idea with some positioning. One technique I used to dress up the company was to put together the private placement memorandum and filed a Reg D with the SEC.

Yes, everyone who invested for the most part knew who I was and what I was capable of—this is where reputation helps. But when it comes to parting with their money, they have to truly believe in the strength of the idea like any good investor. Having these tangibles available was a way to help them visualize the business.

Think about it from their position: When you see a document that looks like an S1 prospectus (IPO filing document) with all the risk factors laid out, detailed budgets, and a clearly defined path to success, you tend to lend the idea a lot more credibility. Beyond this, it also creates transparency by setting clear deadlines for Stage Gates, giving potential investors the information they need to decide whether they are in or out.

Dressing for success in these ways requires a lot of work and intentionality. It's easy to get so wrapped up in the day-to-day of building and scaling your company that you forget to do this. But you really have no reason not to. Even if you never start that second—or third, or fourth—company, dressing for success in these ways will also help you in your current company during your next round of fundraising or at the negotiating table for a successful Exit.

CHAPTER 54

Using Other People's Money to Scale

SINCE WE COVERED lots of elements of raising funds in previous sections, we're not going to rehash it all here. The same formulas and principles apply in Repeat, so instead this chapter will focus on the nuances of how using other people's money may look a bit different in Repeat than in Start or Scale.

Maybe I'm beginning to sound like a broken record, but once again reputation is everything here. Even with every system in place, early ventures can still fail. Remember Shareholder Blockchain back in chapter 7? We had great Systems in place—but not the right People—and had to shut it down.

That's why I tend to make the initial funding myself until the company has proven its concepts and is in a position to scale via other people's money. That way, I take the greatest risk first. You might recall my mom test discussed earlier in Scale. My mother has successfully (and fortunately) invested in several of my companies during the scaling phase, earning quite a handsome profit for herself—but it's only after I have proof that the venture is in a position of a high chance of success do I allow my mother to invest. It's also when I bring in other people's money.

Time for other people's money.

Consider OPM—that is, other people's money. You might be wondering at this point, "But, Colin, if I've already had a successful Exit and have the cash in my pocket, and the new concept is already showing proof, then why not just stay one hundred percent self-funded? Why do this work to go through the painful process of fund-raising all over again? If I'm confident of success, why not be the only investor so that I can keep all the profits?"

Using other people's money—along with yours—reduces the risk for everyone by increasing the oxygen in the tank and giving you time to hit your Stage Gates.

Confidence is the key to success, yes, but even with confidence, I still don't recommend gambling everything on your new venture. Simply put, using other people's money—along with yours—reduces the risk for everyone by increasing the oxygen in the tank and giving you time to hit your Stage Gates.

Remember, change is always around the corner, and you can't control everything that will impact your business. I've known too many entre-preneurs who have lost everything because they had all of their wealth invested in their own company. The other benefit is that you can create a network of investors and informal advisors who work for free. You never know which investor will help you find that next distributor or even lead you to your big break.

Take some chips off the table.

Let's be honest—there's always a bit of a gamble in any venture, no matter how surefire it appears to be. So in gambling terms, you need to take some chips off the table every so often to keep yourself and your loved ones secure.

In other words, take a portion of your wealth from your prior exit and invest it in very conservative instruments where it can earn interest. The first thing I did after my second big exit was to max out my kids' 529 college savings funds. There is a satisfaction knowing that no matter what happens at this stage, even if every business crashes and burns overnight, my kids will have a debt-free education. Likewise, consider setting money aside for your personal home, second home, and/or stocks and bonds. The point is not to put all your eggs in one basket.

In February 2022, Russia invaded Ukraine, setting off a war that brought the front lines within a stone's throw of our main office for GeeksForLess. Thankfully, I had sold some of my stock in the company as a move to take some chips off the table. A couple of my business partners, however, had most of their wealth invested in the company and saw it take a significant hit.

And of course there was the emotional toll of trying to help our employees who were now stuck in a town under siege. We worked to move as many as we could out of harm's way and keep them safe. It truly hurts to watch them suffer throughout this period of uncertainty.

Thankfully, as of the writing of this book, the Ukrainians seem to have repelled the Russians, and our office stands free.

This alone is reason enough to use other people's money when scaling up your next venture. Things will never go perfectly according to plan, so why risk losing everything you just worked for?

Conflicts of interest must be fully disclosed.

Remember, you need to focus on your core business first. I invested eight years on Internet Direct before launching Tucows and Hostopia. I invested another ten years on Hostopia and .CLUB. Never take your eye off the core and give it time to win in the marketplace before launching the next concept. If ideation distracts you from your core business, then don't even think about it. If, however, your core is strong and performing well, I believe that ideation forms the seeds for your later ventures.

On that note, there are times when your core business could end up becoming the funding source for your next venture. Remember when I shared about starting up GeeksForLess and that Hostopia became its first customer? Let's unpack that conflict of interest a bit so that you can see how it played out.

When I launch a new company, it will either have ownership by existing shareholders or no resources except my own personal time that I'm committing to the new entity. In the case of GeeksForLess, I helped fund and find customers for the company, but I was not the CEO. Instead, I partnered with Igor Nikolaichuk over twenty years ago, and he still runs it today.

Whether the first company is public or has a governing board, it needs to be declared by the board if the two companies—old and new—plan to do business together.

When we decided to build GeeksForLess while at Hostopia, we brought the concept to the board, who decided that it wasn't in Hostopia's best interests to outright own an offshore IT company. However, they did vote to allow my partners and me, the majority shareholders, to invest under one condition: the independent board members were to negotiate the contract directly given the conflict of interest.

Likewise, when you're launching a new venture, it's important to disclose all of your potential conflicts of interest to the shareholders on both sides. This can be done in the MD&A portion of your financial statements, in a memo, or in any offering documents.

Think of the reverse strategy for a minute here—and why the board made the decision not to directly invest in the IT firm. Hostopia was a North American publicly traded SaaS platform company. If we decided to use the resources to launch an IT firm, this would have increased the risk for any company looking to invest in or even buy Hostopia. Even though both were broadly in the tech space, the specific concepts were too disparate.

However, if I were to acquire *another* hosting company, this would create an inherent conflict of interest that could not be easily resolved, especially because Hostopia *was* in the market to acquire other hosting companies.

Still, setting up GeeksForLess offshore is one of the key reasons why Hostopia succeeded. It gave Hostopia a real competitive advantage, as the company was now able to hire a trusted source for labor at a fraction of the rate of our competitors, giving us a cost reduction advantage over those companies that relied solely on North American programmers.

GeeksForLess in turn was born from this contract, which allowed the company to break even instantly with Hostopia as a robust customer rather than experience long years of losses. The investment to start was in the millions, as we had to build reliable infrastructure and acquire a substantial piece of real estate to operate it at Western standards. Signing a customer like Hostopia also gave GeeksForLess legitimacy in the eyes of other customers.

It didn't matter that both were controlled by the same shareholders on either side. In fact, by being a customer of our own development center, we had a full understanding of outsourcing challenges, which gave us the experience and know-how to help other companies outsource successfully.

Scarcity can strengthen your offering.

One side note to this is that filing with the SEC also supports the perception among the investors that this train is leaving the station, so jump on board! Creating this perception with a clear deadline is the key.

I once sent out a morning email about a raise five days before the deadline, stating that we were almost 90 percent sold out. By 6:00 p.m., not only did we sell out of the shares but also the demand wouldn't relent for some days to follow, as those who were too late kept reaching out, hoping to get in.

In prior raises, I put myself on the line by investing in a portion of the offering. In addition, I agreed to take zero salary until the company started to generate revenues and earnings. The shareholder agreement disclosed my salary, but I said I would defer it for a period of time to allow the company to gain traction. This is another advantage of taking some chips off the table—you can afford to do this when needed.

Not taking a salary does two things. It reduces your personal out-of-pocket expenses to Uncle Sam, and it sends a very strong signal to your investors. Don't get me wrong—it's not a charity. When the companies start to perform, I begin taking a salary. But the last thing I wanted to do was take a salary and have to pay taxes on it while the company was losing money.

I am well aware that taking no salary is likely not an option for first-time entrepreneurs, but for serial entrepreneurs who have the money, it can be a powerful tool to encourage OPM to come to the table. Where entrepreneurs make the money is on the lift in valuation when raising money, which is also smart from a tax perspective, as that income will be taxed as capital gains down the road when the company ultimately sells. Focus on the lift in value versus salary.

Focus on the lift in value versus salary.

SYSTEMS

Use Copy and Paste Systems

RICHARD POLLACK, WHO RUNS Direct Colors, which I mentioned in Start, has several other companies and is one of my partners at Paw. com. He acquires smaller businesses, applies his skills and systems to scale the companies to the next level, and then sells them off for a nice profit.

Beyond that, his area of expertise is in digital marketing. With his knowledge, he helps other companies ramp up quickly through his digital marketing systems. It's a win-win for everyone because these companies also become his customers for his marketing company, but they get the benefit of copying and pasting his systems to accelerate their own growth. If you have a particular expertise or assets that you can use to help your own companies grow, how can that expertise or asset support your ability to manage and launch multiple companies?

If you've built your first company, funded it, scaled it, and sold it, it's now time to take all of those learnings, build systems around them, and then use those to launch more successful ventures. You can learn both from what worked and from what didn't work, but your systems are what can help you scale as a serial entrepreneur and avoid being a one-hit wonder.

> **Your systems are what can help you scale as a serial entrepreneur and avoid being a one-hit wonder.**

Today, I have nine companies in which I'm a principal shareholder and another six or so that I've invested in and actively work with. In those companies, we deploy strategic planning, goal setting, coaching, profiling, hiring practices, sales playbooks, and other systems that we have learned in the past. Basically, everything we talked about in this book. Once you achieve a level of knowledge and expertise, you can begin to apply that knowledge to others so that they can also find success through your systems.

CHAPTER 56

Make a Difference

ONE OF MY PERSONAL VALUES is to make a difference. It's the reason I set up a 501(c) Help for Ukraine Club to help the population of Mykolaiv, Ukraine, by funding education for the children of fallen soldiers, some of whom were our employees at the time Russia invaded the country.

Sometimes entrepreneurs gain a negative reputation as being selfish because of a few bad eggs who make headlines. As serial entrepreneurs, though, we have a unique opportunity to use our influence and resources to make a difference in the world—through our companies and also as leading voices for causes we care about.

For me, making a difference means sharing with others everything I have learned about entrepreneurship. It's the whole reason behind this book and the live show and podcast *Serial Entrepreneur: Secrets Revealed!*, not to mention the driving force behind Startup Club, which is over one million members strong.

Give to get.

As a member of EO (Entrepreneurs' Organization) for over twenty-five years, I have been absorbed into a culture of success helping other entrepreneurs succeed with no expectation of reciprocation. Others have done the same, which is part of what I love about the EO culture. It's a circle of trust, energy, and support.

Joining an entrepreneur organization of your peers will not only help you run your company better but also help you become a successful serial entrepreneur so that you can Start, Scale, Exit, and Repeat over and over again. Hoarding information and only receiving isn't just selfish; it ends up being unprofitable. Being part of a community, serving one another, and sharing success multiplies success for all.

Being part of a community, serving one another, and sharing success multiplies success for all.

No one finds success alone. In the ups and downs of the entrepreneurship roller coaster, you need others around you who will understand. Times will come when you offer help to others—and times will come when you need to receive help.

The Toll of Entrepreneurial Life

WE SET OUT on this journey to crack the code of what it takes to Start, Scale, Exit, Repeat, and I believe we have uncovered a number of those key actions that serial entrepreneurs do to be successful. What we haven't talked about is something most startup books never take the time to address: the toll of entrepreneurial life.

We tend to be so company-focused that we don't talk about the physical and mental rigors faced by the entrepreneur as an individual or the impact on relationships that the startup founder endures.

Earlier I complimented Zappos for putting together one of the best cultures of any company in recent memory. Like everyone, I was saddened to hear when Zappos founder, Tony Hsieh, died in a fire—either intentionally or unintentionally. As of the writing of this book, the situation is still under investigation, but it's been suggested by some sources that drug use could have played a part.

With leaders of successful startups, we often see a steady, confident, controlled person. They always seem to have it together. They have a lot of wealth, friends, and even a lucky few have beautiful families. But the fact is, they are human. Underneath the tough exterior and behind closed doors, there is a real person who has issues like everyone else.

Michael A. Freeman, MD, is a psychiatrist and executive coach who founded Econa around this idea of entrepreneurial mental health. In his article "Are Entrepreneurs 'Touched with Fire,'" he reports some of his findings:

Self-reported mental health concerns were present across 72% of the entrepreneurs in this sample, a proportion that was significantly higher than that of the comparison group … 49% reported having one or more lifetime mental health conditions, 32% reported having two or more lifetime mental health conditions, 18% reported having three or more lifetime mental health conditions, and 23% reported being asymptomatic members of highly symptomatic families. The entrepreneurs were significantly more likely to report a lifetime history of depression (30%), ADHD (29%), substance use conditions (12%) and bipolar diagnosis (11%) than were comparison participants.[21]

21   Michael A. Freeman, Sheri L. Johnson, Paige J. Staudenmaier, and Mackenzie R. Zisser, "Are Entrepreneurs 'Touched with Fire'?," Econa, April 17, 2015, https://econa.net/wp-content/uploads/2020/08/Are-Entrepreneurs-Touched-with-Fire.pdf.

Find a community of support.

Entrepreneurs, including myself, live on the edge. We have extreme personalities, and we constantly need to get the next fix—the high that comes from closing a deal, launching a new product, registering a domain name, or making that next million. Like any addiction, it can be a dangerous way to live, and it not only impacts us but also all **Entrepreneurship is a drug.** those around us. A very good friend of mine, Goran Dragoslavic, came to this country forty years ago with nothing and, over time, acquired a real estate portfolio of over one thousand rental units in Fort Lauderdale. He recently admitted to me that he cannot stop—he loves the thrill of the buy. Most serial entrepreneurs are no different, including myself. Entrepreneurship is a drug.

We also need to find ways to cope with the roller-coaster ride—the ups and downs, the failures and the successes.

The first thing I will say is that you're not alone—although sometimes it feels like it. And I understand that you can't always have talks with your friends or family about what you're going through because maybe they just don't get it. But you *can* connect with others in a deep and meaningful way.

EO was founded in 1987 by Verne Harnish and twenty-two other entrepreneurs to help entrepreneurs find a way to tackle the isolation most of us feel. They believed there was a great need to open communications among one another, and today the organization has over seventeen thousand members worldwide. They also have an accelerator program, though their qualifications make it less accessible than other accelerator groups you may find.

Every month, I meet with seven other individuals and share my personal, family, and business issues in a safe and nonjudgmental group. My EO group has seen and helped me every step of the way throughout all of my startups since I joined in 1996—from every new business plan, to improving my pitch the day before my IPO, to helping me exit a number of companies. Beyond these business efforts, my forum has done more to support me as a human being.

In 2017, my forum confronted me about my life. See, at that time I was very successful, but I was a workaholic. My entire identity was based on my companies, and I was ignoring other areas of my life. Thankfully, my family stuck through the challenges and continued to support me, but I had let my health deteriorate, traveled way too much, drank a little too much wine to numb the stress, and continued to work day and night on my businesses.

Even if you're in startup mode, it's worthwhile to connect yourself with some type of a community. We've talked about the idea of joining an incubator multiple times, but the more we are connected, the more we can get help—and not just on business matters. We run a weekly show on Startup Club via Clubhouse called *The Complete Entrepreneur*, hosted by Michael Gilmour, which you can listen to on Startup.club or even join us live and participate in the session. It's a great place to vent, receive encouragement, and learn from others facing similar challenges.

Find routines that help you shift out of work mode.

Next, I think it's important to understand that the way we are at work isn't the way we should be at home. Easier said than done,

I know, especially when certain stages of your company's life cycle can dominate your time. I have been told on a number of occasions that sometimes when I get home, I speak to my family like they're employees, issuing orders in a staccato fashion.

Understanding that we should operate differently at work than at home is an important first step. The next step is to find a routine that gives you the space to switch from work mode to home mode. This can be a particular challenge for those who already work from home.

For me, settling back in the hot tub puts me in a very different mindset and calms me down. For you, it may be a change of clothes, putting on a different a pair of shoes, listening to music, going to work out, taking a shower, or some other routine. Whatever it is for you, it's important to find ways to make that mental shift so that your friends, family, and other loved ones don't have to perpetually live with the "work" you.

Delegate responsibilities, not tasks.

Delegate responsibilities, not tasks. I know I'm repeating this one from previous points, but that should tell you how important this really is. When you can effectively delegate responsibilities—or even companies—instead of just tasks, it makes a huge difference in the amount of mental energy you spend on different areas of your life. And I'm not referring just to the time you spend thinking about the problem but also the hours of thought that go through your mind on issues *outside* of work, night and day.

By giving up responsibilities for major areas of the company, the company itself, or even responsibilities in your personal life, you are no longer the primary person trying to solve *all* the challenges. And you can reallocate your personal skills and talents to areas where you know that you can make more of a direct impact. Is there something you don't absolutely love doing? Then it's time to delegate that area to someone who will.

Fire negativity and hire positivity.

Lastly, let go of your failures, stop reliving the past, and learn to celebrate your successes. Remove the negative people around you who drain you of your energy. Learn to say no, fire your worst customers, and, most importantly, enjoy yourself. In an interview at a conference, I asked Joe from Rebook, "What advice would you give other entrepreneurs?"

> **If you think of your mind as a workplace, you can essentially choose to fire the negative comments and hire the positive ones.**

His response was, "Three things: have fun, have fun, have fun." Great advice we could all benefit from.

Life's too short not to love what you do, and while not every day of entrepreneurial life will be fun, we can all be more proactive in *making* it fun. Likewise, you can't control what the naysayers say or when they come around, but you *can* choose how much control their words have over you. If you think of your mind as a workplace, you can essentially choose to fire the negative comments and hire the positive ones.

Some of my fondest memories come from when we were building Internet Direct in the 1990s and Hostopia in the 2000s. Since then, I've traveled to over fifty countries, meeting so many different people in the 2010s while promoting .CLUB, coaching other CEOs, giving back by running Startup Club, speaking at universities and cohorts to the next generation of entrepreneurs, and running the podcast *Serial*

Entrepreneur: Secrets Revealed! And I would say that all of these have been *fun*.

Entrepreneurship can be quite a wild ride—a real roller coaster given all its ups, downs, twists, and turns. Along the way, don't forget to stop and smell success every once in a while to help you remember why you love it in the first place. You've worked hard, and you deserve to be happy.

START.
SCALE.
EXIT.
REPEAT.

CHAPTER 58

Final Thoughts

THIS BOOK HAS BEEN A TRUE JOY to put together. I have spent thirty years as a serial entrepreneur and, during that time, ten years working on this book. Again, it seems like it always takes ten years to become an "overnight" success.

When we took on the writing of this book, it seemed like a herculean task. How could a book cover the entire scope of entrepreneurship? Even with dozens of interviews from serial entrepreneurs, authors, experts, and my own career, this book still only scratches the surface in so many ways. But hopefully it's a place to start. If you want to continue to sharpen your skills and improve your trade as an entrepreneur, consider the authors and experts mentioned in this book. Listen to our podcast, or any podcast you can, and join us on Startup Club.

Forgive me for the following analogy I'm about to use—I know it may be a little out there for some. I love *Star Wars* and even have the original *Star Wars* pinball machine at my house, which I bought after I sold my first company in 1998. With this pinball game, you start out as a Padawan and then through practice (and a lot of play) and learning, you can achieve Jedi Knight status. With more practice, you can be elevated to Jedi Master. And then the final level is a Jedi Spirit. It's tough, but after years of practice, I continue to amaze my kids that I can pull it off.

Being an entrepreneur is a bit like being in the Jedi Order. In your entrepreneur career, you launch your first startup and learn so much as a Padawan. You finally get to the point where you sell your first company successfully and become a Jedi Knight. Then after launching and selling several other companies, you get to call yourself a serial entrepreneur, which is analogous to being a Jedi Master.

Looking back, it's been an incredible journey. We began that scrappy startup in 1993 on a pile of debt and dreams. We hit adversity, surfed the waves of new technology paradigms, and sold companies the right way *and* the wrong way. We launched new companies within existing businesses, and eventually I was able to step back as CEO to become chairman and principal investor in the companies. I'm no longer the day-to-day startup player but a coach for many in my family office.

The failure rate of family offices started by entrepreneurs is quite high. What drives us as entrepreneurs—risk-taking, hard work, leadership—isn't as necessary to be successful at running a larger group of companies. Instead of the leader, we become the *coach*. Instead of working twelve hours a day, we become very strategic with our time. And instead of only taking risks, we begin to measure risk. This is when I usually say, "It's time to take off the entrepreneur's hat and put on the banker's hat." Easier said than done, as it's tough to make that transformation.

I am new to running a family office where everything I have learned can be applied to many different companies. I find myself starting out all over again. I have much to learn still, as I have experienced a number of failures in this new role, but thankfully my successes have outweighed my losses. I am still learning and honing my skills as a coach in this new phase as a Jedi Spirit, so to speak.

> **" Entrepreneurship is a trade like any other, and continuous learning is the key to achieve better and better results. "**

Always remember that your title is not CEO, or cofounder, or executive—it's always entrepreneur. That *is* the job. Entrepreneurship is a trade like any other, and continuous learning is the key to achieve better and better results.

Where are you on your journey as an entrepreneur?

What is the next thing you need to do so that you can Start, Scale, Exit, and Repeat?

Acknowledgments

WHAT AN INCREDIBLE JOURNEY it has been putting this book together. I am so thankful to the authors, serial entrepreneurs, experts, and members of Startup Club who we interviewed to make this happen. I am also very grateful to the many coaches and mentors I have had over the years, in particular Patrick Thean, for helping me start out on the journey of writing this book. When it comes to launching a startup, it truly takes a village. We can't do it alone. And in writing this book, I couldn't do without all the contributors.

I would like to thank my comoderators on *Serial Entrepreneur: Secrets Revealed!*, Michele Van Tilborg and Jeffrey Sass, who helped me conduct hundreds of interviews.

I would also like to acknowledge the authors and experts who have inspired me so much throughout my career and who joined us on our weekly show, including Verne Harnish, who wrote *Scaling Up*; John Mullins, who wrote *The Customer-Funded Business*; Joe Foster, founder of Reebok and author of *Shoemaker*; George Walther, who wrote *Power Talking*; Jenny Kassan, who wrote *Raise Capital on Your Own Terms*; Jack Daly, who wrote the *Sales Playbook* and *Hyper Sales*

Growth; Patrick Thean (again), who wrote *Rhythm*; and lastly Geoffrey Moore, who wrote *Crossing the Chasm* and *Inside the Tornado*.

There are so many entrepreneurs and investors who contributed to this book and who helped us decode the formula that serial entrepreneurs use to Start, Scale, Exit, Repeat over and over again. These are my longtime business partners, including my brother, William Campbell, Igor Nikolaichuk, Dirk Bhagat, Peter Kostandenou, David Gimes, and Richard Pollack. I am also grateful for the expertise provided by Peter LaMantia, Lance Tracey, Michael Cytrynbaum, Andrew Allemann, Gordon Stula, Oscar DiVeroli, Jesse Berger, Jim Bennet, Jeffrey Wolf, Goran Dragoslavic, Ron White, David Rae, David Reeve, Brian Hansell, Rick Eastwood, Dean Allison, Marcia Reese, Reena and Nina Sood, John Lee, Norm Farrar, Mathew George, Lil Roberts, Michael Gilmour, Howard Bell, Elliot Noss, Ed Nusbaum, Lee Schram, Carrie Purcell, John Wensveen, Bill Birgen, Daniel Fiske, Richard Hanbury, Adam Khatib, Mimi Ostrander, Olivia Valdés, Cindy Santa Cruz, Sheel Mohnot, and, of course, my father and dear mother, Kenneth and Lillian Campbell.

I would also like to thank Forbes Books for believing in such a grand vision.

I'm very grateful to our illustrator, Erika Francisco, and my book coach, Jonathan Jordan, and to Olivia Valdés and Michele Van Tilborg for their creative direction.

Lastly, a book like this and the career that I have had could never have occurred if it wasn't for my lovely wife, Kim. In addition, it is my hope that one day both my kids, Kiersten and Quinn, will pick this book up and learn from it as much as I have learned from all those who contributed to it.